# i-Ready® Classroom Mathematics

## Grade 5 • Volume 1

Curriculum Associates®

## NOT FOR RESALE

978-1-4957-8040-0

©2020–Curriculum Associates, LLC

North Billerica, MA 01862

No part of this book may be reproduced
by any means without written permission
from the publisher.

All Rights Reserved. Printed in USA.

9 10 11 12 13 14 15      21

# Contents

# UNIT 2

# Decimals and Fractions
## Place Value, Addition, and Subtraction

## UNIT

# 3

# More Decimals and Fractions
## Multiplication and Division

# UNIT
# 4

# Measurement, Data, and Geometry
## Converting Units, Using Data, and Classifying Figures

NEXT
3 km

## UNIT 5

# Algebraic Thinking and the Coordinate Plane

## Expressions, Graphing Points, Patterns and Relationships

# Whole Number Operations and Applications:

## Volume, Multiplication, and Division

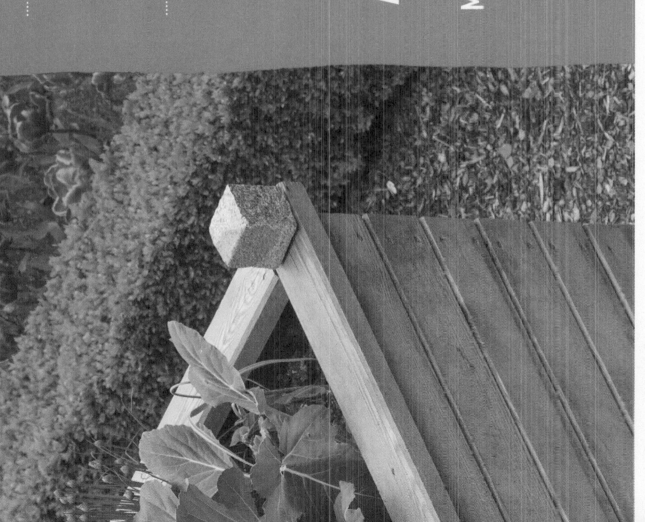

## ✓ SELF CHECK

**Before starting this unit, check off the skills you know below. As you complete each lesson, see how many more skills you can check off!**

| I can . . . | Before | After |
|---|---|---|
| Find the volume of a solid figure by counting unit cubes. | ☐ | ☐ |
| Find volume by using a formula. | ☐ | ☐ |
| Break apart a solid figure into rectangular prisms to find its volume. | ☐ | ☐ |
| Multiply multi-digit whole numbers, for example: $410 \times 16 = 6{,}560$. | ☐ | ☐ |
| Divide a multi-digit whole number by a two-digit number, for example: $2{,}812 \div 38 = 74$. | ☐ | ☐ |

# Build Your Vocabulary

## Math Vocabulary

**Fill in the blank boxes using the review words.**

| | × | |
| ☐ | × | ☐ |
| | = | |
| ☐ | = | ☐ |

| | ÷ | |
| ☐ | ÷ | ☐ |
| | = | |
| ☐ | = | ☐ |

**Using the review words, complete the sentence.**

When you divide the ........................ 72 by the ........................ 8,

the ........................ is 9.

## Academic Vocabulary

**Place a check next to the academic words you know. Then use the words to complete the sentences.**

☐ reasonable     ☐ result     ☐ reason

☐ justify

**1** You must ........................ your answer to prove it is correct.

**2** The ........................ of multiplying two numbers is called the product.

**3** She is a ........................ person; she is fair and sensible.

**4** When you make sense of a problem, you ........................ and use what you know to help solve it.

# Understand Volume

## Dear Family,

### This week your child is exploring volume.

**Volume** is the amount of space inside a **solid figure**. A **unit cube** is a cube, 1 unit on each edge, used to measure volume.

Your child has already learned to find the area of a **plane figure**, such as a rectangle, by covering it with **unit squares**. Area is the number of square units needed to cover a plane figure.

Area = 4 square units

Now your child is learning to find the volume of a solid figure, such as a cube, by filling it with unit cubes. Volume is the number of unit cubes needed to fill a solid figure. The cube at the right has a volume of 8 **cubic units**.

Volume = 8 cubic units

Each unit cube in the solid figures A and B at the right has a volume of 1 cubic unit.

A

B

To find which figure has a greater volume, you can count the unit cubes. Figure A has a volume of 25 cubic units. Figure B has a volume of 9 cubic units. Figure A has a greater volume than Figure B because 25 > 9.

Invite your child to share what he or she knows about volume by doing the following activity together.

# ACTIVITY VOLUME OF A RECTANGULAR PRISM

**Do this activity with your child to explore volume.**

A solid figure with six rectangular sides is called a rectangular prism. Work together with your child to find the volume of the rectangular prisms below.

- Each solid figure below is a rectangular prism made of unit cubes. Each unit cube has a volume of 1 cubic unit.

- Ask your child to explain how to find the volume of each rectangular prism. Then write the volume.

- Challenge! Look at all the solid figures below. Which two figures have the same volume? What is the same about the figures? What is different?

Volume = .............. cubic units

Volume = .............. cubic units

Volume = .............. cubic units

Volume = .............. cubic units

# Explore Volume

## What does volume measure?

## MODEL IT

**Complete the problems below to compare _area_ and _volume_.**

1 A **plane figure** is a two-dimensional figure. Explain how to measure the area of the plane figure using the **unit square**.

plane figure

1 unit
1 unit

unit square

2 A **solid figure** is a three-dimensional figure. The **volume** of a solid figure is the amount of space inside the figure.

A **unit cube** is a cube that has side lengths of 1 unit. How do you think you could use unit cubes to measure the volume of the solid figure?

solid figure

1 unit
1 unit
1 unit

unit cube

## DISCUSS IT

- Compare how you answered the questions about area and volume with your partner. How were your explanations alike and different?

- I think finding the volume of a solid figure is like finding the area of a plane figure because . . . .

# MODEL IT

## Complete the problems below.

**3** A rectangular prism is a solid figure with six rectangular sides, or faces. The two boxes shown below are identical rectangular prisms with unit cubes inside them.

Circle the diagram that you think shows the correct way to use unit cubes to measure the volume of the rectangular prism. Cross out the incorrect way. Then explain your choice.

**1 unit cube**

**Way 1**

**Way 2**

...............................................................

...............................................................

**4** A unit cube is said to have one **cubic unit** of volume. Cubic units are used to measure the volume of a solid figure.

**a.** What is the volume of each unit cube inside the rectangular prism you circled in problem 3? ............... cubic unit(s)

**b.** What is the volume of the rectangular prism?

............... cubic unit(s)

**5** REFLECT

Why do you use cubic units instead of square units to find the volume of a solid figure?

...............................................................

...............................................................

...............................................................

...............................................................

## DISCUSS IT

- How did you and your partner each select the way to measure volume?

- I think when you measure volume with unit cubes, it is important to . . .

Name: _____

# Prepare for Volume

1. Think about what you know about units of measure. Fill in each box. Use words, numbers, and pictures. Show as many ideas as you can.

| What Is It? | What I Know About It |
|---|---|

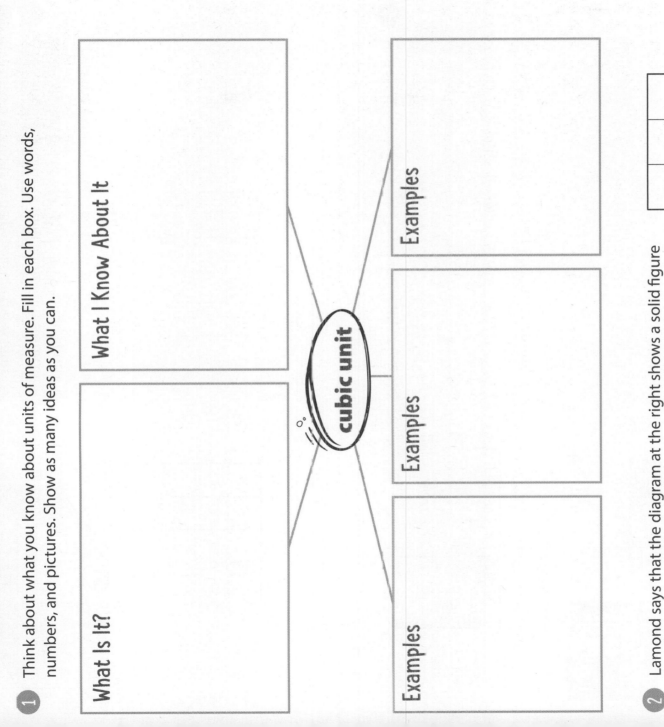

cubic unit

Examples

Examples

Examples

2. Lamond says that the diagram at the right shows a solid figure with a volume of 6 cubic units. Is he correct? Explain.

## Solve.

③ Mai uses unit cubes to help measure the volume of a box. She thinks the volume of the box is 8 cubic units. Do you agree? Explain.

④ What is the volume of the rectangular prism?

........... cubic unit(s)

# Develop Understanding of Volume

## MODEL IT: ADD TO FIND VOLUME

**Try these two problems.**

**1** The rectangular prism shown below is made of unit cubes with no gaps or overlaps between the cubes.

**1 unit cube**

**a.** Write an addition equation to find the volume of the prism.

**b.** Explain what each number in your addition equation represents.

**2** Suppose you add another layer of cubes on top of the rectangular prism in problem 1. What would be your addition equation for the new rectangular prism? What would be the new volume?

## DISCUSS IT

- How did you and your partner figure out how many cubes are in the whole prism if you cannot see them all?

- I think you can use addition to help you measure volume of a rectangular prism because . . . .

# MODEL IT: MULTIPLY TO FIND VOLUME

**Use multiplication to find volume.**

**3** The rectangular prism shown is made of unit cubes with no gaps or overlaps between the cubes.

1 unit cube

**a.** Write a multiplication equation to find the volume of the rectangular prism.

**b.** Explain what each number in your multiplication equation represents.

**DISCUSS IT**

· Did you write the same multiplication equation as your partner?

· I think you can use multiplication to help you measure volume because . . .

# CONNECT IT

**Complete the problems below.**

**4** How are the addition and multiplication strategies for finding volume alike? How are they different?

**5** Figure A and Figure B are built with unit cubes of the same size. Explain how to use the volume of Figure A to find the volume of Figure B.

A

B

# Practice with Volume

**Study how the Example shows counting unit cubes to find the volume of a rectangular prism. Then solve problems 1–8. Each figure shown is built with unit cubes.**

## EXAMPLE

Peter stacks unit cubes to build this rectangular prism. What is the volume of the figure?

There are 4 unit cubes in 1 layer. There are 5 layers.

$4 + 4 + 4 + 4 + 4 = 20$

$5 \times 4 = 20$

There are 20 unit cubes.

Volume = 20 cubic units

1 layer

① Look at Figure A and fill in the blanks below.

There are _____ layers and _____ unit cubes in each layer.

_____ × _____ cubes = _____ unit cubes.

The volume of Figure A is _____ cubic units.

A

B

② What is the volume of Figure B? Tell how you know.

....................................................................

③ Elena stacks 2 layers of 4 unit cubes to fill a small box.

How many cubes are in the box? ....................................

What is the volume of Elena's box? ................................

4  Look at Figure C and fill in the blanks below.

C

There are .............. layers and .............. unit cubes in each layer.

.............. × .............. cubes = .............. unit cubes.

The volume of Figure C is .............. cubic units.

5  What is the volume of Figure D?

D

...........................................

6  Figures D and E are made from unit cubes of the same size. How many of Figure D does it take to fill Figure E? How does the volume of Figure E relate to the volume of Figure D? Explain.

E

7  A prism has a volume of 36 cubic units. It has 9 layers of unit cubes. How many unit cubes are in each layer?

...........................................

8  Draw or describe Box F that has a volume of 5 cubic units. Then draw or describe a box that has 3 times the volume of Box F. What is the volume of the second box?

**Solution** ...........................................

...........................................

# Refine Ideas About Volume

## APPLY IT

**Complete these problems on your own.**

### ① INFER

Eli is stacking unit cubes in a box. He partially fills the box, pauses, and says, "The volume of this box is 18 cubic units."

Explain how Eli found the volume of the box.

### ② EXPLAIN

Zoe says that a box that is 1 unit wide, 2 units long, and 3 units tall has a greater volume than a box that is 2 units wide, 3 units long, and 1 unit tall. Is she correct? Explain your answer.

### ③ COMPARE

Each cube in Figures A and B has a volume of 1 cubic unit. Which figure has less volume, Figure A or Figure B? Explain your answer.

A

B

**PAIR/SHARE**

Discuss your solutions for these three problems with a partner.

**Use what you have learned to complete problem 4.**

**4** Niles uses 16 blocks, each having a volume of 1 cubic unit, to build a rectangular prism.

**Part A** Draw or build a model to represent the situation.

**Part B** Look at your model. Describe the number of layers and the number of blocks in each layer. Then describe a different rectangular prism that also has a volume of 16 cubic units.

**5** MATH JOURNAL

Heather builds a rectangular prism with 3 layers of unit cubes. Each layer of her prism has 10 unit cubes. Explain why the volume of Heather's prism is said to be 30 cubic units.

# Find Volume Using Unit Cubes

## Dear Family,

### This week your child is learning to find volume using unit cubes.

Suppose you want to find the volume of the rectangular prism shown at the right. One way to find the volume is to fill it with unit cubes that each have a volume of 1 cubic centimeter.

3 cm

2 cm

3 cm

1 cm
1 cm 1 cm

**1 cubic centimeter**

You can count all the cubes to find the volume. The prism has a volume of 18 cubic centimeters.

3 cm

2 cm

3 cm

Another way to find the volume is to count the cubes in each layer and then add.

There are 6 cubes in each layer and 3 layers in all.

$6 + 6 + 6 = 18$ cubes

**One layer**          **3 total layers**

The volume of the rectangular prism is 18 cubic centimeters. Using either method, the volume is the same.

Your child is also learning that unit cubes can be different sizes. So, it is important to know the size of the cube you are using when you find the volume of a figure.

- A unit cube with side lengths of 1 centimeter has a volume of 1 cubic centimeter.

- A unit cube with side lengths of 1 inch has a volume of 1 cubic inch.

- A unit cube with side lengths of 1 foot has a volume of 1 cubic foot.

Invite your child to share what he or she knows about different ways to find volume by doing the following activity together.

# ACTIVITY FIND VOLUME USING UNIT CUBES

**Do this activity with your child to find volume with unit cubes.**

***Materials*** scissors, tape, household containers shaped like rectangular prisms, such as cereal boxes and tissue boxes

- Cut out the cube pattern below on the solid lines. Fold on the dotted lines and tape into a cube. This cube represents 1 cubic unit of volume.

- Have your child use the unit cube to estimate the volume of one household container (the number of cubes that fit in the container). Because your child is finding an approximate volume, discuss that the cubes do not need to fill the length, width, and height of the container completely (with no gaps).

- Ask your child the questions below:

  *How many cubes would fit in the bottom of the box?*
  *How many layers of cubes would fit in the box?*
  *What is the approximate volume of the box?*

- Repeat for another container.

# Explore Finding Volume Using Unit Cubes

Previously, you learned that you can fill a solid figure with unit cubes to find its volume. Use what you know to try to solve the problem below.

**Carl filled the clear box shown below with unit cubes to find its volume. The unit cubes Carl used all have side lengths of 1 foot. What is the volume of the box?**

1 ft
1 ft
1 ft

## Learning Targets

- Measure volumes by counting unit cubes, using cubic cm, cubic in, cubic ft, and improvised units.
- Find the volume of a right rectangular prism with whole-number side lengths by packing it with unit cubes, and show that the volume is the same as would be found by multiplying the edge lengths, equivalently by multiplying the height by the area of the base. Represent threefold whole-number products as volumes.

**SMP** 1, 2, 3, 4, 5, 6, 7

 **Math Toolkit**

- unit cubes
- grid paper
- isometric dot paper
- square sticky notes

## TRY IT

## DISCUSS IT

**Ask your partner:** How did you get started?

**Tell your partner:** I started by . . .

# CONNECT IT

## 1 LOOK BACK

Describe the measurement unit Carl should use and explain how he can find the volume of the box.

........................................................................................

........................................................................................

........................................................................................

## 2 LOOK AHEAD

Volume is measured in cubic units. Here are some cubic units you might use to measure volume.

| Unit of Volume | cubic inch | cubic centimeter | cubic foot |
|---|---|---|---|
| Unit Cube | 1 in.<br>1 in.<br>1 in. | 1 cm<br>1 cm<br>1 cm | 1 ft<br>1 ft<br>1 ft |

Carl has another box as shown below. What is its volume? ........................................

1 in.
1 in.
1 in.

## 3 REFLECT

What is the same and what is different about the volume of Carl's two boxes?

........................................................................................

........................................................................................

........................................................................................

# Prepare for Finding Volume Using Unit Cubes

1 Think about what you know about solid figures. Fill in each box.
Use words, numbers, and pictures. Show as many ideas as you can.

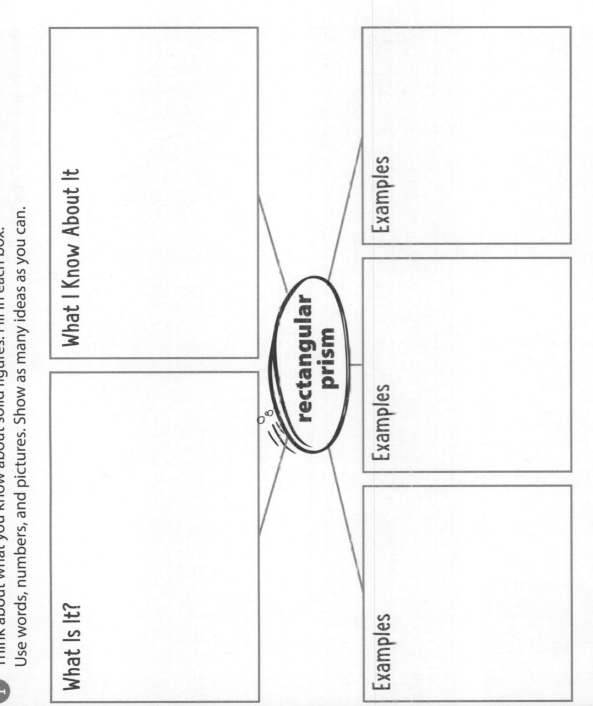

| What Is It? | What I Know About It |
|---|---|

rectangular prism

| Examples | Examples | Examples |
|---|---|---|

2 Instead of using cubic units to measure volume, Paulina wants to measure volume using boxes of pencils. What is the volume of this rectangular prism using boxes of pencils as the unit of measure?

3 Solve the problem. Show your work.

**Jan filled the box shown below with unit cubes to find its volume. The unit cubes Jan used all have side lengths of 1 centimeter. What is the volume of the box?**

1 cm
1 cm
1 cm

4 Check your answer. Show your work.

*Solution* .....................................................

# Develop Finding Volume Using Unit Cubes

Read and try to solve the problem below.

**Abigail uses cardboard to build a rectangular prism like the one shown below. What is the volume of the prism?**

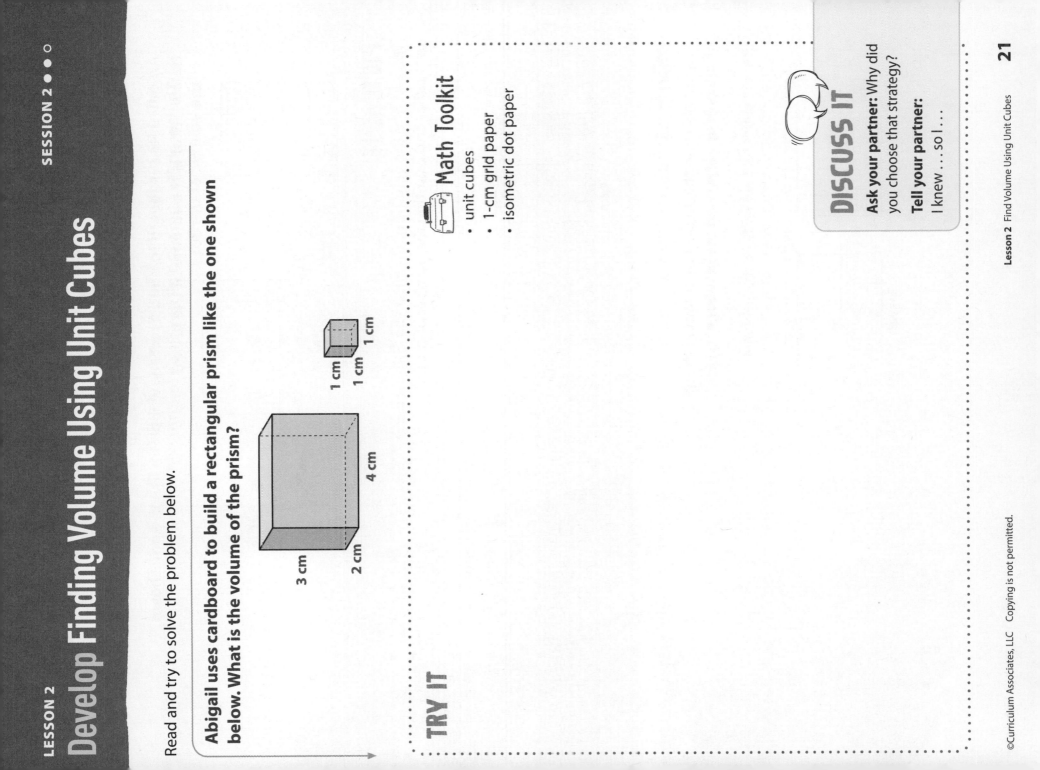

3 cm

4 cm

2 cm

1 cm
1 cm
1 cm

## TRY IT

**Math Toolkit**
- unit cubes
- 1-cm grid paper
- isometric dot paper

**DISCUSS IT**

**Ask your partner:** Why did you choose that strategy?

**Tell your partner:** I knew . . . so I . . . .

Explore different ways to understand finding the volume of a rectangular prism.

**Abigail uses cardboard to build a rectangular prism like the one shown below. What is the volume of the prism?**

3 cm

2 cm

4 cm

1 cm
1 cm
1 cm

## PICTURE IT

**You can find the volume of the prism by filling it with unit cubes and counting the number of cubes.**

Use unit cubes that are each 1 cubic centimeter.

3 cm

2 cm

4 cm

## MODEL IT

**You can also find the volume by counting the number of cubes in one layer and the number of layers.**

Use unit cubes that are each 1 cubic centimeter.

1 layer

3 layers

## CONNECT IT

**Now you will use the problem from the previous page to help you understand how to find the volume of a rectangular prism.**

**1** Look at the model in **Picture It** on the previous page. Count the number of cubes

in one layer. There are ............... cubes in one layer.

**2** How could you find the number of cubes in one layer without counting the cubes?

**3** Once you know how many cubes are in one layer, what else do you need to know to find the volume?

**4** There are 8 cubes in each layer and there are 3 layers. What multiplication

expression can you write to find the volume of the prism? ...............

**5** What is the volume of Abigail's rectangular prism?

**6** Explain how you can use multiplication to find the volume of a rectangular prism.

**7 REFLECT**

Look back at your **Try It**, strategies by classmates, and **Picture It** and **Model It**. Which models or strategies do you like best for finding the volume of a rectangular prism? Explain.

...............................................................

...............................................................

...............................................................

...............................................................

# APPLY IT

## Use what you just learned to solve these problems.

**8** What is the volume of the rectangular prism at the right? Show your work.

1 in.
1 in.
1 in.

**Solution** ..........................................................................

**9** Mr. Wong finds the volume of a box by filling it with 1-foot unit cubes, as shown below. What is the volume of Mr. Wong's box? Show your work.

**Solution** ..........................................................................

**10** Jamila wants to find the volume of the rectangular box at the right. What is the volume of the box?

1 cm
1 cm
1 cm

2 cm

3 cm

6 cm

Ⓐ 18 cubic units

Ⓑ 30 cubic centimeters

Ⓒ 36 cubic centimeters

Ⓓ 36 cubic inches

**Solution** ..........................................................................

# Practice Finding Volume Using Unit Cubes

**Study the Example showing how to use layers to find the volume of a rectangular prism. Then solve problems 1–7.**

## EXAMPLE

Keith uses this box to store his colored markers.
What is the volume of the box?

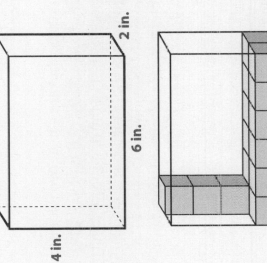

6 in.

4 in.

2 in.

Think about filling the box with 1-inch cubes.
One layer has 2 rows of 6 cubes, or 12 cubes.
There are 4 layers of cubes.

$12 + 12 + 12 + 12 = 48$, or $12 \times 4 = 48$

The volume of the box is 48 cubic inches.

1 Prism G is filled with unit cubes that have side length 1 centimeter.

G

There are ............. layers with ............. cubes in each layer.

............. cubes + ............. cubes = ............. cubes

The volume is ............. .

2 Prism H is filled with unit cubes that have side length 1 foot.

H

There are ............. layers with ............. cubes in each layer.

............. × ............. cubes = ............. cubes

The volume is ............. .

**3** What is the volume of the rectangular prism at the right? Show your work.

2 ft

4 ft

2 ft

**Solution** ....................

**4** Jenn noticed that she can fit two juice boxes side by side on the bottom of this box. She can make two more layers like the one shown to fill the box. Using a juice box as a measure of volume, what is the volume of the larger box?

**Solution** ....................

**5** A box is 2 inches long, 1 inch wide, and 6 inches tall. What is the relationship between the volume of this box and the one in problem 4? Tell how you know.

**6** Box D and Box E are made from unit cubes of the same size. Which has a greater volume, Box D or Box E? Explain.

**7** Add a layer to Box D and compare the volume of the new Box D to the volume of Box E.

D

E

# Refine Finding Volume Using Unit Cubes

**Complete the Example below. Then solve problems 1–9.**

## EXAMPLE

**Pedro has a storage box with a volume of 36 cubic feet. He knows that the box is 4 feet long and 3 feet wide. How high is the box?**

Look at how you could show your work using a drawing and multiplication facts.

The student started by finding the number of cubes in the bottom layer.

$4 \times 3 = 12$

$12 \times \square = 36$

$12 \times 3 = 36$

3 ft    4 ft

**Solution**

**PAIR/SHARE**
Could you solve this problem another way?

## APPLY IT

**1** A box measures 6 centimeters long, 2 centimeters wide, and 4 centimeters high. What is the volume of the box? Show your work.

4 cm    6 cm    2 cm

How many layers of cubes will there be in the box?

**Solution**

**PAIR/SHARE**
Can you use multiplication to solve this problem?

**2** Kamala made the figure below using cubes. What is the volume of Kamala's figure? Show your work.

1 in.
1 in.
1 in.

How many cubes are there in each layer?

**PAIR/SHARE**
How did you decide which method to use to solve the problem?

**Solution** ...........................................................

**3** What is the volume of the rectangular prism below?

1 ft
1 ft
1 ft

Ⓐ 6 square feet

Ⓑ 6 cubic feet

Ⓒ 8 square feet

Ⓓ 8 cubic feet

Nam chose Ⓓ as the correct answer. How did he get that answer?

There is more than one way to find the volume of a rectangular prism.

**PAIR/SHARE**
Does Nam's answer make sense?

4 How many 1-centimeter unit cubes are in the bottom layer of the rectangular prism at the right?

Ⓐ 3

Ⓑ 6

Ⓒ 12

Ⓓ 24

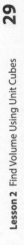

1 cm
1cm
1 cm

5 Which expressions can be used to find the volume, in cubic feet, of the rectangular prism at the right?

Ⓐ 30 × 4

Ⓑ (5 + 6) × 4

Ⓒ 30 + 30 + 30 + 30

Ⓓ 5 + 6 + 4

Ⓔ 30 + 4

1 ft
1 ft   1 ft

6 Flora has a rectangular gift box that has a volume of 24 cubic inches. The box is 2 inches tall. Determine if the gift box could have the given length and width.

| | Yes | No |
|---|---|---|
| Length: 11 inches; Width: 11 inches | Ⓐ | Ⓑ |
| Length: 4 inches; Width: 3 inches | Ⓒ | Ⓓ |
| Length: 10 inches; Width: 2 inches | Ⓔ | Ⓕ |
| Length: 6 inches; Width: 2 inches | Ⓖ | Ⓗ |
| Length: 12 inches; Width: 1 inch | Ⓘ | Ⓙ |

**7** Both figures are filled with unit cubes of the same size. Which rectangular prism has the greater volume, Figure A or Figure B? Show your work.

........... has the greater volume.

**8** **Part A** Mato drew the rectangular prism shown below. Draw and label a different rectangular prism with the same volume as Mato's prism.

4 cm
2 cm
5 cm

**Part B** Explain how you know that the volume of your prism is the same as the volume of Mato's prism.

**9** **MATH JOURNAL**

Jorge uses 1-centimeter cubes to make a rectangular prism. Each layer of his prism is 5 cubes long and 2 cubes wide. His prism has 6 layers. Explain two ways to find the volume of Jorge's prism.

☑ **SELF CHECK** Go back to the Unit 1 Opener and see what you can check off.

# Find Volume Using Formulas

## Dear Family,

### This week your child is learning to find the volume of a solid figure using a formula.

You can use a formula to find the volume of a rectangular prism if you know its length, width, and height. The picture shows a gift bag that is 4 inches long, 2 inches wide, and 3 inches high. The model beside the bag shows the number of 1-inch cubes that would fill the bag.

3 in.

2 in.

4 in.

Using the model, you can find the volume of the cube by multiplying the number of cubes in each layer by the number of layers.

$$\text{volume} = \underset{\text{in each layer}}{\text{number of cubes}} \times \underset{\text{of layers}}{\text{number}}$$

The equation to the right shows that multiplying the number of cubes in each layer by the number of layers is the same as multiplying length, width, and height. This is one of the volume formulas your child is learning to use.

Volume = length × width × height
Volume = 4 inches × 2 inches × 3 inches
       = (8 × 3) cubic inches
       = 24 cubic inches

The volume of the gift bag is 24 cubic inches.

Invite your child to share what he or she knows about finding volume using a formula by doing the following activity together.

Lesson 3  Find Volume Using Formulas

# ACTIVITY USE A VOLUME FORMULA

**Do this activity with your child to find volume using a formula.**

Work with your child to use a formula to find the volume of the L-shaped solid figure shown at the right.

9 cm
10 cm
6 cm
4 cm
10 cm

• The figure is composed of two rectangular prisms. Ask your child to talk about different ways to break the figure apart into two smaller rectangular prisms.

• Choose two ways to break the figure into rectangular prisms. Have your child draw pictures of the two ways to break up the figure and label the lengths, widths, and heights.

• Start with one of the ways your child broke up the figure. Have him or her use the volume formula below to find the volume of each of the smaller rectangular prisms. Then add the volumes to find the volume of the original figure.

  Volume = length × width × height

• Repeat for the other way your child broke up the figure.

• Have your child compare the two volumes he or she found for the figure. They should be the same. Ask your child: *Suppose there were a third way to break the figure into two other rectangular prisms. Would the volume of the figure be the same?*

# Explore Finding Volume Using Formulas

Previously, you learned how to find volume by counting unit cubes and by using addition and multiplication strategies. Now you will learn how to find volume using a formula. Use what you know to try to solve the problem below.

**Becky uses 1-inch cubes to create a model for a small paper gift bag she is making. Her model is a rectangular prism. What is the volume of Becky's model?**

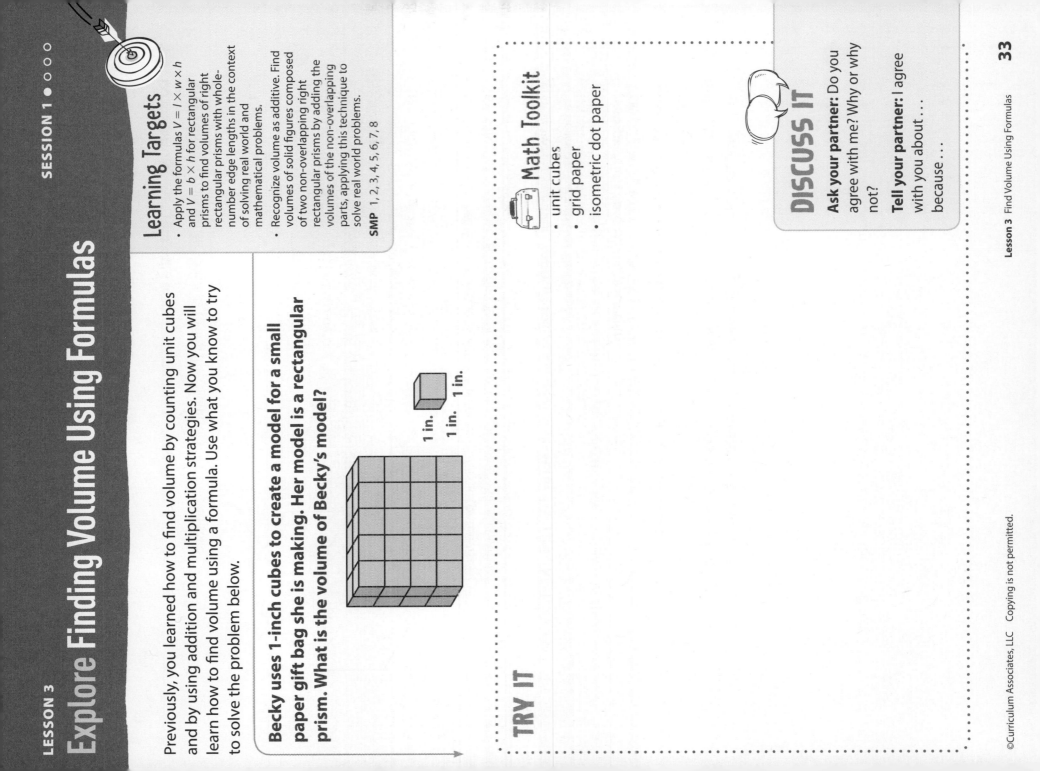

1 in.

1 in.   1 in.

## Learning Targets

- Apply the formulas $V = l \times w \times h$ and $V = b \times h$ for rectangular prisms to find volumes of right rectangular prisms with whole-number edge lengths in the context of solving real world and mathematical problems.

- Recognize volume as additive. Find volumes of solid figures composed of two non-overlapping right rectangular prisms by adding the volumes of the non-overlapping parts, applying this technique to solve real world problems.

**SMP** 1, 2, 3, 4, 5, 6, 7, 8

## TRY IT

### Math Toolkit
- unit cubes
- grid paper
- isometric dot paper

## DISCUSS IT

**Ask your partner:** Do you agree with me? Why or why not?

**Tell your partner:** I agree with you about . . . because . . .

# CONNECT IT

## 1 LOOK BACK

Explain how you can find the volume of Becky's model without counting each cube.

..................................................................................

..................................................................................

..................................................................................

## 2 LOOK AHEAD

Becky's finished gift bag is shown below. You can find the volume with a formula.
Use the letters ℓ, *w*, and *h* to represent the **length**, **width**, and **height**.

*h* = **4 in.**

*w* = **2 in.**

ℓ = **5 in.**

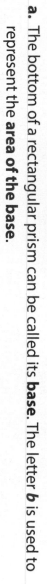

**a.** The bottom of a rectangular prism can be called its **base**. The letter *b* is used to
represent the **area of the base.**

Write an equation using the area of the base to find the bag's volume **V**. Then
complete the formula with a letter.

**V** = .............. × ..............

**V** = ............ *b* × ............

**b.** Use the letters shown in the formula below to help you complete another
equation for the volume of the bag. Then complete the formula.

.............. = .............. × .............. × ..............

**V** = ℓ × *w* × ..............

## 3 REFLECT

How are the two volume formulas you wrote above alike? How are they different?

..................................................................................

..................................................................................

..................................................................................

# Prepare for Finding Volume Using Formulas

1  Think about what you know about formulas. Fill in each box. Use words, numbers, and pictures. Show as many ideas as you can.

| In My Own Words | My Illustrations |
|---|---|
|  |  |

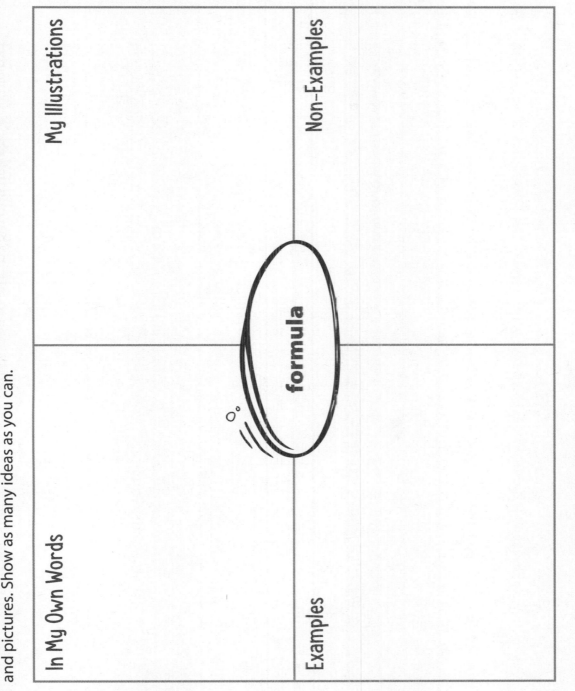

formula

| Examples | Non-Examples |
|---|---|
|  |  |

2  Find the volume of the rectangular prism. Explain.

1 unit cube

3  Solve the problem. Show your work.

**Adrien uses 1-inch cubes to create a model for a small box he is making. His model is a rectangular prism. What is the volume of Adrien's model?**

1 in.
1 in.
1 in.

4  Check your answer. Show your work.

*Solution*

·················································································

# Develop Finding Volume Using Formulas

Read and try to solve the problem below.

> **Gareth has a rectangular pencil cup on his desk. The cup is 3 inches long, 2 inches wide, and 5 inches high. What is the volume of the pencil cup?**

## TRY IT

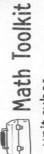

**Math Toolkit**
- unit cubes
- grid paper
- isometric dot paper

Explore different ways to understand using the dimensions of a rectangular prism to find its volume.

**Gareth has a rectangular pencil cup on his desk. The cup is 3 inches long, 2 inches wide, and 5 inches high. What is the volume of the pencil cup?**

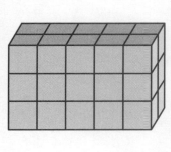

## PICTURE IT

You can picture the pencil cup as a rectangular prism made up of 1-inch cubes.

## MODEL IT

You can draw a model of the pencil cup and label its dimensions. Then use a volume formula.

5 in.

2 in.

3 in.

$V = \ell \times w \times h$   or   $V = b \times h$

# CONNECT IT

**Now you will use the problem from the previous page to help you understand and use formulas to find volume.**

1 Explain how you can find the volume of the pencil cup using the prism shown in **Picture It**. Find the volume.

2 Explain how the area of the base of the prism shown in **Model It** relates to the prism in **Picture It**.

3 Explain how you can use the prism in **Model It** to find the volume of the pencil cup.

4 Use the volume formulas shown in **Model It** to write two different multiplication equations you can use to find the volume of the pencil cup.

5 Explain how you can use the dimensions of a rectangular prism to find its volume.

6 **REFLECT**

Look back at your **Try It**, strategies by classmates, and **Picture It** and **Model It**. Which models or strategies do you like best for using the dimensions of a rectangular prism to find its volume? Explain.

# APPLY IT

**Use what you just learned to solve these problems.**

**7** What is the volume of a rectangular jewelry box with a length of 12 centimeters, a width of 7 centimeters, and a height of 5 centimeters? Show your work.

*Solution* ......................

**8** How much space is taken up by a book that is 12 inches long, 10 inches wide, and 1 inch tall? Show your work.

*Solution* ......................

**9** A rectangular prism has a volume of 100 cubic meters. One of the dimensions is 5 meters. Which pairs of measurements could be the other two dimensions of the prism?

Ⓐ 1 meter, 20 meters

Ⓑ 5 meters, 10 meters

Ⓒ 10 meters, 10 meters

Ⓓ 4 meters, 5 meters

Ⓔ 20 meters, 20 meters

# Practice Finding Volume Using Formulas

**Study the Example showing how to use formulas to find the volume of a rectangular prism. Then solve problems 1–7.**

## EXAMPLE

Gwen puts her leftover food in a rectangular container. The container is 6 inches long, 5 inches wide, and 2 inches tall. What is the volume of the container?

Use the formula *volume = length × width × height.*

$V = \ell \times w \times h = 6 \times 5 \times 2$, or 60 cubic inches

Or use the formula *volume = area of the base × height.*

The *area of the base* is the same as the *length × width.*

**b = 6 × 5, or 30**

$V = b \times h = 30 \times 2$, or 60 cubic inches

1  Ted's box is 4 inches tall, 3 inches long, and 1 inch wide.

**a.** Label the picture of the box with its dimensions.

**b.** What is the volume of the box? Show your work.

......... in.

......... in.

......... in.

*Solution* ............................................................

2  A rectangular prism has a square base with sides that are 2 feet long. The height of the prism is 5 feet. What is the volume of the prism? Show your work.

*Solution* ............................................................

**3** Elon's shed is 10 feet long, 6 feet wide, and 8 feet tall.
What is the volume of the shed? Show your work.

**Solution**

**4** The base of a rectangular prism has a length of 4 centimeters and has
a width of 2 centimeters. The height of the prism is 3 centimeters.
What is the volume of the prism? Show your work.

**Solution**

**5** What is the volume of a box that is 8 inches long, 2 inches wide, and
6 inches tall? Show your work.

**Solution**

**6** The base of a rectangular prism is a rectangle that is 7 inches long and
5 inches wide. Its height is 10 inches. Write two different equations that you can
use to find the volume.

**7** Jin has two boxes. Box A has dimensions of 6 centimeters, 5 centimeters, and
9 centimeters. Box B has dimensions of 4 centimeters, 10 centimeters, and
7 centimeters. Which box holds more? Explain.

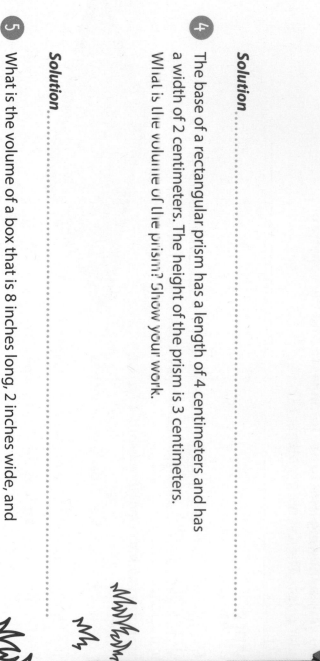

# Develop Breaking Apart Figures to Find Volume

Read and try to solve the problem below.

**Bethany has a raised garden bed. The diagram shows its measurements. All the corners are right angles. If she fills the bed to the top with soil, how many cubic feet of soil will Bethany need?**

## TRY IT

🚌 **Math Toolkit**
- unit cubes
- grid paper
- isometric dot paper

**DISCUSS IT**

**Ask your partner:** Can you explain that again?

**Tell your partner:** I knew . . . so I . . . .

Explore different ways to understand finding the volume of a solid figure by breaking it apart into two rectangular prisms.

**Bethany has a raised garden bed. The diagram shows its measurements. All the corners are right angles. If she fills the bed to the top with soil, how many cubic feet of soil will Bethany need?**

## MODEL IT

**You can break the garden bed into two rectangular prisms this way.**

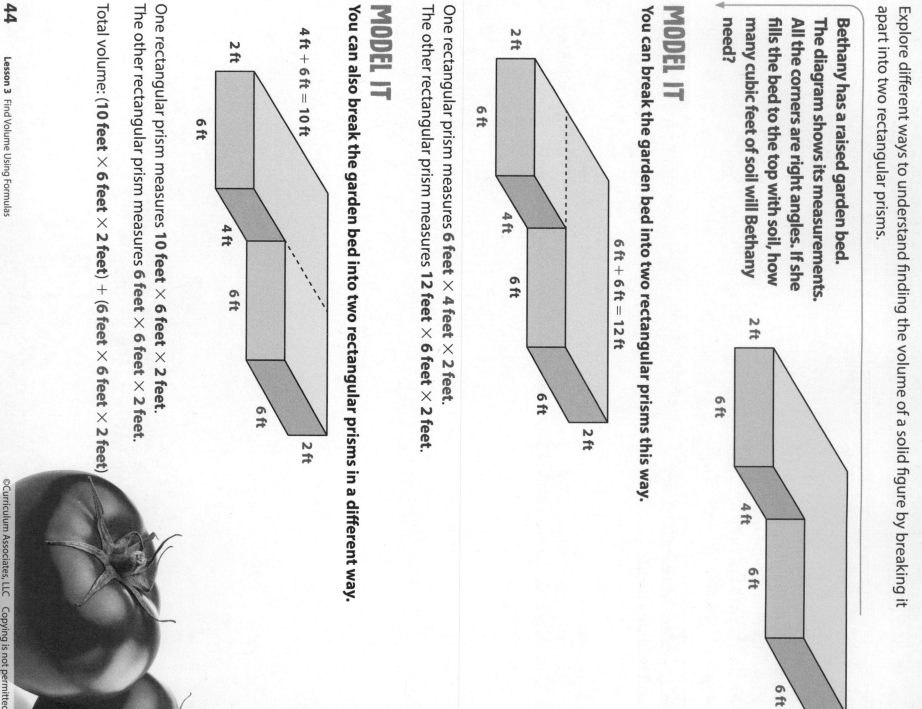

One rectangular prism measures 6 feet × 4 feet × 2 feet.
The other rectangular prism measures 12 feet × 6 feet × 2 feet.

## MODEL IT

**You can also break the garden bed into two rectangular prisms in a different way.**

4 ft + 6 ft = 10 ft

One rectangular prism measures 10 feet × 6 feet × 2 feet.
The other rectangular prism measures 6 feet × 6 feet × 2 feet.

Total volume: (10 feet × 6 feet × 2 feet) + (6 feet × 6 feet × 2 feet)

## CONNECT IT

**Now you will use the problem from the previous page to help you understand ways to break apart a solid figure to find its volume.**

1. Look at the first **Model It.** How can you find the volume of each rectangular prism?

2. How can you find the volume of the entire garden bed?

3. What is the volume of the entire garden bed? Show your work.

4. Now look at the second **Model It.** Show how to use the expression to find the volume of the garden bed if you break it apart this way. When you evaluate an expression, do the operations in the parentheses first.

5. Do you need to break apart a solid figure in a certain way to find its volume? Use the problem from the previous page to explain your reasoning.

## REFLECT

Look back at your **Try It,** strategies by classmates, and **Model Its.** Which models or strategies do you like best for breaking apart solid figures to find volume? Explain.

## APPLY IT

**Use what you just learned to solve these problems.**

**7** The Recreation Center has an L-shaped pool. One part of the pool is 8 meters by 6 meters. The other part is 12 meters by 6 meters. The whole pool is 4 meters deep. What is the volume of the entire pool? Show your work.

Solution .................................................................................................................................

**8** What is the volume of the solid figure below? Show your work.

30 cm

30 cm

10 cm

20 cm

30 cm

Solution .................................................................................................................................

**9** What is the volume of the solid figure below? Show your work.

3 ft

4 ft

8 ft

2 ft

6 ft

Solution .................................................................................................................................

# Practice Breaking Apart Figures to Find Volume

**Study the Example showing how to break apart a solid figure into rectangular prisms and find its volume. Then solve problems 1–8.**

## EXAMPLE

Molly wants to know how much soil she needs to fill her two-tiered planter, shown below. What is the volume of the planter?

You can break the figure into two rectangular prisms in different ways.

Prism A measures 6 ft × 3 ft × 2 ft.
Volume of Prism A = 36 cubic feet

Prism B measures 8 ft × 3 ft × 2 ft.
Volume of Prism B = 48 cubic feet

Volume of planter = 36 + 48, or 84
The volume is 84 cubic feet.

Prism A measures 9 ft × 3 ft × 2 ft.
Volume of Prism A = 54 cubic feet

Prism B measures 5 ft × 3 ft × 2 ft.
Volume of Prism B = 30 cubic feet

Volume of planter = 54 + 30, or 84
The volume is 84 cubic feet.

1 Show how to find the volume of Prism D.

2 Find the volume of Prism C.

3 What is the volume of the whole figure?

**4** Draw lines in Figures A and B to separate them into two rectangular prisms. Do each in a different way.

**5** Show how to find the volume of Figure A.

**6** Show how to find the volume of Figure B.

**7** What is the volume of Figure X? Show your work.

**8** Show how to break Figure S into three rectangular prisms. Then find the volume of Figure S. Show your work.

*Solution* ............................................................................

*Solution* ............................................................................

# Refine Finding Volume Using Formulas

**Complete the Example below. Then solve problems 1–9.**

## EXAMPLE

**Coen is making a clay vase. He wants the interior of the vase to be a rectangular prism with base 3 inches long and 3 inches wide. He wants the vase to hold 45 cubic inches of water. How tall should Coen make the vase?**

Look at how you could use a formula to solve the problem.

Volume = $\ell \times w \times h$

$45 = 3 \times 3 \times h$

$45 = 9 \times h$

$45 \div 9 = h$

$5 = h$

*Solution*

The student wrote an equation using the formula for volume.
The height is the unknown.

**PAIR/SHARE**
Did you and your partner solve the problem the same way?

## APPLY IT

**1** The diagram shows the dimensions of a cement walkway, where all of the sides meet at right angles. What is the total volume of cement needed to make the walkway? Show your work.

8 ft
1 ft
2 ft
10 ft
2 ft

After you break apart the figure, how will you find the missing measurements?

**PAIR/SHARE**
How did you and your partner decide how to break apart the solid figure?

*Solution*

Lesson 3  Find Volume Using Formulas

**2** The rectangular prism shown below has a volume of 42 cubic meters. What is the length of the prism? Show your work.

3 m

2 m

ℓ

What dimensions are labeled on the prism?

**Solution** .................................................

PAIR/SHARE
How could you check your answer?

**3** A cube is a rectangular prism whose side lengths are all the same. What is the volume of a cube with a side length of 2 feet?

Ⓐ 4 cubic feet

Ⓑ 6 cubic feet

Ⓒ 8 cubic feet

Ⓓ 12 cubic feet

Danny chose Ⓑ as the correct answer. How did he get that answer?

Each side of a cube is a square.

PAIR/SHARE
Does Danny's answer make sense?

**4** A rectangular prism has a square base with side lengths of 5 centimeters and a height of 7 centimeters. What is the volume of the prism?

Ⓐ 35 cubic centimeters

Ⓑ 140 cubic centimeters

Ⓒ 175 cubic centimeters

Ⓓ 245 cubic centimeters

**5** The diagram below shows the measurements of a mold used to make sandcastles. Which expressions can be used to find the volume of the mold, in cubic inches?

2 in.

3 in.

5 in.

6 in.

7 in.

Ⓐ (5 × 2 × 3) + (5 × 5 × 3)

Ⓑ (5 × 2 × 3) + (7 × 5 × 3)

Ⓒ (5 × 2 × 6) + (5 × 5 × 3)

Ⓓ (5 × 2 × 6) + (7 × 5 × 3)

Ⓔ (5 × 2 × 3) + (7 × 5 × 6)

**6** The diagram shows the dimensions of two identical rectangular prisms joined together. What is the combined volume, in cubic meters, of the two prisms?

10 m

5 m

11 m

**7** A cardboard box has a volume of 60 cubic feet. Give three different sets of measurements that could be the dimensions of the box.

............ feet × ............ feet × ............ feet

............ feet × ............ feet × ............ feet

............ feet × ............ feet × ............ feet

**8** Rami designed a small pond for a restaurant. The diagram below shows the measurements of the pond. How many cubic feet of water are needed to fill the pond? Show your work.

4 ft

12 ft

18 ft

6 ft

2 ft

............ cubic feet

**9** MATH JOURNAL

Describe a real-world object that can be modeled by a rectangular prism and give its dimensions. Use a formula to find the volume of the object.

☑ **SELF CHECK** Go back to the Unit 1 Opener and see what you can check off.

# Multiply Multi-Digit Numbers

## Dear Family,

## This week your child is learning to multiply multi-digit numbers.

One way to find 124 × 25 is to set up the problem vertically to find partial products that can be added to find the total product.

First, multiply each digit in 124 by the 5 ones in 25.

```
    124
  ×   5
     20
    100
  + 500
    620
```

Then multiply each digit in 124 by the 2 tens in 25.

```
     124
  ×   20
      80
     400
  + 2,000
   2,480
```

partial product

Lastly, add the partial products to find the product: 124 × 25 = **620** + **2,480** = **3,100**.

Partial products are the basis of the standard algorithm for multiplying multi-digit numbers. An algorithm is a set of routine steps used to solve problems.

Your child is learning how to record the steps of the standard algorithm in a condensed format, with regrouping shown above the problem.

Notice how the partial products appear as steps in the standard algorithm.

```
     124
  ×   25
      20
     100
     500
      80
     400
  + 2,000
   3,100
```

```
     1 2
     124
  ×   25
     620
  + 2,480
   3,100
```

Another way your child is learning to multiply is with an area model, which gives a visual representation of the multiplication.

Invite your child to share what he or she knows about multiplying multi-digit numbers by doing the following activity together.

# ACTIVITY MULTIPLY MULTI-DIGIT NUMBERS

**Do this activity with your child to multiply multi-digit numbers.**

*Materials* magazine or newspaper

Work with your child to find a real-life example of using multiplication that involves the number of words in a magazine or newspaper article.

Sometimes a reporter has to write a story with a certain number of words, for example, 500 words. Multiplication is a good way to find the number of words in a story.

- Have your child choose an article from a magazine or newspaper.

- Ask your child to count the number of words in one paragraph and record the number on a sheet of paper.

- Then count the number of paragraphs in the article.

- Ask your child the following questions.

1. Suppose each paragraph has the same number of words. How could you find how many words are in the article? How many words are in the article?

2. If each paragraph has a different number of words, is the answer to the previous question an exact answer or an estimate for the total number of words in the article?

**Answers:**

1. Multiply the number of words in a paragraph by the number of paragraphs.
2. It is an estimate because the number of words in each paragraph varies.

## EXPLORING MARS

Have you ever thought about exploring Mars? Even if you haven't, other people certainly have. Mars was first explored by telescope in the 1700s. Early astronomers observed ice caps, dust clouds, and dark streaks. They wondered if there could be life on Mars.

In modern times, the United States, the former Soviet Union, and other countries have sent spacecraft to gather more information about the "red planet." The first missions to Mars flew near the planet. In November 1964, the U.S. National Aeronautics and Space Administration (NASA) launched Mariner 4. This spacecraft flew past Mars in July 1965 and took the first close-up photographs. The pictures were blurry, but they helped scientists learn what Mars looked like.

Then new technology allowed the United States to get even closer. In 1975, the United States launched Viking 1 and Viking 2. Viking 1 landed on the surface of Mars on July 19, 1976. Viking 2 followed on September 3, 1976. ...

NASA also built space rovers that could ... is a solar-powered vehicle that is operated fro... NASA spacecraft have carried rovers to Mars. landed the first Mars rover, Sojourner, in 1997 photographs back to Earth and collected soil s...

Two more rovers were launched in 2003. ... rovers Spirit and Opportunity discovered evide... lost contact with Spirit in 2010. But, as of April collecting data.

Finally, on November 26, 2011, NASA laun... named Curiosity. Since landing in 2012, this Ma... planet has ever been able to support life. Curios... rocks and soil.

Over the past 50 years, scientists have learn... For example, they have a better understanding ... its atmosphere. With future missions, they hope ... red planet.

The Viking 2 spacecraft took this photograph of the Martian surface in 1976. Mars is red because its surface is known as rust.

# Explore Multiplying Multi-Digit Numbers

You know how to multiply a two-digit number by a two-digit number. Now you will multiply greater multi-digit numbers. Use what you know to try to solve the problem below.

## Learning Target

- Fluently multiply multi-digit whole numbers using the standard algorithm.

SMP 1, 2, 3, 4, 5, 6, 8

**A mall has a rectangular outdoor space that is 127 feet by 46 feet. There is a grassy section with a width of 40 feet and a cement sidewalk with a width of 6 feet. What is the area of the outdoor space in square feet?**

## TRY IT

### Math Toolkit

- base-ten blocks
- base-ten grid paper
- grid paper
- index cards
- multiplication models

## DISCUSS IT

**Ask your partner:** Can you explain that again?

**Tell your partner:** The strategy I used to find the answer was . . .

# CONNECT IT

### 1 LOOK BACK

The area of the outdoor space is $127 \times 46$. How can you find this product?

### 2 LOOK AHEAD

When you multiply with multi-digit numbers, you need to pay special attention to place value. To help, you can use patterns in the number of 0s in the factors of a product and the number of 0s in the product.

a. Look at the partial products used to find the product of 512 and 24. Compare the number of zeros in each partial product to the number of zeros in its factors. Look at both red and blue zeros. Describe any patterns you see.

$$
\begin{array}{r}
512 \\
\times \quad 24 \\
\hline
8 \longrightarrow 4 \times 2 \\
40 \longrightarrow 4 \times 10 \\
2{,}000 \longrightarrow 4 \times 500 \\
40 \longrightarrow 20 \times 2 \\
200 \longrightarrow 20 \times 10 \\
+ \ 10{,}000 \longrightarrow 20 \times 500 \\
\hline
12{,}288
\end{array}
$$

b. Explain why the partial product $4 \times 500$ has three 0s, not just two 0s.

### 3 REFLECT

Why is it important to pay attention to place value when multiplying multi-digit numbers?

# Prepare for Multiplying Multi-Digit Numbers

1 Think about what you know about multiplying multi-digit whole numbers. Fill in each box. Use words, numbers, and pictures. Show as many ideas as you can.

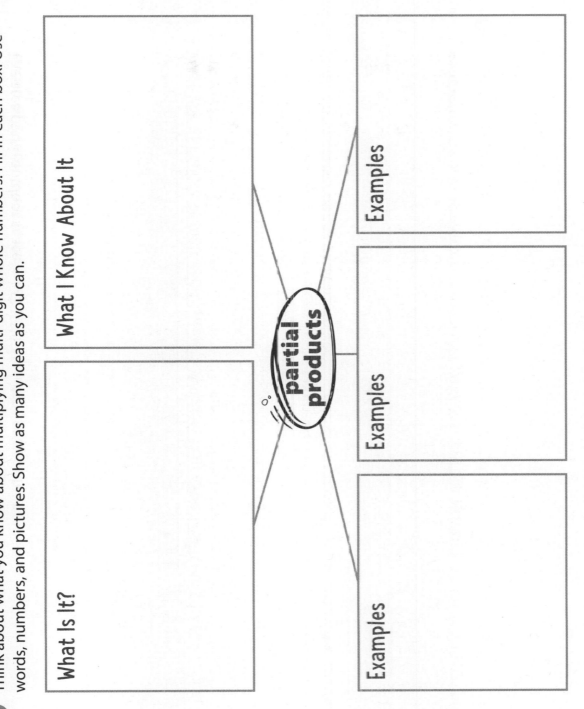

What Is It?

What I Know About It

partial products

Examples

Examples

Examples

Examples

2 Zula multiplied 761 by 5 using partial products. Is she correct? Explain.

```
   761
 ×   5
 -----
     5
    30
+ 3,500
 -----
 3,535
```

**3** Solve the problem. Show your work.

A city has a rectangular park that is 143 feet by 32 feet. There is a grassy field with a width of 30 feet. Next to the field there is a flower bed with a width of 2 feet. What is the area of the park in square feet?

100 ft

40 ft   3 ft

30 ft        3,000 square feet        ?        ?

?                    ?        ?

2 ft        ?

143 ft

32 ft

**4** Check your answer. Show your work.

**Solution** .................................................................

# Develop Multiplying Multi-Digit Numbers

Read and try to solve the problem below.

**There are 128 pens in a full box. How many pens are in 35 full boxes?**

## TRY IT

**Math Toolkit**
- base-ten blocks
- base-ten grid paper
- grid paper
- index cards
- multiplication models

## DISCUSS IT

**Ask your partner:** Why did you choose that strategy?

**Tell your partner:** I knew . . . so I . . . .

Explore different ways to understand multiplying multi-digit whole numbers.

← **There are 128 pens in a full box. How many pens are in 35 full boxes?**

## MODEL IT
**Use an area model to show partial products.**

To find the product 128 × 35, sketch a rectangle with dimensions 128 by 35.

**128** is **100 + 20 + 8.**

**35** is **30 + 5.**

|  | 100 | + | 20 | + | 8 |
|---|---|---|---|---|---|
| 30 | 30 × 100 = 3,000 | | 30 × 20 = 600 | | 30 × 8 = 240 |
| + | | | | | |
| 5 | 5 × 100 = 500 | | 5 × 20 = 100 | | 5 × 8 = 40 |

First row: 3,000 + 600 + 240 = 3,840

Second row: 500 + 100 + 40 = 640

## MODEL IT
**Use the distributive property to find partial products and add them.**

128 × 35 = 128 × (30 + 5)

128 × (30 + 5) = (128 × 30) + (128 × 5)

```
     128              128
   ×  30            ×   5
     240  →  30 × 8       40  →  5 × 8
     600  →  30 × 20     100  →  5 × 20
 + 3,000  →  30 × 100  + 500  →  5 × 100
   3,840                 640
```

## CONNECT IT

**Now you will use the problem from the previous page to help you understand how to multiply multi-digit whole numbers.**

1 Why is the area model divided into six sections?

2 How do the three partial products in each multiplication equation in the second **Model It** relate to the three sections in each row of the area model?

3 Use the partial products 3,840 and 640 to find the product 128 × 35. How many pens are in 35 full boxes?

4 Would the product change if 30 and 5 on the left side of the area model were changed to 20, 10, and 5? Explain.

5 List two different ways you could break up the factors in 239 × 64 to find the product. Explain why the two ways would have the same product.

6 **REFLECT**

Look back at your **Try It**, strategies by classmates, and **Model Its**. Which models or strategies do you like best for multiplying multi-digit whole numbers? Explain.

## APPLY IT

**Use what you just learned to solve these problems.**

**7** Find the product 120 × 25 × 40. Does it matter what order you multiply the numbers? Explain.

**8** Find the volume of the rectangular prism. How is this problem similar to problem 7?

25 cm

40 cm

120 cm

**9** A library bookshelf holds 156 books. There are 15 bookshelves in a certain section of the library. How many books can the library place on these bookshelves? Show your work.

**Solution**

...................................................................

# Practice Multiplying Multi-Digit Whole Numbers

**Study the Example showing how to multiply a three-digit number by a two-digit number using the distributive property. Then solve problems 1–3.**

## EXAMPLE

Find 132 × 26.

Use the distributive property.

$$132 \times \mathbf{26} = 132 \times (\mathbf{20} + \mathbf{6})$$
$$= (132 \times \mathbf{20}) + (132 \times \mathbf{6})$$

Find the partial products.

```
    132                      132
  × 20                     ×  6
     40   (20 × 2)           12   (6 × 2)
    600   (20 × 30)         180   (6 × 30)
+ 2,000   (20 × 100)      + 600   (6 × 100)
  2,640                     792
```

Write the sum of the partial products.     2,640 + 792 = 3,432

So, 132 × 26 = 3,432.

**1** Complete the steps to find 253 × 34.

$$253 \times 34 = 253 \times (30 + 4) = (\text{.........} \times 30) + (\text{.........} \times 4)$$

```
    253                    253
  × 30                   ×  4
     90   (30 × 3)
          (30 × ........)       ........
+ (........ × ........)    + ........
   ........                 ........
```

253 × 34 = 7,590 + 1,012 = ........

**2** You can also use an area model to find the product of 253 × 34.

**a.** Write the missing partial products in the area model.

| | 30 | + | 4 |
|---|---|---|---|
| 200 | 200 × 30 = ............ | | 200 × 4 = ............ |
| + | | | |
| 50 | 50 × 30 = ............ | | 50 × 4 = ............ |
| + | | | |
| 3 | 3 × 30 = ............ | | 3 × 4 = ............ |

**b.** Write the partial products to complete the equations below.

First column: ............ + ............ + ............ = ............

Second column: ............ + ............ + ............ = ............

**c.** 253 × 34 = ............

**3** What is the volume of a box that has length of 24 cm, a width of 11 cm, and a height of 15 cm? Show your work.

**Solution** ....................................................................

**4** Nate's mother drives 225 miles for work each month. How many miles does she drive for work in 1 year? (There are 12 months in one year.) Show your work.

**Solution** ....................................................................

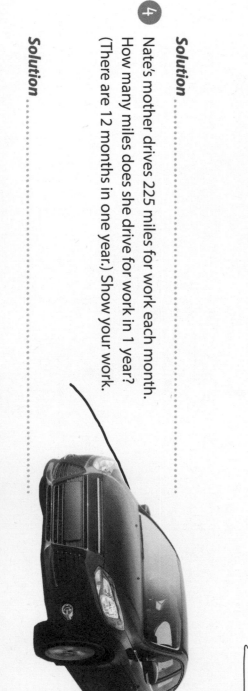

# Develop Multiplying with the Standard Algorithm

Read and try to solve the problem below.

▶ **Find the product 1,429 × 42.**

## TRY IT

**Math Toolkit**
- base-ten blocks
- base-ten grid paper
- grid paper
- index cards
- multiplication models

## DISCUSS IT

**Ask your partner:** Do you agree with me? Why or why not?

**Tell your partner:** I agree with you about.... because....

Explore different ways to understand how to find a product using the standard algorithm for multiplying multi-digit whole numbers.

## Find the product 1,429 × 42.

### MODEL IT
**You can use partial products.**

You can record each partial product in a separate row.

```
      1,429
    ×    42
─────────────
        18
        40
       800 ┐
     2,000 ┘ 2,858
       360
       800 ┐
    16,000 │
 +  40,000 ┘ 57,160
```

Now you can add the partial products to find the product.

### MODEL IT
**You can use the standard algorithm.**

An algorithm is a set of routine steps used to solve problems. With the standard algorithm for multiplication, you multiply by place value, regrouping and adding as you go. You record all the partial sums for each place value in a single row.

**Step 1:** Multiply by **ones.** Regroup as needed. Record the partial product in one row.

```
      1
    1,429
  ×    42
─────────
    2,858 ◁ partial product
```

**Step 2:** Multiply by **tens.** Regroup as needed. Record the partial product in a second row.

```
    1 1 3
      1
    1,429
  ×    42
─────────
    2,858
 + 57,160 ◁ partial product
```

Now you can add the partial products to find the product.

## CONNECT IT

**Now you will use the problem from the previous page to help you understand how to connect partial products to the standard algorithm for multiplication.**

1. Where do you see multiplying by ones and by tens in the first **Model It?**

2. Look at the second **Model It.** How do the partial products 18, 40, 800, and 2,000 relate to the first step of the standard algorithm model?

3. Look at the second **Model It.** How do the partial products 360, 800, 16,000, and 40,000 relate to the second step of the standard algorithm model?

4. Complete the multiplication in each **Model It** by adding the partial products.

   What is 1,429 × 42? ........................................

5. Compare the partial products model and the standard algorithm model.

6. **REFLECT**

   Look back at your **Try It,** strategies by classmates, and **Model Its.** Which models or strategies do you like best for understanding the standard algorithm for multiplying two multi-digit numbers? Explain.

   ........................................................................

   ........................................................................

   ........................................................................

## APPLY IT

**Use what you just learned to solve these problems.**

**7** The base of a storage bin has an area of 504 square inches. Its height is 18 inches. What is the volume of the storage bin? Estimate to check for reasonableness. Show your work.

*Solution*

**8** A school supply store has boxes of markers with 25 markers in each box. There are 1,075 boxes of markers in stock. How many markers does the store have in stock? Show your work.

*Solution*

**9** What is the product 257 × 34? Use the standard algorithm. Show your work.

*Solution*

# Practice Multiplying with the Standard Algorithm

**Study the Example showing how to multiply multi-digit whole numbers using the standard algorithm. Then solve problems 1–5.**

## EXAMPLE

Find the product 6,078 × 32 using the standard algorithm.

Find the first partial product (**2** × 6,078).

$2 \times 8 = 16$ (regroup **1** ten)
$2 \times 70 = 140 + $**10**$ = 150$ (regroup **1** hundred)
$2 \times 0 = 0 + $**100**$ = 100$
$2 \times 6,000 = 12,000$
$12,000 + 100 + 50 + 6 = 12,156$

$$
\begin{array}{r}
\overset{2\ 2}{\underset{1\ 1}{6{,}078}} \\
\times\ \ \mathbf{32} \\
\hline
12{,}156 \quad \longleftarrow \text{partial product} \\
+\ 182{,}340 \quad \longleftarrow \text{partial product} \\
\hline
194{,}496 \quad \longleftarrow \text{product}
\end{array}
$$

Find the second partial product (**30** × 6,078).

$30 \times 8 = 240$ (regroup **2** hundreds)
$30 \times 70 = 2,100 + $**200**$ = 2,300$ (regroup **2** thousands)
$30 \times 0 = 0 + $**2,000**$ = 2,000$
$30 \times 6,000 = 180,000$
$180,000 + 2,000 + 300 + 40 = 182,340$

Add the partial products to find the product: $182{,}340 + 12{,}156 = 194{,}496$.

1 Which expression shows the numbers that are multiplied to find the partial product 12,060?

$$
\begin{array}{r}
\overset{2}{1{,}206} \\
\times\ \ \ 14 \\
\hline
4{,}824 \\
+\ 12{,}060 \\
\hline
16{,}884
\end{array}
$$

Ⓐ 4 × 1,206

Ⓑ 14 × 1,206

Ⓒ 10 × 1,206

Ⓓ 100 × 126

2 Find the product of 512 and 46 using the standard algorithm. Estimate to check for reasonableness. Show your work.

### Solution

.......................................................................................................................

3 When using the standard algorithm to find the product 5,917 × 29, the first step is multiplying 9 ones by 7 ones. Explain why you regroup before the next step.

$$
\begin{array}{r}
^{6}\;\;\\
5{,}91\overset{6}{7} \\
\times \quad 29 \\
\hline
3
\end{array}
$$

.......................................................................................................................

4 What is the value of the regrouped "1" above the multiplication problem?

$$
\begin{array}{r}
^{2}\;\;^{2}\;\; \\
^{1}\;\;\;\; \\
7{,}504 \\
\times \quad\quad 52 \\
\hline
15{,}008 \\
+\;375{,}200 \\
\hline
390{,}208
\end{array}
$$

Ⓐ 1

Ⓑ 100

Ⓒ 1,000

Ⓓ 10,000

5 The base of a garden box has an area of 27,405 square centimeters. Its height is 18 centimeters. What is the volume of the garden box? Use the standard algorithm. Show your work.

### Solution

.......................................................................................................................

# Refine Multiplying Multi-Digit Numbers

**Complete the Example below. Then solve problems 1–9.**

## EXAMPLE

**Find the product 3,606 × 24.**

Look at how you could show your work with the standard algorithm.

```
    1   1
    2   2
    3,606
 ×     24
   14,424
 + 72,120
   86,544
```

*Solution* ....................................................

Why does the product of 3,606 and 2 tens have a 0 in the ones place?

**PAIR/SHARE**
How are the regrouped ones and hundreds used to find the partial products?

## APPLY IT

**1** A certain washing machine uses 29 gallons of water for each load of laundry washed. How many gallons of water would the washing machine use for 156 loads of laundry? Show your work.

What is the role of place value when multiplying two numbers?

**PAIR/SHARE**
Show and explain how to solve this problem using a different method.

*Solution* ....................................................

**2** A container at a construction site is shaped like a rectangular prism. The container is 49 feet long, 45 feet wide, and 25 feet high. What is the volume of the container? Use estimation to check the reasonableness of your answer. Show your work.

How could I estimate the answer to this problem?

**Solution** ....................................................

**PAIR/SHARE**
Is your answer close to your estimate?

**3** Raquel can type 63 words every minute. Rick can type 73 words every minute. How many more words can Rick type than Raquel in 135 minutes?

Ⓐ 1,350

Ⓑ 4,599

Ⓒ 8,505

Ⓓ 9,855

Jared chose Ⓑ as the correct answer. How did he get that answer?

How can I use the difference in the number of words typed by Rick and Raquel every minute to solve this problem?

**PAIR/SHARE**
Does Jared's answer make sense?

4 Mrs. Cady constructs a cube with 216 magnetic blocks. Students in her two classes will each make an identical cube. There are 28 students in one class and 25 students in the other class. How many magnetic blocks does she need for all her students?

Ⓐ 2,160

Ⓑ 5,460

Ⓒ 6,048

Ⓓ 11,448

5 What are the values of the regrouped amounts in the multiplication below?

$$\begin{array}{r} \overset{3}{\phantom{0}}\overset{2}{\phantom{0}}\overset{3}{\phantom{0}} \\ 1,435 \\ \times \quad 17 \\ \hline 10,045 \\ + 14,350 \\ \hline 24,395 \end{array}$$

Ⓐ 3, 2, and 3

Ⓑ 300, 20, and 3

Ⓒ 3,000, 200, and 30

Ⓓ 10,000, 300, and 21

6 Which expressions are equivalent to $179 \times 44$?

Ⓐ $179 \times (4 + 4)$

Ⓑ $(179 \times 40) + (179 \times 4)$

Ⓒ $(100 \times 4) + (70 \times 4) + (9 \times 4)$

Ⓓ $4,000 + 2,800 + 360 + 400 + 280 + 36$

Ⓔ $(100 \times 44) + (70 \times 44) + (9 \times 44)$

**7** Show two different ways to complete the multiplication problem.

```
    3 1 4
  ×    5 □
  ─────────
  1 □ □ 6
```

```
    3 1 4
  ×    5 □
  ─────────
  1 □ □ 6
```

**8** At the start of the day, there are 78 boxes of DVDs in a warehouse. Each box has 116 DVDs. Then 19 of the boxes are shipped. Now how many DVDs are left in the warehouse? Show your work.

.............. DVDs

**9** **MATH JOURNAL**

Write a multiplication word problem using a 3-digit number and a 2-digit number. Use the standard algorithm to solve the problem and explain any regrouping that is needed.

☑ **SELF CHECK** Go back to the Unit 1 Opener and see what you can check off.

# Divide Multi-Digit Numbers

## Dear Family,

**This week your child is learning to divide multi-digit whole numbers by a two-digit number.**

One way to solve a division problem such as 770 ÷ 14 is to set it up vertically.

First divide the hundreds in 770 by 14.
There are **50** groups of 14 in 700.

Then divide the tens in 770 by 14.
There are **5** groups of 14 in 70.

Add the partial quotients to find the quotient.
**50** + **5** = 55
So, 770 ÷ 14 = 55.

```
        55      quotient
         5
      50 )770   partial quotients
      -700
        70
       - 70
         0
```

Another way your child is learning to divide is with an area model, similar to the model used in multiplication.

The area model below shows 770 ÷ 14.

Because multiplication and division are **inverse operations**, or operations that undo each other, use the relationship between them to divide.

```
       770

      770
     -700
       70
```

```
       50        +          5         = 55

(14 × 50 = 700)      (14 × 5 = 70)
      770                   70
     -700                  -70
       70                    0
```

Both methods result in the same quotient, 55. Notice that 50 and 5 appear as partial quotients in each way of dividing.

Invite your child to share what he or she knows about dividing whole numbers by doing the following activity together.

# ACTIVITY DIVISION IN THE WORLD

**Do this activity with your child to divide multi-digit numbers.**

Work with your child to solve real-life problems involving division.

• Choose a favorite book with your child and look at the total number of pages in it. The book should have more than 100 pages. Pick a two-digit number of pages to read each day. Ask: *How many days would it take to read the entire book?*

• Use division to find the answer. For example, suppose the book has 286 pages and the number of pages to be read each day is 15. Divide 286 by 15 to find the number of days it will take to read the book.

• Work together to write and solve the division problem about the book. Encourage your child to use rounding and multiplication to help estimate the quotient first.

• Decide what to do if there is a remainder. Will you read the remaining number of pages on the next day, or will you read the remaining number of pages on the last day of reading?

• Repeat this activity at least 3 more times, either using the same situation or another.

# Explore Dividing Multi-Digit Numbers

## Learning Target

- Find whole-number quotients of whole numbers with up to four-digit dividends and two-digit divisors, using strategies based on place value, the properties of operations, and/or the relationship between multiplication and division. Illustrate and explain the calculation by using equations, rectangular arrays, and/ or area models.

SMP 1, 2, 3, 4, 5, 6, 7, 8

You already know how to divide a multi-digit number by a one-digit divisor. Now you will learn how to divide with two-digit divisors. Use what you know to try to solve the problem below.

**There are 92 fifth graders at Wilson Middle School and 23 students in each fifth-grade classroom. How many fifth-grade classrooms are there at Wilson Middle School?**

## Math Toolkit

- base-ten blocks
- base-ten grid paper
- grid paper
- index cards
- multiplication models

## TRY IT

## DISCUSS IT

**Ask your partner:** Can you explain that again?

**Tell your partner:** I started by . . .

# CONNECT IT

## 1 LOOK BACK

What is 92 ÷ 23? Explain your reasoning.

## 2 LOOK AHEAD

Multiplication and division are called **inverse operations** because they "undo" each other. For example, the related multiplication and division equations 5 × 7 = 35 and 35 ÷ 5 = 7 show that if you multiply a number by 5 and then divide the result by 5, you end up with the number you started with.

Think about the related equations 264 ÷ 12 = **?** and 12 × **?** = 264.

You can use the related multiplication equation to help you divide.

**a.** Start by listing products of the divisor, 12, and **multiples of 10.**

| Multiple of 10 | 10 | 20 | 30 | 40 | 50 |
|---|---|---|---|---|---|
| **12 × Multiple of 10** | 120 | | | | |

**b.** Which row of the table above is related to the dividend in 264 ÷ 12? How could you use the table above to estimate the quotient 264 ÷ 12?

**c.** Start with 12 × **a multiple of 10** to divide 264 by 12 using an area model. Complete the missing numbers.

| 12 | 264 |
|---|---|

? 

12

| 264 | 240 | |
|---|---|---|

20 + ............. = .............

## 3 REFLECT

How can you use the inverse relationship between multiplication and division to check your answer to 264 ÷ 12?

# Prepare for Dividing Multi-Digit Numbers

1 Think about what you know about division. Fill in each box. Use words, numbers, and pictures. Show as many ideas as you can.

| Word | In My Own Words | Example |
|------|-----------------|---------|
| dividend | | |
| divisor | | |
| quotient | | |

2 Label the *dividend, divisor,* and *quotient* of the division equation shown by the area model. Then write the division equation.

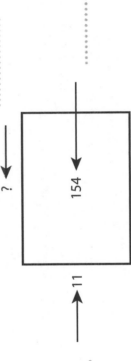

3  Solve the problem. Show your work.

**There are 95 students on a field trip and 19 students on each bus. How many buses of students are there on the field trip?**

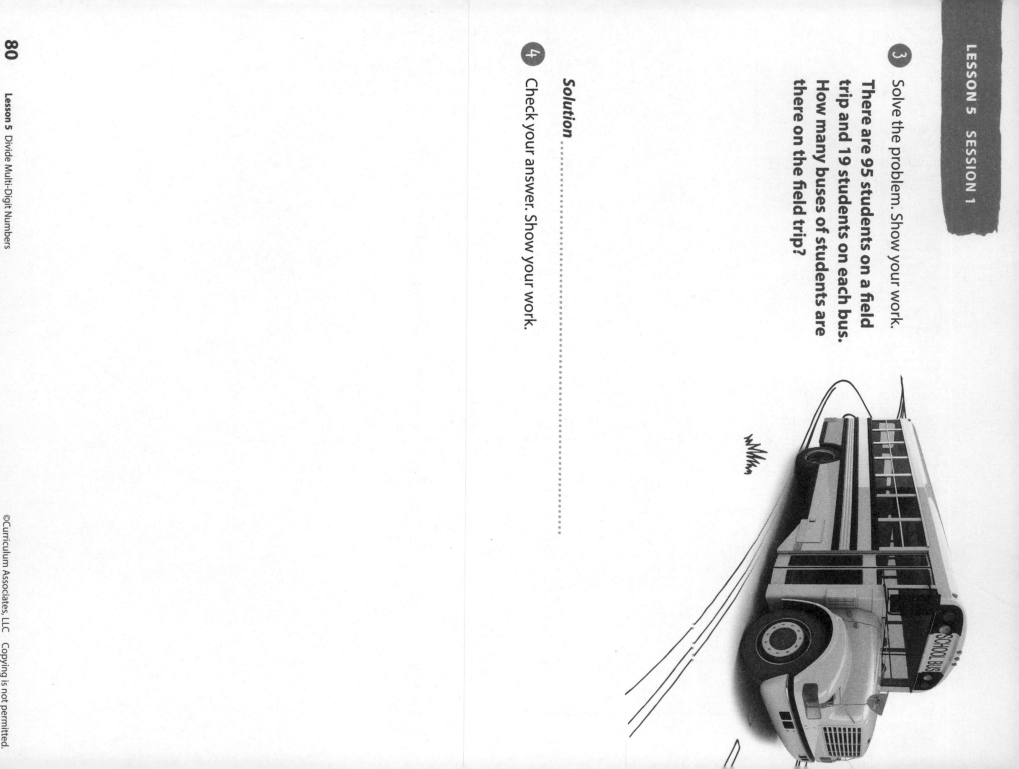

4  Check your answer. Show your work.

*Solution* ....................................................

# Develop Estimating Quotients

Read and try to solve the problem below.

**A toy company packs 504 robots into 21 boxes. Each box has the same number of robots. Show how you could estimate the number of robots in each box.**

## TRY IT

### Math Toolkit
- base-ten blocks
- base-ten grid paper
- grid paper
- index cards
- multiplication models ▲

**DISCUSS IT**

**Ask your partner:** How did you get started?

**Tell your partner:** I knew . . . so I . . . .

Explore different ways to understand how to estimate quotients when dividing whole numbers.

> **A toy company packs 504 robots into 21 boxes. Each box has the same number of robots. Show how you could estimate the number of robots in each box.**

## MODEL IT
**You can use compatible numbers to estimate a quotient.**

*Compatible numbers are numbers close to the values of the actual dividend and divisor that allow you to multiply or divide using basic facts.*

500 and 20 are compatible numbers that are close to 504 and 21.

You can use them to estimate by thinking $500 \div 20 = ?$ means $20 \times ? = 500$.

| 20 | 500 |
|----|-----|

with ? above.

## MODEL IT
**You can use the inverse relationship between multiplication and division to estimate a quotient.**

$504 \div 21 = ?$ or $21 \times ? = 504$

Multiply 21 by multiples of 10. Make a table.

| Number of Robots per Box | Total Number of Robots |
|------|------|
| 10 | $21 \times 10 = 210$ |
| 20 | $21 \times 20 = 420$ |
| 30 | $21 \times 30 = 630$ |

## CONNECT IT

**Now you will use the problem from the previous page to help you understand how to estimate quotients with two-digit divisors.**

1. Look at the first **Model It**. Why are 500 and 20 good choices to use for compatible numbers? Why not round to the nearest thousand and use 1,000 and 20 as compatible numbers?

2. How can you find the quotient 500 ÷ 20? What estimate does this give for the number of robots in each box?

3. Look at the second **Model It**. Why do you multiply 21 by multiples of 10? Could you multiply 21 by multiples of 5 instead of by multiples of 10?

4. Look at the table. Between which two numbers is a good estimate for the number of robots packed in each box? Explain how you know.

5. What do the methods of estimating quotients in the **Model Its** have in common?

## REFLECT

Look back at your **Try It**, strategies by classmates, and **Model Its**. Which models or strategies do you like best for estimating quotients? Explain.

................................................................

................................................................

................................................................

## APPLY IT

**Use what you just learned to solve these problems.**

**7** Estimate the quotient 342 ÷ 38. Show your work.

*Solution* ........................................................................................

**8** Estimate the quotient 1,103 ÷ 23. Show your work.

*Solution* ........................................................................................

**9** Camille arranged 238 chairs into equal rows of 14 chairs. Which of the following is the best estimate for the number of rows she made?

Ⓐ a number close to 30

Ⓑ about 20

Ⓒ a number between 30 and 40

Ⓓ about 10

# Practice Estimating Quotients

**Study the Example showing how to estimate a quotient with a two-digit divisor. Then solve problems 1–4.**

## EXAMPLE

Estimate the quotient $1,474 \div 22$.

Choose compatible numbers that are close to the actual dividend and divisor and easy to multiply and divide using a basic fact.

1,400 and 20 are close to 1,474 and 22.

$2 \times 7 = 14$, $2 \times 70 = 140$, and $20 \times 70 = 1,400$.

$20 \times 70 = 1,400$ is the same as $1,400 \div 20 = 70$.

So, 70 is the estimated quotient for $1,474 \div 22$.

?

| 20 | 1,400 |

1 Look at the Example. You can also multiply 22 by **multiples of 10** to estimate the quotient $1,474 \div 22$.

**a.** Complete the table.

| Multiple of 10 | 10 | 20 | 30 | 40 | 50 | 60 | 70 | 80 |
|---|---|---|---|---|---|---|---|---|
| 22 × Multiple of 10 | 220 | 440 | 660 | 880 | 1,100 | | | |

**b.** Complete the statement below with two numbers from the table.

The dividend 1,474 is between ............... and ............... .

**c.** What is a good estimate for the quotient $1,474 \div 22$?

2  Which of the following is the best estimate for the quotient 713 ÷ 31?

Ⓐ  a number between 10 and 20

Ⓑ  a number close to 40

Ⓒ  a number close to 35

Ⓓ  a number between 20 and 30

3  A beverage company makes 1,008 bottles of water and packs them into boxes. The company packs 24 bottles in each box. Estimate how many boxes of water bottles the company packs. Show your work.

*Solution* .....................................................................................................................................

4  Marcus builds 2,744 kites for a 14-day summer kite festival.
He plans to give away about the same number of kites each day.
He gives away 492 kites the first two days. Did Marcus stick to his plan?
Use estimation to explain. Show your work.

*Solution* .....................................................................................................................................

# Develop Using Estimation and Area Models to Divide

Read and try to solve the problem below.

A factory produces 768 buses and puts them in 24 buildings. Each building has the same number of buses. How many buses are in each building? Estimate and then solve.

## TRY IT

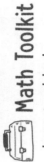 **Math Toolkit**
- base-ten blocks
- base-ten grid paper
- grid paper
- index cards
- multiplication models

**DISCUSS IT**

**Ask your partner:** Do you agree with me? Why or why not?

**Tell your partner:** I agree with you about.... because....

Explore different ways to understand how to divide multi-digit numbers using estimation and area models.

> A factory produces 768 buses and puts them in 24 buildings. Each building has the same number of buses. How many buses are in each building? Estimate and then solve.

## MODEL IT

**You can use the relationship between multiplication and division to estimate the quotient.**

$768 \div 24 = $ **?** and $24 \times $ **?** $= 768$

Multiply 24 by **multiples of 10** to estimate the quotient. You can organize your work in a table.

| Number of Buses in Each Building | Total Number of Buses |
|---|---|
| 10 | 240 |
| 20 | 480 |
| 30 | 720 |
| 40 | 960 |

The quotient is between **30** and **40**.

## MODEL IT

**You can use an area model to solve a division problem with a two-digit divisor.**

The area model breaks up the problem $768 \div 24$ into parts.

| 24 | 768 |
|---|---|

$\longrightarrow$ 24

| | 30 | + | 2 |
|---|---|---|---|
| 24 | $(24 \times 30 = 720)$ | | $(24 \times 2 = 48)$ |

$$\begin{array}{r} 768 \\ -720 \\ \hline 48 \end{array} \qquad \begin{array}{r} 48 \\ -48 \\ \hline 0 \end{array}$$

# CONNECT IT

**Now you will use the problem from the previous page to help you understand how to divide multi-digit numbers using estimation and area models.**

**1** In the first **Model It**, how do you know the quotient is between 30 and 40?

**2** Look at the second **Model It**. The number 24 is multiplied by which estimate, 30 or 40, to start the area model work? Why do you think the other number was not used?

**3** What does the expression 30 + 2 above the area model represent?

**4** Explain why the numbers 30 and 2 can be called *partial quotients*.

**5** Explain how an area model can help you break apart a division problem to make it easier to solve.

**6** REFLECT

Look back at your **Try It**, strategies by classmates, and **Model Its**. Which models or strategies do you like best for dividing whole numbers? Explain.

.............................................................................................

.............................................................................................

## APPLY IT

**Use what you just learned to solve these problems.**

**7** In the problem on the previous page, 768 ÷ 24, you first estimated and then used an area model to find the quotient. Describe how can you use multiplication to check that you have the correct quotient.

Show your work for the check.

**8** Dante has 468 cards in his sports card collection. He buys cards in packages of 12. Complete the table and give an estimate for how many packages of cards Dante has bought.

| Number of packages | 10 | 20 | 30 | 40 | 50 |
|---|---|---|---|---|---|
| Number of sports cards | | | | | |

**Solution**

**9** Refer to the situation in problem 8. Complete the area model to find the quotient 468 ÷ 12. How many packages of sports cards did Dante buy?

$$(12 \times 30 = \text{.........})$$
468
−
108

$$(12 \times \text{.........} = 108)$$
108
−
0

................. + ................. = .................

**Solution**

# Practice Using Estimation and Area Models to Divide

**Study the Example showing how to estimate and use area models to divide. Then solve problems 1–4.**

## EXAMPLE

A donut shop sells donuts in boxes that each contain 13 donuts. If 728 donuts were sold in one day, how many boxes of donuts were sold?

Multiply 13 by multiples of 10 to help you estimate the quotient. Make a table.

| Number of boxes | 10 | 20 | 30 | 40 | 50 | 60 |
|---|---|---|---|---|---|---|
| Number of donuts | 130 | 260 | 390 | 520 | 650 | 780 |

Because 728 is between 650 and 780, the quotient is between 50 and 60.

Use 50 as the first partial quotient in an area model for 728 ÷ 13.

```
          50              +        6            = 56
     ┌──────────────┐    ┌──────────────┐
     │ (13 × 50 = 650)│   │ (13 × 6 = 78)  │
13   │                │   │                │
     │      728       │   │      78        │
     │     − 650      │   │     − 78       │
     │   ─────────    │   │   ─────────    │
     │       78       │   │        0       │
     └──────────────┘    └──────────────┘
```

```
     ┌──────────────┐
13   │              │ ──→ 13
     │     728      │
     │              │
     └──────────────┘
       ?
```

728 ÷ 13 = 56.  The donut shop sold 56 boxes of donuts.

1 The area model in the Example shows how to break apart the problem 728 ÷ 13 into parts.

**a.** What was 13 multiplied by first? ......................................

**b.** What equation in the area model shows this? ......................................

**c.** Why do you subtract 650 from 728? ......................................

**d.** What is the second partial quotient? ......................................

**2** The table can be used to estimate the quotient 851 ÷ 37. Which of the following is the best estimate of the quotient?

| Multiple of 10 | 10 | 20 | 30 | 40 |
|---|---|---|---|---|
| 37 × Multiple of 10 | 370 | 740 | 1,110 | 1,480 |

Ⓐ a number between 30 and 40

Ⓑ about 15

Ⓒ a number between 20 and 30

Ⓓ about 42

**3** Complete the steps for using an area model to find the quotient 851 ÷ 37.

851 ÷ 37 is the same as ............... × ? = ............... .

37 | 851

?

851 ÷ 37 = ...............

(37 × 20 = ...............)
851
−
_____

+

(37 × 3 = ...............)
− 111
_____

= ...............

37

**4** Which of the following equations cannot be used to represent the area model?

Ⓐ 42 × ? = 4,326

Ⓑ 42 + 4,326 = ?

Ⓒ 4,326 ÷ ? = 42

Ⓓ 4,326 ÷ 42 = ?

42 | 4,326

?

# Develop Using Area Models and Partial Quotients to Divide

Read and try to solve the problem below.

> **A grocery store only sells eggs by the dozen. There are 12 eggs in 1 dozen. If there are 1,248 eggs in stock, how many dozens of eggs are there?**

## TRY IT

 **Math Toolkit**
- base-ten blocks
- base-ten grid paper
- grid paper
- index cards
- multiplication models

## DISCUSS IT

**Ask your partner:** Why did you choose that strategy?

**Tell your partner:** I knew . . . so I . . . .

Explore different ways to record partial products when dividing multi-digit whole numbers.

> **A grocery store only sells eggs by the dozen. There are 12 eggs in 1 dozen. If there are 1,248 eggs in stock, how many dozens of eggs are there?**

## MODEL IT

**You can use an area model to record partial quotients.**

Estimate to determine the first partial quotient for $1,248 \div 12$.

1,200 and 12 are compatible numbers close to the dividend and divisor.

$12 \times 100 = 1,200$, so you can use 100 as the first partial quotient in an area model.

|  | 100 | + | 4 |
|---|---|---|---|
| 12 | $(12 \times 100 = 1,200)$ | | $(12 \times 4 = 48)$ |
| | $\begin{array}{r} 1,248 \\ -1,200 \\ \hline 48 \end{array}$ | | $\begin{array}{r} 48 \\ -48 \\ \hline 0 \end{array}$ |

```
12 [        1,248        ]
              |
              v
             12
```

```
?
```

## MODEL IT

**You can use a vertical format to record partial quotients.**

```
        4    ←── second partial quotient
      100    ←── first partial quotient
12)1,248     ←── How many groups of 12 in 1,200?
  −1,200
      48     ←── How many groups of 12 in 48?
     −48
       0
```

## CONNECT IT

**Now you will use the problem from the previous page to help you understand how to record partial products in a vertical format.**

1 Look at the second **Model It**. How many hundreds are in the dividend? ............

How many groups of 12 are in 1,200? ............

Notice that this first partial quotient is written above the bar.

2 After writing the first partial quotient above the bar, you write the number 1,200 under the dividend. What equation in the area model shows where the number

1,200 comes from?

3 Why is 1,200 subtracted from 1,248?

4 How does the area model relate to finding the second partial quotient?

5 Explain how to use the partial quotients to find 1,248 ÷ 12. How many dozens of eggs does the grocery store have?

6 Describe how to divide using partial quotients.

7 **REFLECT**

Look back at your **Try It**, strategies by classmates, and **Model Its**. Which models or strategies do you like best for recording partial products? Explain.

# APPLY IT

**Use what you just learned to solve these problems.**

**8** What is the quotient 583 ÷ 11? Show your work.

*Solution* ..........................................................................................................

**9** Carlos has 1,134 pennies. He puts an equal number of pennies into 27 different glass jars. How many pennies are in each jar? Show your work.

*Solution* ..........................................................................................................

**10** Which of the following pairs of numbers are partial quotients for 594 ÷ 18?

Ⓐ 50 and 5

Ⓑ 40 and 4

Ⓒ 30 and 3

Ⓓ 20 and 15

# Practice Using Area Models and Partial Quotients to Divide

**Study the Example showing division with a two-digit divisor using partial quotients. Then solve problems 1–5.**

## EXAMPLE

Find 1,386 ÷ 22.

To divide using partial quotients, estimate a number that can be multiplied by the divisor to get a product less than or equal to the dividend. Then subtract the product from the dividend. Repeat these steps until you reach a number less than the divisor.

$$
\begin{array}{r}
\mathbf{3} \\
\mathbf{60} \\
22\overline{)1,386} \\
-1,320 \\
\hline
66 \\
-66 \\
\hline
0
\end{array}
$$

→ How many groups of 20 in 1,200? **60**
→ 22 × 60
→ How many groups of 22 in 66? **3**
→ 22 × 3

1,386 ÷ 22 = 63

1  Look at the Example. For the first step, Jaime thought: *How many groups of 20 in 1,400? There are 70.* If he continues with the division steps, when will he know that his first estimate of 70 is too high?

2  Multiply 14 by multiples of 10 to complete the table.

| Multiple of 10 | 10 | 20 | 30 | 40 | 50 | 60 |
|---|---|---|---|---|---|---|
| 14 × Multiple of 10 | 140 | 280 | | | 700 | |

Write a multiple of 10 from the table to show the greatest partial quotient to start with for each division problem below.

a.  ☐
    14)462

b.  ☐
    14)350

c.  ☐
    14)798

d.  ☐
    14)588

**3** Use an area model to find the quotient 504 ÷ 14.

14

```
┌──────────────┐          ┌─────────────────────────────┐
│              │          │ (14 × 30 = ·········· )  +  (14 × 6 = ·········· ) =  ········
│      ?       │   → 14   │                                            │
│ ·········    │          │        504                    ··········    ··········
│              │          │    −  ··········              −   84        ··········
│              │          │       ··········             ──────────     ──────────
└──────────────┘          │       ──────────                            ··········  │
                          └─────────────────────────────┘
```

504 ÷ 14 = ··········

**4** A rectangular box has a volume of 504 cubic inches. The width of the box is 7 inches, and the height of the box is 6 inches. Use the partial quotient method shown in the example to find the length of the box. Show your work.

**Solution** ......................................................................

**5** A hunger relief program ships boxes that hold 25 pounds of food. How many boxes will 2,350 pounds of food fill? Show your work.

DONATION BOX

**Solution** ......................................................................

# Refine Dividing Multi-Digit Numbers

**Complete the Example below. Then solve problems 1–8.**

## EXAMPLE

**Each package has 21 pieces of chalk. How many packages can be made with 1,701 pieces of chalk?**

Look at how you could show your work using partial quotients.

```
        1
       80
   21)1,701
   - 1,680  ←— 21 × 80
        21
    -   21  ←— 21 × 1
         0
```

Why is 80 a good number to use as a first partial quotient?

**Solution**

PAIR/SHARE
How can you use multiplication to check that the quotient is correct?

## APPLY IT

1 A water cooler holds 1,284 ounces of water. How many more 6-ounce glasses than 12-ounce glasses can be filled from a full cooler? Show your work.

You can first estimate how many glasses of each size can be filled.

PAIR/SHARE
Explain how you found your estimate.

**Solution**

**2** Each student needs 35 craft sticks for an art project. The art teacher has 7,140 craft sticks. The art teacher starts a division problem to determine how many students can get craft sticks from him. He was interrupted before he could complete the problem.

His partial work is shown below. Fill in the blanks to complete his work. Write your answers in the blanks.

```
      .......  ← quotient
      .......  ← partial quotient
      .......  ← partial quotient
35)7,140
  − 7,000
      140
  −   140
        0
```

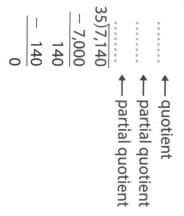

What numbers can I use to estimate the quotient?

**PAIR/SHARE**
Explain how to check the answer to a division problem.

**3** Harrison creates balloon animals for different events. He has 6,440 balloons. He wants to use the same number of balloons for each of 28 events. How many balloons can Harrison use at each event?

Ⓐ 23

Ⓑ 203

Ⓒ 230

Ⓓ 2,030

Tina chose Ⓐ as the correct answer. How did she get that answer?

What will be the greatest place in the quotient?

**PAIR/SHARE**
Does Tina's answer make sense?

4 Mr. Kovich writes the problem $32 \times \triangle = 1,696$ on the board. Write a division equation that can be used to find the value of the triangle. Then find the value of the triangle. Show your work.

*Solution* ........................................................................................

5 Vera makes a table to help her find the area of the base of a rectangular box with a volume of 672 cubic inches and a height of 16 inches.

| 10 | 20 | 30 | 40 | 50 | 60 |
|-----|-----|-----|-----|-----|-----|
| 160 | 320 | 480 | 640 | 800 | 960 |

Choose the correct option to fill in each blank below.

The area of the base is between _____

Ⓐ 20    Ⓑ 30    Ⓒ 40    Ⓓ 60

and _____ square inches.

Ⓐ 30    Ⓑ 40    Ⓒ 50    Ⓓ 60

6 Lisa's camera has 2,048 megabytes of memory for storing pictures. She has already used half this amount. A high-quality picture uses 16 megabytes of memory. How many high-quality pictures can Lisa store with the remaining memory?

**7** Mr. Sullivan is organizing teams for the middle school's annual field day. There are 8 classes at the school and 21 students in each class.

**Part A** What is the total number of students at the school?

............ students

**Part B** Mr. Sullivan wants to have 12 students on each team. How many teams will there be?

............ teams

**Part C** How many fewer students will be on each team if he decides to have 24 teams? Explain your answer using diagrams, pictures, mathematical expressions, and/or words.

............ fewer students

**8** **MATH JOURNAL**

Explain what you would do first to divide 1,260 by 28. Tell why it would be your first step.

**SELF CHECK** Go back to the Unit 1 Opener and see what you can check off.

# Self Reflection

## In this unit you learned to . . .

| Skill | Lesson |
|---|---|
| Find the volume of a solid figure by counting unit cubes. | 1, 2 |
| Find volume by using a formula. | 3 |
| Break apart a solid figure into rectangular prisms to find its volume. | 3 |
| Multiply multi-digit whole numbers, for example: $410 \times 16 = 6,560$. | 4 |
| Divide a multi-digit whole number by a two-digit number, for example: $2,812 \div 38 = 74$. | 5 |

## Think about what you have learned.

**Use words, numbers, and drawings.**

**1** Two important things I learned are . . .

**2** I would like to learn more about how to . . .

**3** I still need to work on . . .

# Solve Multiplication and Division Problems

**SMP 1** Make sense of problems and persevere in solving them.

## Study an Example Problem and Solution

**Read this problem about multiplying multi-digit numbers. Then look at Beau's solution to this problem.**

### Worm Farm

Beau likes to recycle. He is going to have a fair to show recycling ideas. One of his ideas is to start a worm farm where he can recycle kitchen scraps from people in his school. He gathers this information.

#### My Data

- 2,000 worms can eat about 1 pound of food in 1 day.
- I can collect 195 to 215 pounds of scraps each week.

Show how to find the number of worms Beau needs for this amount of scraps.

- Tell how many and what size packages Beau can buy to get this many worms.

- Give the total cost of buying the worms.

**RED WORM PRICES**

| | |
|---|---|
| 1,050 worms | $25 |
| 2,950 worms | $72 |

**Read the sample solution on the next page. Then look at the checklist below. Find and mark parts of the solution that match the checklist.**

☑ PROBLEM-SOLVING CHECKLIST

- ☐ Tell what is known.
- ☐ Tell what the problem is asking.
- ☐ Show all your work.
- ☐ Show that the solution works.

a. **Circle** something that is known.

b. **Underline** something that you need to find.

c. **Draw a box around** what you do to solve the problem.

d. **Put a checkmark** next to the part that shows the solution works.

# BEAU'S SOLUTION

Hi, I'm Beau. Here's how I solved this problem.

- **I already know** that the amount of kitchen scraps is between 195 to 215 pounds. I'll use 200 pounds to make an estimate.

- **I need to find** about how many worms are needed to recycle 200 pounds of scraps each week.

- **I also know** that 2,000 worms eat 1 pound of scraps in 1 day. That means 2,000 worms eat 7 pounds of scraps in 7 days, or 1 week.

- **I can estimate** that 200 is about 30 times 7. So, I need about 30 times 2,000 worms for 200 pounds of scraps.

  $2,000 \times 30 = 60,000$

  I need about 60,000 worms.

Since the amount of kitchen scraps is not exact, I can estimate.

- **Now I can look for ways to get about 60,000 worms.** 2,950 is about 3,000 and $3,000 \times 20 = 60,000$.

- **I'll start with 20 packages of 2,950 worms.**

$$\begin{array}{r} 2,950 \\ \times\ \ 20 \\ \hline 59,000 \end{array}$$

Here I used the exact number of worms in the package.

- **Then, I'll subtract to find how many more worms I need.**

  $60,000 - 59,000 = 1,000$

  I need 1 package of 1,050 worms to get 1,000 more worms.

  The total number of worms is $59,000 + 1,250$, or 60,250.

  This is close to 60,000.

There may be more than 200 pounds of scraps some months. It's okay to have more worms.

- **Multiply to find the total cost.**

$\$25 \times 1\ =\ \ \ \ \$25$
$\$72 \times 20\ =\ \underline{+\ \$1,440}$
$\$1,465$

# Try Another Approach

There are many ways to solve problems. Think about how you might solve the Worm Farm problem in a different way.

## Worm Farm

Beau likes to recycle. He is going to have a fair to show recycling ideas. One of his ideas is to start a worm farm where he can recycle kitchen scraps from people in his school. He gathers this information.

### My Data

- 2,000 worms can eat about 1 pound of food in 1 day.

- I can collect 195 to 215 pounds of scraps each week.

Show how to find the number of worms Beau needs for this amount of scraps.

- Tell how many and what size packages Beau can buy to get this many worms.

- Give the total cost of buying the worms.

RED WORM PRICES

1,050 worms . . . . . . . . . . . . . . . $25
2,950 worms . . . . . . . . . . . . . . . $72

## PLAN IT

**Answer these questions to help you start thinking about a plan.**

**A.** Will you use a lesser or greater amount of kitchen scraps to estimate the number of worms? Explain why.

**b.** How could you solve the problem by finding the amount of kitchen scraps there will be in 1 day?

# SOLVE IT

**Find a different solution for the Worm Farm problem. Show all your work on a separate sheet of paper.**

You may want to use the Problem-Solving Tips to get started.

⌐ PROBLEM-SOLVING TIPS

● **Models** You might want to use . . .

- partial products.
- area models.

● **Word Bank**

| estimate | total | about |
|---|---|---|
| multiply | subtract | close to |

● **Sentence Starters**

- To make an estimate, I can use _____

- There are _____ worms in _____

☑ PROBLEM-SOLVING CHECKLIST

Make sure that you . . .

- ☐ tell what you know.
- ☐ tell what you need to do.
- ☐ show all your work.
- ☐ show that the solution works.

# REFLECT

**Use Mathematical Practices** As you work through the problem, discuss these questions with a partner.

- **Be Precise** Why is it appropriate to use an estimate with this problem?

- **Make an Argument** Why did you choose the numbers you did for your estimates?

# Discuss Models and Strategies

**Read the problem. Write a solution on a separate sheet of paper.**
**Remember, there can be lots of ways to solve a problem!**

## Goldfish Pool

Sweet T is helping design a small goldfish pool to be built for the fair.

The pool will be shaped like the diagram shown. The two ends are the same depth. The middle section is deeper.

### Pool Plans

- The total length is between 10 and 16 feet.
- The width is between 6 and 8 feet.
- The deepest part of the pool is no more than 4 feet deep.
- The total volume is 300 cubic feet or less.

What should the dimensions of the pool be? What will the volume of the pool be?

# PLAN IT AND SOLVE IT

**Find a solution to the Goldfish Pool problem.**

- Find the dimensions of the pool.

- Verify that the lengths, widths, and depths you chose meet all of the requirements in the pool plans.

- Find the volume of the pool.

## PROBLEM-SOLVING TIPS

● **Questions**

- How deep will the shallow section be? The deep section?

- How can you divide the solid figure into rectangular prisms?

● **Word Bank**

| | | |
|---|---|---|
| rectangular prism | length | volume |
| solid figure | width | cubic feet |

✓ **PROBLEM-SOLVING CHECKLIST**

Make sure that you . . .

☐ tell what you know.

☐ tell what you need to do.

☐ show all your work.

☐ show that the solution works.

## REFLECT

**Use Mathematical Practices** As you work through the problem, discuss these questions with a partner.

- **Use a Model** How can the model help you find appropriate dimensions?

- **Be Precise** What measurement units will you use when you work out the solution? Explain.

# Persevere On Your Own

**Read the problems. Write a solution on a separate sheet of paper.**

## Robot Area

Beau plans to bring his recycled robots to the fair. Guests can buy tickets to play with the robots. Beau needs to rope off an area of the fairgrounds to keep his robots in sight. Read his notes.

### Robot Area Notes

- The area should be rectangular.
- It needs to be more than 100 feet long and less than 100 feet wide.
- The area needs to be between 7,500 and 10,000 square feet.

What dimensions should the robot area have?

## SOLVE IT

**Describe an area that Beau can rope off for his robots.**

- Give the length and width of the area.
- Give the area in square feet.
- Explain why your measurements work.

## REFLECT

**Use Mathematical Practices** After you complete the task, choose one of these questions to discuss with a partner.

- **Use Structure** How did you use place-value ideas to think about numbers that would work?

- **Persevere** Did you try different combinations of numbers before deciding on a final answer? Explain.

## Layered Dessert

Sweet T is making his favorite layered dessert to bring to the fair. Read his notes.

### Layered Dessert Notes

• Cut brownies, marshmallows, and cake into cubes.

• First layer is brownie cubes.

• Second layer is marshmallow cubes.

• Third layer is cake cubes.

• Use more than 3 layers.

• You choose the thickness of each layer.

• Repeat layers as many times as you want to fill the bowl.

9 in.

12 in.

8 in.

The picture above shows the container Sweet T uses to make the dessert. How many layers should Sweet T use? How thick should each layer be?

## SOLVE IT

**Help Sweet T make a plan.**

• Tell which item is in each layer.

• Give the length, width, and volume of each layer.

• Find the total volume of the completed dessert.

## REFLECT

**Use Mathematical Practices** After you complete the task, choose one of these questions to discuss with a partner.

• **Use a Model** What models did you use and how did they help you find a solution?

• **Persevere** What did you do to get through any difficult parts of the solution?

**1** Which unit of measure can be used to express the volume of the prism?

Ⓐ unit squares

Ⓑ square units

Ⓒ cubic units

Ⓓ units

**2** Kyle has an aquarium in the shape of a rectangular prism. The aquarium is 24 inches long and has a height of 10 inches. The volume of the aquarium is 2,880 cubic inches. What is the width, in inches, of the aquarium? Record your answer on the grid. Then fill in the bubbles.

**3** The solid figure below is made up of two rectangular prisms.

20 in.

7 in.

30 in.

4 in.

11 in.

[not drawn to scale]

What is the volume of the solid figure? Explain how you found your answer.

**4** Which expressions are equivalent to 562 × 42? Choose all the correct answers.

Ⓐ 562 × (40 + 2)

Ⓑ (562 × 4) + (562 × 2)

Ⓒ (500 × 42) + (60 × 42) + (2 × 42)

Ⓓ (500 × 40) + (500 × 2) + (60 × 40) + (60 × 2) + (2 × 40) + (2 × 2)

Ⓔ (5 × 40) + (5 × 2) + (6 × 40) + (6 × 2) + (2 × 40) + (2 × 2)

**5** A theater has 3,150 seats. All of the seats are arranged in 42 equal rows. How many seats are in each row? Show your work.

*Solution*..............................................................................................

**6** Decide if each expression can be used to find the volume, in cubic centimeters, of the rectangular prism below.
*Choose Yes or No for each expression.*

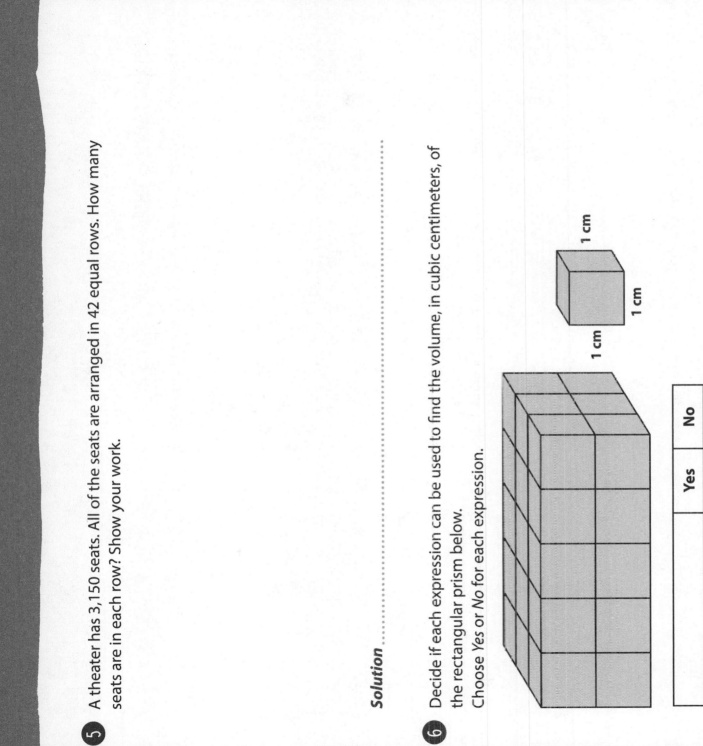

1 cm
1 cm
1 cm

|  | Yes | No |
|---|---|---|
| 15 × 2 | Ⓐ | Ⓑ |
| (5 + 3) × 2 | Ⓒ | Ⓓ |
| 15 + 15 | Ⓔ | Ⓕ |
| 5 + 3 + 2 | Ⓖ | Ⓗ |
| 15 + 2 | Ⓘ | Ⓙ |

## Performance Task

**Answer the questions and show all your work on separate paper.**

Jack wants to make a terrarium for the science fair. The first steps of the instructions are shown below.

### How to make a terrarium:

**Step 1** Fill the bottom of the tank with a 2-inch layer of small rocks.

**Step 2** Add a layer of soil. There should be 5 inches from the top of the soil to the top of the tank.

Jack already has one cubic foot (1,728 cubic inches) of soil and 576 cubic inches of small rocks to use. Now he has to choose a tank. Which of the tanks below can he use without having to buy more rocks and soil?

**Tank A:** 18 inches long, 15 inches wide, 15 inches tall

**Tank B:** 24 inches long, 12 inches wide, 12 inches tall

**Tank C:** 21 inches long, 18 inches wide, 10 inches tall

### REFLECT

**Use Mathematical Practices** After you complete the task, choose one of the following questions to answer.

- **Use Reasoning** Why is the height of the soil layer different for each tank?

- **Model** How does drawing and labeling a diagram help you solve the problem?

# Vocabulary

**Draw or write to show examples for each term.**

**base (of a prism)** one side of a prism, usually considered to be the side shown as the bottom of the prism. In the volume formula $V = b \times h$, $b$ represents the area of the base of the prism.

**My Example**

**cubic unit** the volume of a unit cube.

**My Example**

**distributive property** when one of the factors of a product is written as a sum, multiplying each addend by the other factor before adding does not change the product. For example, $3 \times 12 = (3 \times 10) + (3 \times 2)$.

**My Example**

**inverse operations** operations that undo each other. For example, addition and subtraction are inverse operations, and multiplication and division are inverse operations.

**My Example**

**plane figure** a two-dimensional figure, such as a circle, triangle, or rectangle.

**My Example**

**solid figure** a three-dimensional figure.

**My Example**

**unit cube**   a cube with side lengths of 1 unit. A unit cube is said to have one cubic unit of volume, and can be used to measure the volume of a solid figure.

**My Example**

**unit square**   a square with side lengths of 1 unit. A unit square is said to have one square unit of area, and can be used to measure the area of a plane figure.

**My Example**

**volume**   the amount of space inside a solid figure. Volume is measured in cubic units such as cubic inches.

**My Example**

**My Word:** _____

**My Example**

**My Word:** _____

**My Example**

**My Word:** _____

**My Example**

## ☑ SELF CHECK

**Before starting this unit, check off the skills you know below. As you complete each lesson, see how many more skills you can check off!**

| I can . . . | Before | After |
|---|---|---|
| Recognize that a digit in one place represents 10 times as much as it represents in the place to its right and $\frac{1}{10}$ of what it represents in the place to its left. | ☐ | ☐ |
| Use patterns to understand multiplying and dividing whole numbers and decimals by powers of 10. | ☐ | ☐ |
| Read and write decimals in different forms, for example: $80.63 = (8 \times 10) + \left(6 \times \frac{1}{10}\right) + \left(3 \times \frac{1}{100}\right)$. | ☐ | ☐ |
| Compare decimals, for example: $3.47 > 3.096$. | ☐ | ☐ |
| Round decimals, for example: 6.274 rounded to the nearest tenth is 6.3. | ☐ | ☐ |
| Add and subtract decimals, for example: $20.08 + 5.15 = 25.23$. | ☐ | ☐ |
| Add and subtract fractions with unlike denominators. | ☐ | ☐ |
| Estimate sums and differences of fractions or decimals. | ☐ | ☐ |

# Build Your Vocabulary

## Math Vocabulary

**Complete the blank boxes with the corresponding vocabulary terms.**

4　5　6　5　.　8　2

Write the number above in expanded form.

Write the word form of the number.

## Academic Vocabulary

**Place a check next to the academic words you know. Then use the words to complete the sentences.**

☐ analyze　☐ defend　☐ format　☐ relationship

1　You can .................................................................

2　Sometimes you have to ................................................ a problem by examining its parts carefully.

3　In STEM classes, you can examine the ................................ your answer to show why it is correct.

4　It's important to use the correct ................................ between science, technology, engineering, and math.

.................................. when setting up a division problem.

# Understand Decimal Place Value

## Dear Family,

### This week your child is exploring place value in whole numbers and decimal numbers.

We use a number system called **base ten**. It is based on a pattern of tens. The models below show the pattern of tens in whole numbers and decimals. Each place value is 10 times the place value to its right.

| Thousands | Hundreds | Tens | Ones |
|---|---|---|---|
| 1 thousand is **10 times 1 hundred** | 1 hundred is **10 times 1 ten** | 1 ten is **10 times 1 one** | 1 one |

| 1,000 | 100 | 10 | 1 |

| Ones | Tenths | Hundredths |
|---|---|---|
| 1 whole is **10 times 1 tenth** | 1 tenth is **10 times 1 hundredth** | 1 hundredth |
| 1 | 0.1 | 0.01 |

Understanding place value helps your child think about and use different ways to add, subtract, multiply, and divide numbers.

Invite your child to share what he or she knows about place value by doing the following activity together.

## ACTIVITY DECIMAL PLACE VALUE

**Do this activity with your child to explore decimal place-value relationships.**

Work together with your child to shade models to understand decimal place value.

• Have your child shade in the decimal grids below to represent the number that is shown below each grid.

• Ask your child to explain how each pair of grids shows that the number on the right is 10 times the number on the left grid.

Each grid represents 1 whole.

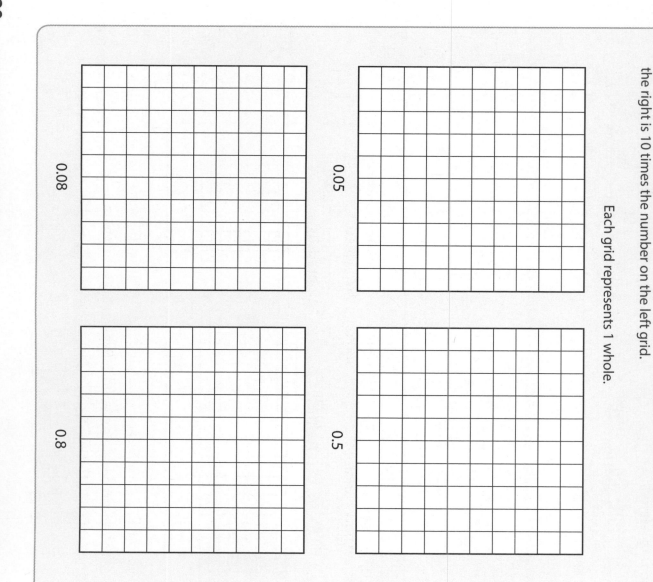

0.05

0.5

0.08

0.8

# Explore Decimal Place Value

## How is place value related to the number 10?

### Learning Target

- Recognize that in a multi-digit number, a digit in one place represents 10 times as much as it represents in the place to its right and $\frac{1}{10}$ of what it represents in the place to its left.

SMP 1, 2, 3, 4, 5, 6, 7, 8

## MODEL IT

**Complete the problems below.**

1 Look at the place-value models for whole numbers. Write the missing factor in each equation to show how ones, tens, hundreds, and thousands are related.

| Thousands | Hundreds | Tens | Ones |
|---|---|---|---|
| $1,000 = \underline{\hspace{1cm}} \times 100$ | $100 = \underline{\hspace{1cm}} \times 10$ | $10 = \underline{\hspace{1cm}} \times 1$ | $1$ |

2 Write the missing numbers in the equations below these place-value models for decimals to show how hundredths, tenths, and ones are related.

| Ones | Tenths | Hundredths |
|---|---|---|
| $1.0 = \underline{\hspace{1cm}} \times 0.1$ | $0.1 = \underline{\hspace{1cm}} \times 0.01$ | $0.01$ |

3 Look at your equations in problems 1 and 2. Explain how the value of each place compares to the value of the place to its right.

## DISCUSS IT

- How are relationships between decimal place values like relationships between whole number place values?

- I think we call our number system **base ten** because . . .

## MODEL IT

**Complete the problems below.**

**4** Fill in the blanks in the diagram to show how the values of the numbers change from row to row in the table. Extend the pattern to fill in the top and bottom rows.

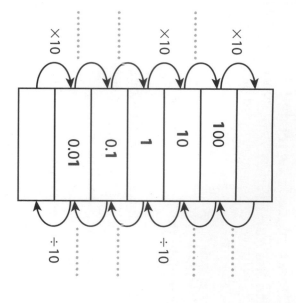

**5** What happens to the position and value of the digit **1** when you multiply by 10?

**6** What happens to the position and value of the digit **1** when you divide by 10?

**7** What do you think is the value of the digit 1 in the number you wrote in the last row of the table? Explain.

**8** Dividing a number by 10 is the same as finding $\frac{1}{10}$ of the number. Use the phrase "$\frac{1}{10}$ of" or the phrase "10 times" to complete each statement about 1 **thousandth**.

0.001 is .............. 0.01.

$\frac{1}{100}$ is .............. $\frac{1}{1,000}$.

**9** **REFLECT**

In which number does the digit 5 have a greater value, 0.05 or 0.005? How many times as great is the value? Explain how you know.

..........

..........

..........

### DISCUSS IT

• How are your descriptions of the patterns in the position and value of the digit **1** similar to your partner's? How are they different?

• I think you would show 0.001 on a decimal grid by shading $\frac{1}{10}$ of one small square because . . .

Name: _____

# Prepare for Place Value

1 Think about what you know about place value. Fill in each box.
Use words, numbers, and pictures. Show as many ideas as you can.

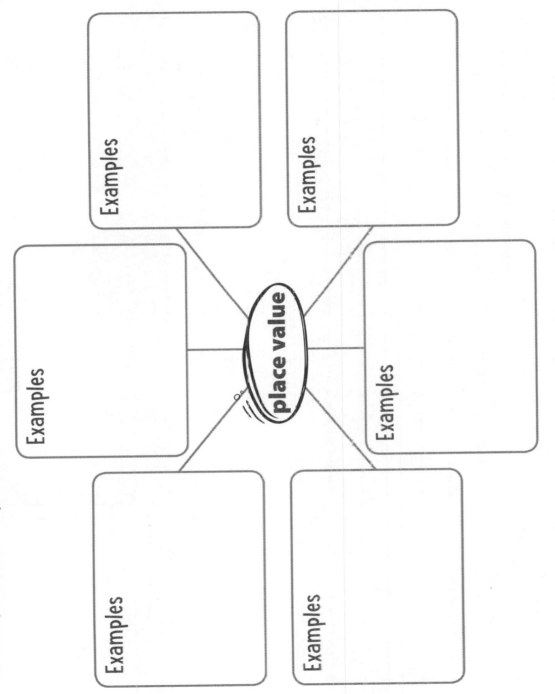

| Examples | Examples |
|---|---|

**place value**

| Examples | Examples |
|---|---|

| Examples | Examples |
|---|---|

2 Complete each statement with the phrase "$\frac{1}{10}$ of" or the
phrase "10 times."

$\frac{1}{10}$ is ............... $\frac{1}{100}$.

0.01 is ............... 0.1.

## Solve.

3  Write the missing number in each sentence below the base-ten models to show how ones, tens, hundreds, and thousands are related.

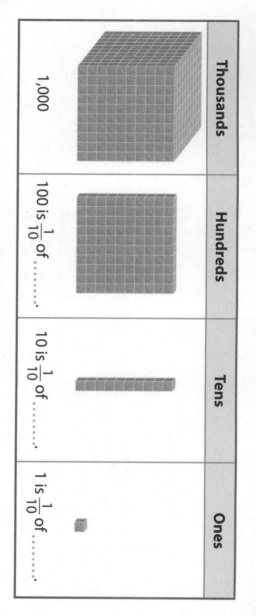

| Thousands | Hundreds | Tens | Ones |
|---|---|---|---|
| 1,000 | 100 is $\frac{1}{10}$ of ............ . | 10 is $\frac{1}{10}$ of ............ . | 1 is $\frac{1}{10}$ of ............ . |

4  Write the missing number in each sentence below the decimal grid models to show how hundredths, tenths, and ones are related.

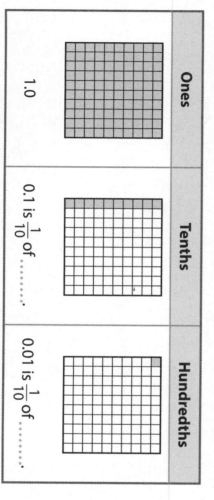

| Ones | Tenths | Hundredths |
|---|---|---|
| 1.0 | 0.1 is $\frac{1}{10}$ of ............ . | 0.01 is $\frac{1}{10}$ of ............ . |

5  Look at your sentences in problems 3 and 4. Explain how the value of each place compares to the value of the place to its left.

# Develop Understanding of Decimal Place Value

## MODEL IT: DECIMAL GRIDS

**Try these three problems.**

**1** Each decimal grid in models *A*, *B*, and *C* represents 1 whole. Shade each model to show the decimal number below the model.

*A*

3.0

*B*

0.3

*C*

0.03

**2** Complete four different equations that show relationships between the numbers shown in models *A*, *B*, and *C* above.

$\times$ 10 = ...............

$\times$ 10 = ...............

$\div$ 10 = ...............

$\div$ 10 = ...............

**3** Finding $\frac{1}{10}$ of a number is the same as multiplying the number by 0.1. Complete each sentence and then write the sentence as a multiplication equation.

**a.** 0.03 is $\frac{1}{10}$ of ...............

*Equation* ...............

**b.** ............... is $\frac{1}{10}$ of 3.0.

*Equation* ...............

## DISCUSS IT

- How did you and your partner figure out what numbers to use in the equations?

- I think the value of the 3 in 0.3 is greater than the value of the 3 in 0.03 because . . .

# MODEL IT: NUMBER LINES

**Use a number line to show how decimal place values are related.**

**4**  **a.** Fill in the missing labels for the red tick marks on the number lines below.

**b.** Place a point for the whole number 1 on the first number line, the decimal 0.1 on the second number line, and the decimal 0.01 on the last number line.

0                               1

0   0.1     0.3   0.4     0.7   0.9   1.0

0   0.20   0.30    0.50   0.60    0.80   0.90

**5**  How does the distance from 0 to 1 compare to the distance from 0 to 0.1? to the distance from 0 to 0.01?

## CONNECT IT

**Complete the problems below.**

**6**  How do decimal grids and number lines help you understand the relationship between adjacent place values in our number system?

## DISCUSS IT

• How did you and your partner decide where 0.01 is on the last number line?

• I think you can use a number line to show any decimal value because . . .

**7**  How many times as great is the value of 1.5 than the value of 0.15? Explain.

# Practice with Decimal Place Value

**Study how the Example shows place-value patterns. Then solve problems 1–8.**

## EXAMPLE

Show how the numbers 1, 0.1, and 0.01 are related.

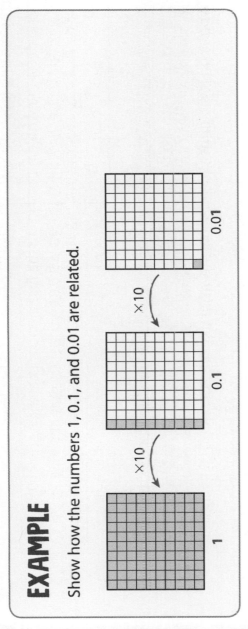

1          ×10 →        0.1          ×10 →        0.01

1 Use the ×10 pattern from the Example to complete each equation.

   1 = ............. × 10

   0.1 = ............. × 10

2 The pattern can also be described using division. Use the decimal grids in the Example to complete the equations.

   1.0 ÷ 10 = .............

   0.1 ÷ 10 = .............

3 Use the ÷ 10 pattern to fill in the blanks.

   400 ............. ............. 0.4 ............. .............

        ↰ ÷ 10

4 How are the decimals 0.009 and 0.09 related? Explain.

**5** Is the expression equivalent to 0.07?

| | Yes | No |
|---|---|---|
| 0.007 × 10 | Ⓐ | Ⓑ |
| 0.7 ÷ 10 | Ⓒ | Ⓓ |
| 0.07 × 10 | Ⓔ | Ⓕ |
| 0.007 ÷ 10 | Ⓖ | Ⓗ |

**6** **a.** Label the red tick marks on the number line below.

**b.** Place a point on the number line to show the value that is $\frac{1}{10}$ of 0.5.

0 ————————————————————————— 1.00

**c.** $\frac{1}{10}$ of 0.5 is ................ .

**d.** Write the sentence in part c as a multiplication equation.

**7** Ethan says that the value of 40.7 is 10 times the value of 4.07. Is he correct? Explain.

**8** Mya says the value of the 6 in 0.006 is $\frac{1}{10}$ of the value of the 6 in 0.6. Is she correct? Explain.

# Refine Ideas About Decimal Place Value

## APPLY IT

**Complete these problems on your own.**

**① CREATE**

Shade the models at the right to show how the value of 0.04 is related to the value of 0.4. Then write a division equation to represent the relationship.

*Equation* ........................................................

**② ANALYZE**

Kiran showed 0.08 with the model below.

0 ————————————————————————→ 1

What is wrong with Kiran's model? Describe how the length she shaded relates to the length that she should have shaded. How can Kiran change her model to show 0.08?

**③ COMPARE**

How does the value of the digit 8 in 1.8 compare to the value of the digit 8 in 486? Explain.

**PAIR/SHARE**
Discuss your solutions for these three problems with a partner.

## Use what you have learned to complete problem 4.

**4** An ant has a mass of 0.005 gram. A small bee has a mass of 0.05 gram. A grasshopper has a mass of 0.5 gram.

**Part A** Write each measurement in the place-value chart below.

| Object | Tens | Ones | . | Tenths | Hundredths | Thousandths |
|--------|------|------|---|--------|------------|-------------|
| ant | | | | | | |
| bee | | | | | | |
| grasshopper | | | | | | |

**Part B** Shade the models to compare the mass of the bee to the mass of the grasshopper. Then write a sentence to describe the relationship between the two masses.

Bee

Grasshopper

**Part C** Explain how many ants it would take to equal the mass of 1 grasshopper. Then write an equation using the measurements to show your answer.

**5** MATH JOURNAL

What is the number that has a value 10 times the value of 0.009? Explain.

# Understand Powers of 10

## Dear Family,

## This week your child is exploring powers of 10.

Your child is learning that numbers such as 10, 100, or 1,000 can be written as products of the number 10.

These numbers are called **powers of 10**. The **exponent** tells how many times to use 10 as a factor.

$10 = \mathbf{10} = 10^1$

$100 = \mathbf{10 \times 10} = 10^2$

$1,000 = \mathbf{10 \times 10 \times 10} = 10^3$

When you multiply a decimal by a power of 10, the digits in the product will be to the left of where they were in the factor and will have a new value.

Multiply by 10.

$0.03 \times 10 = 0.3$

The digit in the hundredths place is now in the tenths place.

Multiply by 100 (10 × 10).

$0.005 \times 100 = 0.5$

The digit in the thousandths place is now in the tenths place.

When you divide a decimal by a power of 10, the digits in the quotient will be to the right of where they were in the dividend and will have a new value.

Divide by 10.

$0.3 \div 10 = 0.03$

The digit in the tenths place is now in the hundredths place.

Divide by 100 (10 × 10).

$0.5 \div 100 = 0.005$

The digit in the tenths place is now in the thousandths place.

Invite your child to share what he or she knows about powers of 10 by doing the following activity together.

# ACTIVITY MULTIPLY AND DIVIDE BY POWERS OF 10

**Do this activity with your child to explore multiplying and dividing by a power of 10.**

Work together with your child to show how the value of the product or quotient changes when you multiply or divide a decimal number by a power of 10.

- Have your child write the number 12345 with large digits on a separate sheet of paper or use the number below. Have your child read the five-digit number aloud.

- Have your child place his or her finger between the 3 and 4. Your child's finger represents the decimal point. Have your child read the new number aloud.

- Ask your child to multiply the number from the previous step by 100 and show the product by moving his or her finger to show the placement of the decimal point. (Your child should move his or her finger two places to the right.) Ask your child to explain the relationship between the factor 100, the placement of the decimal point, and the value of each digit in the product.

- Ask your child to divide the number from the previous step by 10 and show the quotient by moving his or her finger to show the placement of the decimal point. (Your child should move his or her finger one place to the left.) Again, have your child read the new number aloud and then explain the relationship between the divisor 10 and the value of each digit in the quotient.

- Ask your child to show you another multiplication or division by a power of 10. Have your child explain how the power of 10 is related to the placement of the decimal point in the product or quotient.

1 2 3 4 5

# Explore Powers of 10

**What patterns can you find when you multiply or divide by 10, 100, or 1,000?**

## Learning Target

• Explain patterns in the number of zeros of the product when multiplying a number by powers of 10, and explain patterns in the placement of the decimal point when a decimal is multiplied or divided by a power of 10. Use whole-number exponents to denote powers of 10.

SMP 1, 2, 3, 4, 5, 6, 7

## MODEL IT

**Complete the problems below.**

1. Numbers like 10, 100, or 1,000 that can be written as a product of tens are called **powers of 10**. Complete the equations to multiply 3 by a power of 10.

```
      ×10   ×10   ×10   ×10
   3    30    300   3,000   30,000
            ×100
```

a. 3 × 10 × 10 = 3 × ..........

= ..........

b. 3 × 10 × 10 × 10 = 3 × ..........

= ..........

c. 3 × 10 × 10 × 10 × 10 = 3 × ..........

= ..........

2. Complete the equations to divide 30,000 by a power of 10.

```
      ÷10   ÷10   ÷10   ÷10
   3    30    300   3,000   30,000
            ÷100
            ÷100
```

30,000 ÷ 100 = ..........

30,000 ÷ 10,000 = ..........

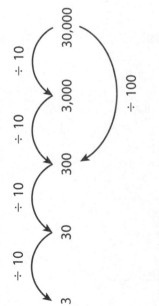

## DISCUSS IT

• How did you and your partner determine the product or quotient in the equations?

• Patterns help me understand how to multiply or divide by numbers like 10, 100, or 1,000 because . . .

## MODEL IT

**Complete the problems below.**

3. You can write a power of 10 using an **exponent**.

The exponent **4** means to use the **base 10** as a factor 4 times.

$$10^4 = 10 \times 10 \times 10 \times 10$$

Complete the table to show different ways to write the first three powers of 10.

| Standard Form | Product of Tens | Exponent Form |
|---|---|---|
| 10 | 10 | $10^1$ |
| 100 | | $10^2$ |
| | $10 \times 10 \times 10$ | |

**DISCUSS IT**

- What patterns do you notice in multiplying by powers of 10?

- Using exponent form helps me understand place-value relationships because . . .

4. Complete the table to show different ways to write 300, 3,000, and 30,000.

| Standard Form | Using a Power of 10 | Using Factors of 10 | Exponent Form |
|---|---|---|---|
| 300 | $3 \times \mathbf{100}$ | $3 \times \mathbf{10 \times 10}$ | $3 \times 10^2$ |
| 3,000 | $3 \times 1,000$ | $3 \times$ | $3 \times$ |
| 30,000 | $3 \times$ | $3 \times 10 \times 10 \times 10 \times 10$ | $3 \times$ |

5. **REFLECT**

How do you know how many zeros are in the product $5 \times 10^4$? What is the product?

# Prepare for Powers of 10

1 Think about what you know about powers of 10. Fill in each box.
Use words, numbers, and pictures. Show as many ideas as you can.

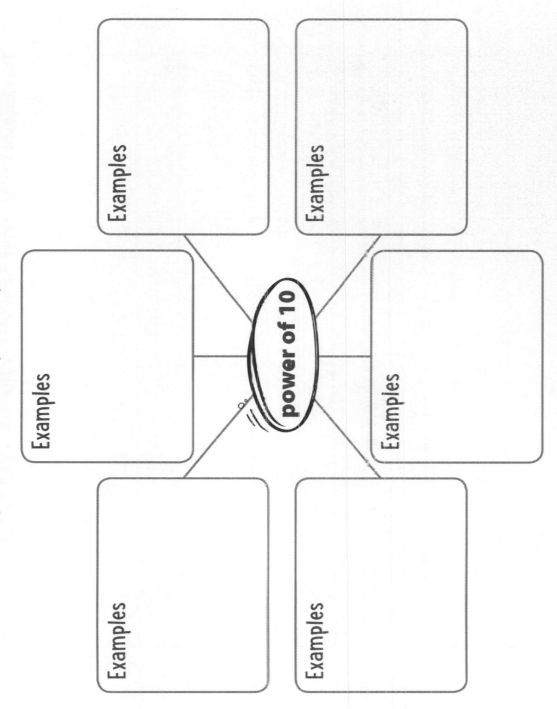

Examples

Examples

Examples

power of 10

Examples

Examples

Examples

2 Use the diagram to help you find each product.

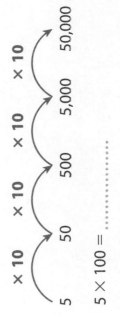

$\times 10$   $\times 10$   $\times 10$   $\times 10$

5    50    500    5,000    50,000

$5 \times 100 =$ ..................

$5 \times 10,000 =$ ..................

## Solve.

**3** Complete the table showing different ways to write powers of 10.

| Standard Form | Product of Tens | Exponent Form |
|---|---|---|
| 100 | $10 \times 10$ | $10^2$ |
| 1,000 | | $10^3$ |
| 10,000 | $10 \times 10 \times 10 \times 10$ | |

**4** Complete the table to show different ways to write 500, 5,000, and 50,000.

| Standard Form | Using a Power of 10 | Using Factors of 10 | Exponent Form |
|---|---|---|---|
| 500 | $5 \times \mathbf{100}$ | $5 \times \mathbf{10} \times \mathbf{10}$ | $5 \times 10^2$ |
| 5,000 | $5 \times 1,000$ | 5 | $5 \times$ |
| 50,000 | $5 \times$ | $5 \times 10 \times 10 \times 10 \times 10$ | $5 \times$ |

**5** Rewrite each division equation to show the power of 10 in exponent form. Use the first pair of equations as an example.

$5,000 \div 10 = 500 \longrightarrow 5,000 \div 10^1 = 500$

$5,000 \div 100 = 50 \longrightarrow 5,000 \div \text{.............} = 50$

$5,000 \div 1,000 = 5 \longrightarrow 5,000 \div \text{.............} = 5$

# Develop Understanding of Powers of 10

## MODEL IT: DECIMAL POINT PATTERNS

**Try these two problems.**

1. The diagrams below show patterns in the placement of the decimal point each time you multiply or divide a decimal by 10.

Complete the missing numbers in each diagram. The decimal point for each missing number is already placed for you.

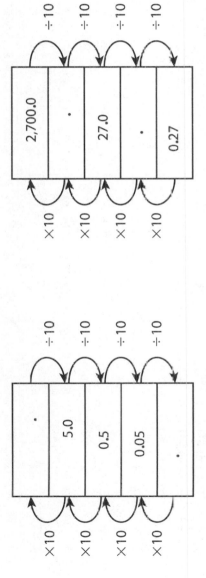

×10      ÷10
    .

×10      ÷10
    5.0

×10      ÷10
    0.5

×10      ÷10
    0.05
    .

×10      ÷10
    2,700.0

×10      ÷10
    .

×10      ÷10
    27.0

×10      ÷10
    .

×10      ÷10
    0.27

2. Use the decimal point pattern diagrams above to help you find each product or quotient.

$0.5 \times 100 =$ ............

$0.5 \times 10^2 =$ ............

$5 \div 100 =$ ............

$5 \div 10^2 =$ ............

$0.27 \times 1,000 =$ ............

$0.27 \times 10^3 =$ ............

$2,700 \div 1,000 =$ ............

$2,700 \div 10^3 =$ ............

## DISCUSS IT

• What happens to the value of a number when you multiply or divide by a power of 10? Why?

• I think patterns in the placement of the decimal point help you multiply by 1,000 because . . .

## MODEL IT: PLACE-VALUE CHARTS

Use place-value charts to show multiplying and dividing by powers of 10.

**3** Complete each row with the product shown to the right of that row.

| Ones | . | Tenths | Hundredths | Thousandths | | |
|------|---|--------|------------|-------------|---|---|
| 0 | . | 0 | 0 | 5 | | 0.005 × 10¹ |
| 0 | . | 0 | 0 | 5 | | 0.005 × 10² |
| | . | | | | | 0.005 × 10³ |

**4** Complete each row with the quotient shown to the right of that row.

| Ones | . | Tenths | Hundredths | Thousandths | | |
|------|---|--------|------------|-------------|---|---|
| 5 | . | 0 | 0 | 0 | | 5 ÷ 10¹ |
| 5 | . | 0 | 0 | 0 | | 5 ÷ 10² |
| 5 | . | 0 | 0 | 0 | | 5 ÷ 10³ |

**DISCUSS IT**

• How do the values of the digits and the placement of the decimal point change when you multiply or divide any decimal by a power of 10?

• I think place-value charts show the pattern of multiplying and dividing by powers of 10 because . . .

## CONNECT IT
**Complete the problems below.**

**5** Look at the first decimal point pattern diagram and the place-value charts. How do the position and the value of the digit 5 change when multiplying and dividing by 10?

**6** Show how to find the product 0.19 × 10³.

# Practice with Powers of 10

**Study how the Example shows multiplying a decimal number by a power of 10. Then solve problems 1–7.**

## EXAMPLE

Find $10^2 \times 0.004$.

Break $10^2$ into the product of tens.

$10^2 \times 0.004 = 10 \times \mathbf{10 \times 0.004}$
$\qquad\qquad\quad = 10 \times \mathbf{0.04}$
$\qquad\qquad\quad = 0.4$

The value of the digit 4 increases by moving one place to the left for each factor of 10.

$10^2 \times 0.004 = 0.4$

### Vocabulary

**power of 10** a number that can be written as a product of tens.

$10 = 10$
$100 = 10 \times 10$
$1,000 = 10 \times 10 \times 10$

**exponent** the number in a power that tells how many times to use the base as a factor.

$10^2 \longleftarrow$ exponent
$\uparrow$
base

$10^2 = 10 \times 10$, or 100

1  Write the missing power of 10 in exponential form.

a. $0.04 \times$ ............... $- 0.4$     $0.004 \times$ ............... $= 4$

b. ............... $\times 0.006 = 0.6$     ............... $\times 0.006 = 6$

c. $0.007 \times$ ............... $= 7$     $0.07 \times$ ............... $= 7$

2  Complete the equations to find each product.

a. $8 \times 100 = 8 \times 10^2 =$ ...............

b. $8 \times 1,000 = 8 \times$ ............... $=$ ...............

c. $2 \times$ ............... $= 2 \times 10^1 =$ ...............

d. $0.02 \times 100 = 0.02 \times$ ............... $=$ ...............

3  Complete the equations.

a. $0.03 \times 1,000 =$ ...............

b. $0.18 \times 100 =$ ...............

**4** Use the place-value chart to show dividing 9 by powers of 10. Complete each row with the quotient shown to the right of the row.

| Ones | · | Tenths | Hundredths | Thousandths | | |
|------|---|--------|------------|-------------|---|---|
| 9 | · | 0 | 0 | 0 | | $9 \div 10$ |
| | · | | | | | $9 \div 10^2$ |
| | · | | | | | $9 \div 10^3$ |

**5** Match each expression with its quotient.

**a.** $5.2 \div 10$           0.052

**b.** $520 \div 10^2$         0.52

**c.** $52 \div 10^3$           5.2

**d.** $5,200 \div 10^1$       52

                       520

                       5,200

**6** Describe how the placement of the decimal point changes when you multiply a number by a power of ten. How is this the same and different for division?

**7** Is multiplying by $10^3$ the same as multiplying by 10 factors of 3? Explain.

# Refine Ideas About Powers of 10

## APPLY IT

**Complete these problems on your own.**

### 1 COMPARE

Complete the place-value chart with the products and quotients shown to the right of the chart. Then write a sentence to compare the value of $0.8 \times 10^2$ to the value of $0.8 \div 10^2$.

| Tens | Ones | . | Tenths | Hundredths | Thousandths | |
|------|------|---|--------|------------|-------------|---|
|  |  | . |  |  |  | $0.8 \times 10^2$ |
|  |  | . |  |  |  | $0.8 \times 10^1$ |
|  | 0 | . | 8 |  |  | $0.8 \div 10^1$ |
|  |  | . |  | 0 | 0 | $0.8 \div 10^2$ |

### 2 INSPECT

Max says that the product $30 \times 10^4$ has exactly four zeros. Is he correct? Explain.

### 3 EXPLAIN

How do you determine the value of the unknown exponent in the equation $9{,}700 \div 10^? = 0.97$?

**PAIR/SHARE**

Discuss your solutions for these three problems with a partner.

## Use what you have learned to complete problem 4.

**4** Jaime claims that when you multiply a whole number or a decimal by $10^2$, the placement of the decimal point in the product is always two places to the right of where it was in the factor.

Salome argues that the placement of the decimal point changes two places to the right only when you multiply a decimal by $10^2$. Salome says that when you multiply a whole number by $10^2$, you can put two extra zeros after the whole number to find the product.

**Part A** Explain each student's point of view with examples.

**Part B** Which student is correct? Justify your answer.

**5 MATH JOURNAL**

Find the value of $80 \div 10^4$. Explain the change in value between 80 and $80 \div 10^4$.

# Read and Write Decimals

## Dear Family,

### This week your child is learning how to read and write decimals.

The table below shows different ways to represent the number 5.387.

| Standard Form | 5.387 |
|---|---|
| Word Form | five and three hundred eighty-seven thousandths |
| Place-Value Chart | <table><tr><th>Ones</th><th>.</th><th>Tenths</th><th>Hundredths</th><th>Thousandths</th></tr><tr><td>5</td><td>.</td><td>3</td><td>8</td><td>7</td></tr></table> |
| Decimal Expanded Form | 5 + 0.3 + 0.08 + 0.007 <br> or <br> 5 + (3 × 0.1) + (8 × 0.01) + (7 × 0.001) |
| Fraction Expanded Form | $5 + \frac{3}{10} + \frac{8}{100} + \frac{7}{1,000}$ <br> or <br> $5 + \left(3 \times \frac{1}{10}\right) + \left(8 \times \frac{1}{100}\right) + \left(7 \times \frac{1}{1,000}\right)$ |
| Mixed Number | $5\frac{387}{1,000}$ |

Understanding different ways to read and write decimals helps prepare your child for comparing decimals and solving problems with decimals.

Invite your child to share what he or she knows about reading and writing decimals by doing the following activity together.

# ACTIVITY   READING AND WRITING DECIMALS

**Do this activity with your child to read and write decimals.**

*Materials* number cube

- Use the two tables below, one for you and one for your child. Have your child roll the number cube. You and your child each write the digit shown on the cube in one place in your place-value chart. You should each write the digit in a different place in your chart.

- Have your child roll the number cube three more times. Write each digit rolled in your place-value charts. For example, if the digits 1, 3, 5, and 6 are rolled, you might write 3.615 and your child might write 5.361.

- Now, write the decimal in word form and in standard form in your charts.

- Ask your child to explain why the order of the digits matters when writing decimals.

| Place-Value Chart | | | | | |
|---|---|---|---|---|---|
| | **Ones** | **.** | **Tenths** | **Hundredths** | **Thousandths** |
| | | . | | | |
| **Word Form** | | | | | |
| **Standard Form** | | | | | |

| Place-Value Chart | | | | | |
|---|---|---|---|---|---|
| | **Ones** | **.** | **Tenths** | **Hundredths** | **Thousandths** |
| | | . | | | |
| **Word Form** | | | | | |
| **Standard Form** | | | | | |

# Explore Reading and Writing Decimals

## Learning Target

- Read and write decimals to thousandths using base-ten numerals, number names, and expanded form, e.g., 347.392 = $3 \times 100 + 4 \times 10 + 7 \times 1 + 3 \times \frac{1}{10} + 9 \times \frac{1}{100} + 2 \times \frac{1}{1000}$.

**SMP** 1, 2, 3, 4, 5, 6, 7

In previous lessons, you learned about decimal place value. Use what you know to try to solve the problem below.

**Jessica reads aloud from a science website.**

**She comes across the measurement 0.32 meter.**

**How should she read this measurement aloud? Explain how you know.**

## TRY IT

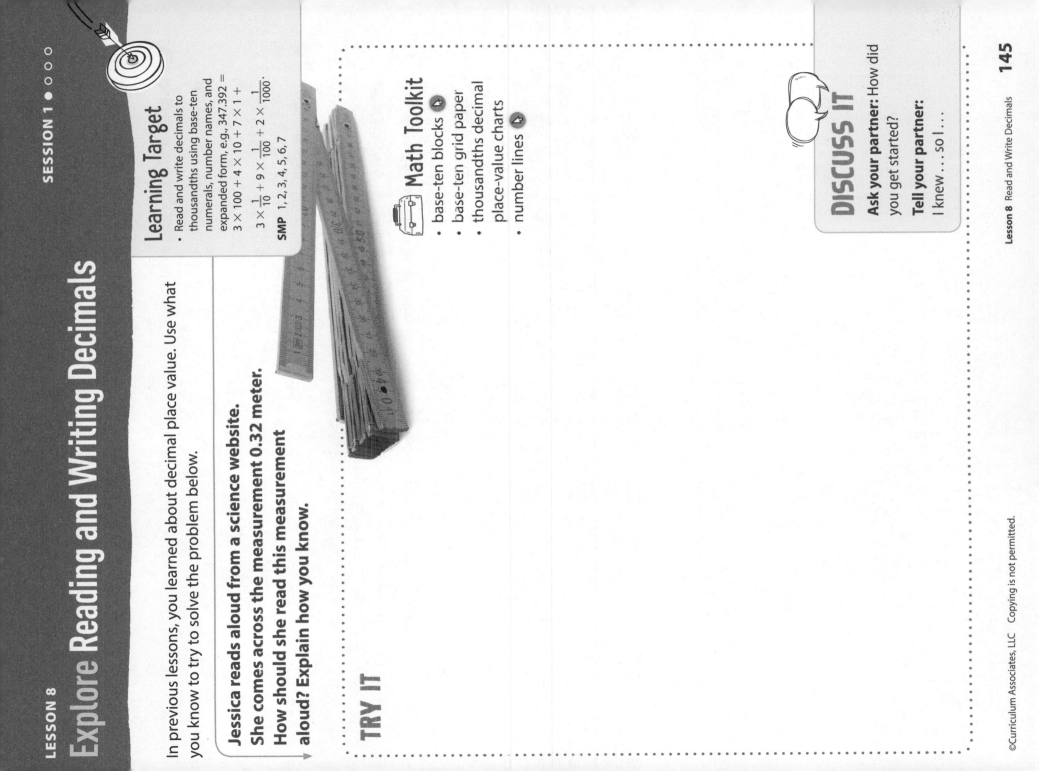

**Math Toolkit**
- base-ten blocks
- base-ten grid paper
- thousandths decimal place-value charts
- number lines

## DISCUSS IT

**Ask your partner:** How did you get started?

**Tell your partner:** I knew . . . so I . . .

## CONNECT IT

### 1 LOOK BACK

Explain how to read 0.32 aloud.

.................................................................................................

.................................................................................................

.................................................................................................

.................................................................................................

### 2 LOOK AHEAD

On the previous page, you used words to say the standard form of the decimal 0.32. You can also use **expanded form** to break apart a decimal by place value. You can use either decimals or fractions to write the expanded form of a decimal.

**a.** Complete each missing number to show two ways to write 0.32 in expanded form using decimals.

$0.32 = $ ..................... $+$ .....................

$0.32 = $ ..................... $\times 0.1 + $ ..................... $\times 0.01$

**b.** Complete each missing number to show two ways to write 0.32 in expanded form using fractions.

$0.32 = \dfrac{\boxed{\phantom{0}}}{10} + \dfrac{\boxed{\phantom{0}}}{100}$

$0.32 = $ ..................... $\times \dfrac{1}{10} + $ ..................... $\times \dfrac{1}{100}$

### 3 REFLECT

How are the different expanded forms of 0.32 alike and different?

.................................................................................................

.................................................................................................

.................................................................................................

# Prepare for Reading and Writing Decimals

1 Think about what you know about expanded form. Fill in each box. Use words, numbers, and pictures. Show as many ideas as you can.

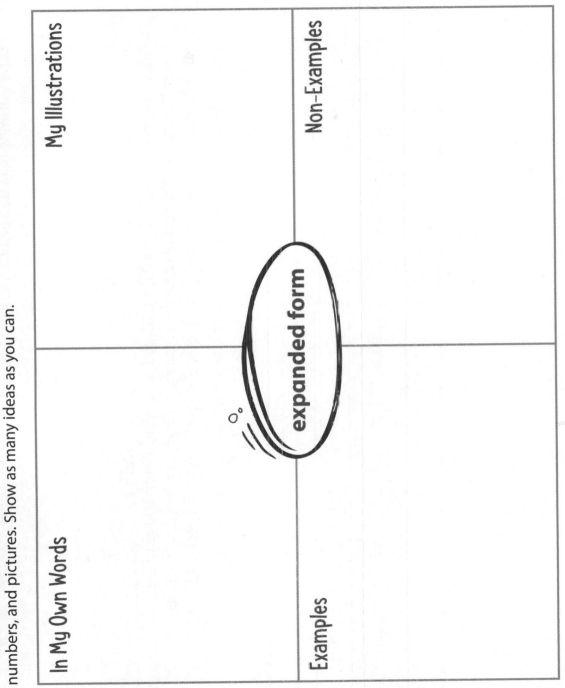

In My Own Words

My Illustrations

expanded form

Examples

Non-Examples

2 You can show the value of each digit in a number as the digit times its place value. Write the expanded form of 0.45 in this way, using fractions and using decimals.

$0.45 = $ .............. $\times \frac{1}{10} + 5 \times$ ..............

$0.45 = 4 \times$ .............. $+$ .............. $\times 0.01$

**3** Solve the problem. Show your work.

**Ajay reads aloud from a sports magazine. He comes across the measurement 0.63 kilometer. How should he read this measurement aloud? Explain how you know.**

*Solution* ..........................................................................................

........................................................................................................

**4** Check your answer. Show your work.

# Develop Reading a Decimal in Word Form

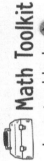

Read and try to solve the problem below.

> Josh uses a kitchen scale to weigh some blueberries.
> The blueberries weigh 0.604 pound. Josh's mom
> wants to know how much the blueberries weigh.
> How does Josh say how much the blueberries weigh?
> Explain your thinking.

## TRY IT

 **Math Toolkit**

- base-ten blocks
- base-ten grid paper
- thousandths decimal
  place-value charts

## DISCUSS IT

**Ask your partner:** Do you
agree with me? Why or
why not?

**Tell your partner:** At first,
I thought . . .

Explore different ways to understand how to read decimals.

> Josh uses a kitchen scale to weigh some blueberries. The blueberries weigh 0.604 pound. Josh's mom wants to know how much the blueberries weigh. How does Josh say how much the blueberries weigh?
>
> **Explain your thinking.**

## MODEL IT

**You can use place-value understanding to write the expanded form of 0.604.**
**You can then write the number as a fraction.**

With decimals:

$$0.604 = 0.6 + 0.004$$

$$= (6 \times 0.1) + (4 \times 0.001)$$

With fractions:

$$0.604 = \left(6 \times \frac{1}{10}\right) + \left(4 \times \frac{1}{1,000}\right)$$

$$= \frac{6}{10} + \frac{4}{1,000}$$

$$= \frac{600}{1,000} + \frac{4}{1,000}$$

$$= \frac{604}{1,000}$$

## MODEL IT

**You can write 0.604 in a place-value chart to show the place value of each digit.**

| Ones | . | Tenths | Hundredths | Thousandths |
|------|---|--------|------------|-------------|
| 0 | . | 6 | 0 | 4 |

The least place value of 0.604 is thousandths.

## CONNECT IT

**Now you will use the problem from the previous page to help you understand how to read decimals.**

1. Look at the place-value chart. What are the names of the four place values in 0.604?

...........................................................

Which of those places has the least value?

...........................................................

2. Look at the expanded form with fractions. How many thousandths are there

altogether in 0.604? ...................

3. What is the word form of 0.604?

...........................................................

4. What is the word form of 1.604?

...........................................................

5. Explain how reading the digits to the right of the decimal point and knowing the name of the least place value help you read a decimal number. Use the examples 0.604 and 1.604 in your explanation.

...........................................................

6. **REFLECT**

Look back at your **Try It**, strategies by classmates, and **Model Its**. Which models or strategies do you like best for reading a decimal? Explain.

...........................................................
...........................................................
...........................................................
...........................................................

# APPLY IT

**Use what you just learned to solve these problems.**

**7** What is the word form of 0.374? Show your work.

*Solution* ....................................................................................................................

**8** A number is written in expanded form as

$7 \times 10 + 5 \times \frac{1}{10} + 1 \times \frac{1}{100} + 6 \times \frac{1}{1,000}$.

What is the word form of the number? Show your work.

*Solution* ....................................................................................................................

**9** What is the word form of 807.0577 Show your work.

*Solution* ....................................................................................................................

# Practice Reading a Decimal in Word Form

**Study the Example showing how to read a decimal. Then solve problems 1–8.**

## EXAMPLE

To read a decimal, you name the place value of the smallest-sized unit, and tell how many of those units there are.

| Ones | . | Tenths | Hundredths | Thousandths |
|------|---|--------|------------|-------------|
| 0 | . | 0 | 7 | 3 |

The least place value of 0.073 is *thousandths*.

There are 73 thousandths.

To read the decimal 0.073, say: *seventy-three thousandths*.

1  Write the decimal 0.24 in the place-value chart.

| Ones | . | Tenths | Hundredths | Thousandths |
|------|---|--------|------------|-------------|
|  | . |  |  |  |

2  Using the chart in problem 1, what is the least place value of 0.24?

3  How do you read the decimal 0.24?

4  Write the word form of each decimal.

**a.** 0.8 ...........................................................

**b.** 0.08 ...........................................................

**c.** 0.008 ...........................................................

**5** The two grids show the same amount shaded. Is the word form of the decimals the same? Explain.

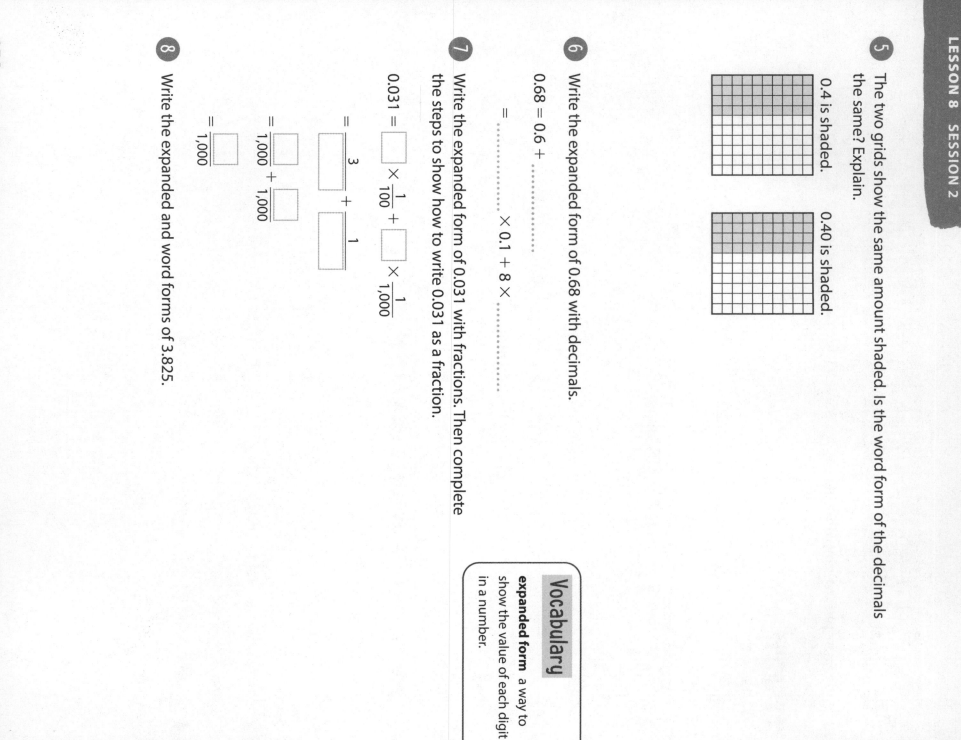

0.4 is shaded.          0.40 is shaded.

**Vocabulary**

**expanded form** a way to show the value of each digit in a number.

**6** Write the expanded form of 0.68 with decimals.

0.68 = 0.6 + ........

= ........ × 0.1 + 8 × ........

**7** Write the expanded form of 0.031 with fractions. Then complete the steps to show how to write 0.031 as a fraction.

$0.031 = \boxed{\phantom{x}} \times \frac{1}{100} + \boxed{\phantom{x}} \times \frac{1}{1,000}$

$= \boxed{\phantom{x}}^{3} + \boxed{\phantom{x}}^{1}$

$= \frac{\boxed{\phantom{x}}}{1,000} + \frac{\boxed{\phantom{x}}}{1,000}$

$= \frac{\boxed{\phantom{x}}}{1,000}$

**8** Write the expanded and word forms of 3.825.

# Develop Writing a Decimal in Standard Form

Read and try to solve the problem below.

A school holds a running race.

- Abha finishes the race one and sixteen thousandths seconds ahead of Nadia.

- Brianne finishes two and thirty-five hundredths seconds ahead of Chandra.

What decimals represent these measurements?

➤ Use a model to support your answer.

## TRY IT

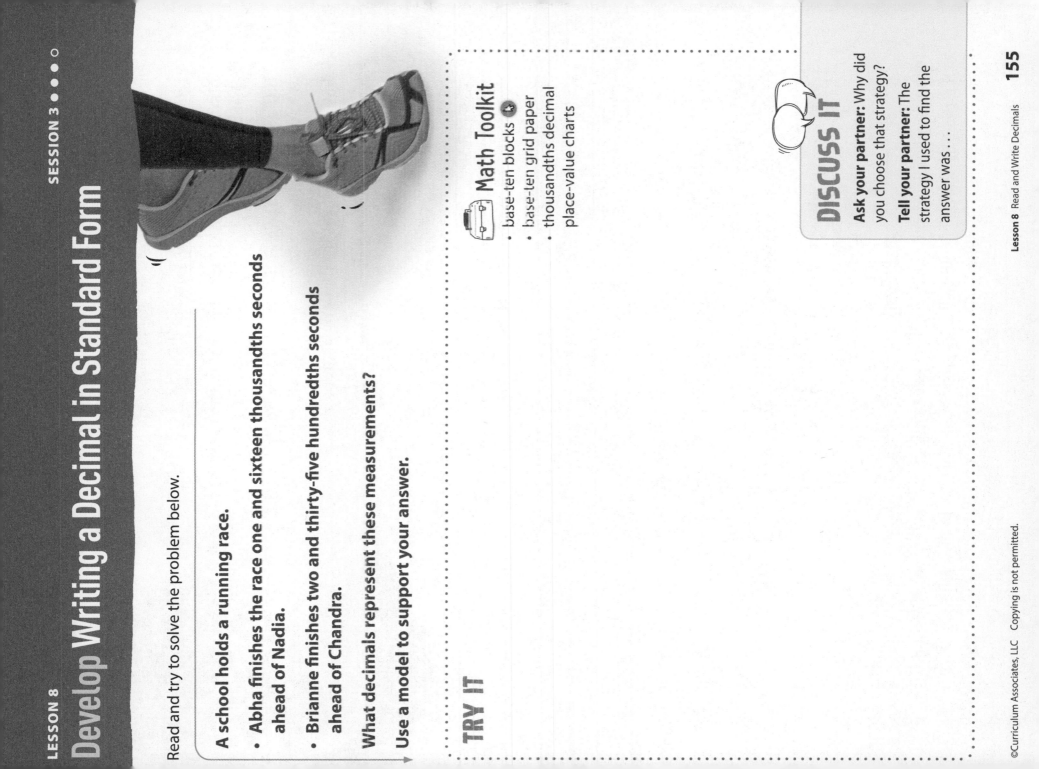

**Math Toolkit**
- base-ten blocks
- base-ten grid paper
- thousandths decimal place-value charts

### DISCUSS IT

**Ask your partner:** Why did you choose that strategy?

**Tell your partner:** The strategy I used to find the answer was . . .

Explore different ways to understand how to write a mixed number given in word form as a decimal in standard form.

**A school holds a running race.**

- **Abha finishes the race one and sixteen thousandths seconds ahead of Nadia.**

- **Brianne finishes two and thirty-five hundredths seconds ahead of Chandra.**

**What decimals represent these measurements?**

← **Use a model to support your answer.**

## MODEL IT

**Model the measurements with mixed numbers and expanded form.**

Write mixed numbers to show the number of whole seconds and the fraction of a second given by each measurement. Then expand.

one and sixteen thousandths

$1\frac{16}{1,000}$

$1 + \frac{16}{1,000}$

$1 + \frac{10}{1,000} + \frac{6}{1,000}$

$1 + \frac{1}{100} + \frac{6}{1,000}$

two and thirty-five hundredths

$2\frac{35}{100}$

$2 + \frac{35}{100}$

$2 + \frac{30}{100} + \frac{5}{100}$

$2 + \frac{3}{10} + \frac{5}{100}$

## MODEL IT

**Use a place-value chart to write the measurements.**

| Ones | . | Tenths | Hundredths | Thousandths |
|------|---|--------|------------|-------------|
| 1 | . | 0 | 1 | 6 |
| 2 | . | 3 | 5 | |

16 thousandths is 10 thousandths and 6 thousandths or 1 hundredth and 6 thousandths.

35 hundredths is 30 hundredths and 5 hundredths or 3 tenths and 5 hundredths.

# CONNECT IT

**Now you will use the problem from the previous page to help you understand how to write a mixed number given in word form as a decimal in standard form.**

**1** Compare the mixed-number and the place-value representations of *one and sixteen thousandths*. How does each model show the number of whole seconds?

**2** Compare the expanded form and the place-value representations of *one and sixteenth thousandths*. How does each model show the fractional part of a second?

**3** How can you write *one and sixteen thousandths* as a decimal? ..............................

**4** How can you write *two and thirty-five hundredths* as a decimal? ..............................

**5** Explain how you can write the standard form of a decimal given in word form.

## REFLECT

**6** Look back at your **Try It**, strategies by classmates, and **Model Its**. Which models or strategies do you like best for writing the standard form of a mixed number given in word form? Explain.

....................................................................................................

....................................................................................................

....................................................................................................

# APPLY IT

**Use what you just learned to solve these problems.**

**7** What decimal represents *ten and seventy-five hundredths*? Show your work.

*Solution* .........................................................................................................................................................

**8** A number is written in expanded form as $9 \times 1,000 + 6 \times 1 + 3 \times \frac{1}{10} + 8 \times \frac{1}{1,000}$.
What decimal represents the number? Show your work.

*Solution* .........................................................................................................................................................

**9** Which decimal represents *six and fifty-four thousandths*?

Ⓐ 60.54

Ⓑ 6.540

Ⓒ 6.054

Ⓓ 0.654

# Practice Writing a Decimal in Standard Form

**Study the Example showing a number written in multiple forms. Then solve problems 1–6.**

## EXAMPLE

| Words | one and forty-six thousandths |
|---|---|
| Mixed Number | $1\frac{46}{1,000}$ |
| Expanded Form | $1 + \frac{46}{1,000} = 1 + \frac{40}{1,000} + \frac{6}{1,000}$ <br> $= 1 + \frac{4}{100} + \frac{6}{1,000}$ <br> $= 1 \times 1 + 4 \times \frac{1}{100} + 6 \times \frac{1}{1,000}$ |
| Decimal | 1.046 |

1 In the Example, what does the 0 in 1.046 mean?

2 Fill in the missing information in the table below.

| Words | three and seventy-two hundredths |
|---|---|
| Mixed Number | $3 + \frac{\boxed{\phantom{0}}}{100}$ |
| Expanded Form | $3 + \frac{72}{100} = 3 + \frac{\boxed{\phantom{0}}}{100} + \frac{\boxed{\phantom{0}}}{100}$ <br> $= 3 + \frac{\boxed{\phantom{0}}}{10} + \frac{\boxed{\phantom{0}}}{100}$ <br> $= \boxed{\phantom{0}} \times 1 + \boxed{\phantom{0}} \times \frac{1}{10} + \boxed{\phantom{0}} \times \frac{1}{100}$ |
| Decimal | |

3  Fill in the blanks with numbers and words to show the values of the digits in the decimal *four and sixty-five hundredths*. Then write *four and sixty-five hundredths* as a decimal.

*Four and sixty-five hundredths* is ............... ones and ............... hundredths.

65 hundredths is 6 ............... and 5 ............... .

The decimal that represents *four and sixty-five hundredths* is ............... .

4  An expanded form of a number is shown below. Write the number in the place-value chart. Then write it as a decimal in standard form.

$$3 \times 1{,}000 + 5 \times 10 + 7 \times \frac{1}{100}$$

| Thousands | Hundreds | Tens | Ones | . | Tenths | Hundredths |
|-----------|----------|------|------|---|--------|------------|
|           |          |      |      | . |        |            |

The decimal form of the number is ............... .

5  When a decimal is written in word form, what indicates whether the number can be written as a mixed number or as a fraction less than 1?

6  The length of an eastern gray tree frog tadpole can be as long as five and twenty-two hundredths centimeters. What is this length written as a decimal? Show your work.

*Solution* ............................................................................................

# Refine Reading and Writing Decimals

**Complete the Example below. Then solve problems 1–9.**

## EXAMPLE

**Coach Roberts is two and fifty-four thousandths meters tall. Write this height as a decimal.**

Look at how you could show your work using expanded form.

Two and fifty-four thousandths is $2\frac{54}{1,000}$

$$\frac{54}{1,000} = \frac{50}{1,000} + \frac{4}{1,000}$$

$$= \left(5 \times \frac{10}{1,000}\right) + \left(4 \times \frac{1}{1,000}\right)$$

$$= \left(5 \times \frac{1}{100}\right) + \left(4 \times \frac{1}{1,000}\right)$$

$$= (5 \times 0.01) + (4 \times 0.001)$$

| Ones | . | Tenths | Hundredths | Thousandths |
|------|---|--------|------------|-------------|
| 2 | . | 0 | 5 | 4 |

*Solution*

What place-value relationship lets me write $\frac{50}{1,000}$ as $\frac{5}{100}$?

**PAIR/SHARE**
Why can you use fractions to represent a decimal number?

## APPLY IT

**1** Aubrey runs the 100-meter dash in 14.895 seconds. What words could you use to read 14.895? Show your work.

How can you write 14.895 as a mixed number?

**PAIR/SHARE**
Is there a different way to use words to represent 14.895?

*Solution*

**2** Paulo measures the length of a sideline on a football field. It is one hundred nine thousandths of a kilometer. Write this length as a decimal and in expanded form. Show your work.

*Solution* ..........................................................................................

How could you represent this number in a place-value chart?

PAIR/SHARE
What other ways could you represent this number?

**3** Which of the following correctly represents 4.082?

Ⓐ $4 + \dfrac{8}{10} + \dfrac{2}{1,000}$

Ⓑ four and eighty-two thousandths

Ⓒ four and eight and two hundredths

Ⓓ $4 + \left(8 \times \dfrac{1}{10}\right) + \left(2 \times \dfrac{1}{100}\right)$

Rachel chose Ⓓ as the correct answer. How did she get that answer?

What are the place values of each digit in 4.082?

PAIR/SHARE
Does Rachel's answer make sense?

4  Daniel ran the 400-meter dash in 89.023 seconds. Which of the following expresses this time in words?

Ⓐ eighty-nine and twenty-three hundredths seconds

Ⓑ eighty-nine and two tenths and three thousandths seconds

Ⓒ eighty-nine and twenty-three thousandths seconds

Ⓓ eighty-nine thousand twenty three seconds

5  What decimal represents the number shown below in expanded form?

$$6 \times 1{,}000 + 2 \times 10 + 3 \times \frac{1}{10} + 5 \times \frac{1}{1{,}000}$$

Ⓐ 6,020.305

Ⓑ 6,200.350

Ⓒ 6,020.035

Ⓓ 6,002.035

6  A guitar string that plays a very low note is eleven hundredths of an inch thick. Does the expression correctly represent eleven hundredths?

| | Yes | No |
|---|---|---|
| $\frac{1}{100} + \frac{1}{1{,}000}$ | Ⓐ | Ⓑ |
| $\frac{1}{10} + \frac{1}{100}$ | Ⓒ | Ⓓ |
| 0.11 | Ⓔ | Ⓕ |
| 0.1 + 0.01 | Ⓖ | Ⓗ |
| 0.01 + 0.001 | Ⓘ | Ⓙ |

**7** Which expressions correctly represent the decimal 57.036?

Ⓐ $57 + \frac{3}{100} + \frac{6}{1,000}$

Ⓑ $57 + 3 \times \frac{10}{1,000} + 6 \times \frac{10}{1,000}$

Ⓒ $57 + 36 \times 0.01$

Ⓓ $57 + 36 \times 0.001$

Ⓔ fifty-seven and thirty-six hundredths

**8** Alex wrote 103.903 in expanded form as shown below.

$1 \times 100 + 3 \times 1 + 9 \times \frac{1}{100} + 3 \times \frac{1}{1,000}$

Explain his mistake. Then tell how to correct it.

**9** MATH JOURNAL

Represent 240.149 in two different ways. Then explain how each way shows the place value of the digits of the number.

---

☑ SELF CHECK Go back to the Unit 2 Opener and see what you can check off.

# Compare and Round Decimals

## Dear Family,

**This week your child is learning to compare and round decimals.**

One way to compare decimals is to use a place-value chart. For example, compare 7.033 and 7.02. Write a 0 in the thousandths column for 7.02. Start by comparing the ones.

| Ones | . | Tenths | Hundredths | Thousandths |
|------|---|--------|------------|-------------|
| 7 | . | 0 | 3 | 3 |
| 7 | . | 0 | 2 | 0 |

7 = 7     0 = 0     3 > 2

The ones digits are the same. The tenths digits are the same. 3 hundredths > 2 hundredths. So, 7.033 > 7.02.

Another way to compare decimals is to write them as mixed numbers. Write the fractions with like denominators.

$$7.033 = 7\frac{33}{1,000} \qquad 7.02 = 7\frac{2}{100} = 7\frac{20}{1,000}$$

$$7\frac{33}{1,000} > 7\frac{20}{1,000}$$

So, 7.033 > 7.02.

Your child is also learning to round decimals using a number line. The number line shows that 0.042 is closer to 0.04 than to 0.05.

0.042 rounded to the nearest hundredth is 0.04.

Invite your child to share what he or she knows about comparing and rounding decimals by doing the following activity together.

## ACTIVITY   COMPARE DECIMALS

**Do this activity with your child to compare decimals.**

Work with your child to find real-world examples that involve comparing decimals.

- Look around the house or through fliers for at least eight numbers that involve a decimal. The wrappers or labels on household items usually show a number. Make a list of the decimals as you find them. You do not need to write the units.

- Examples: a 3.17-ounce bar of soap, an 8.5-ounce bottle of lotion, a 7.4-ounce box of snack bars, a 7.9-ounce box of crackers.

- Take turns. One person marks two numbers for the other person to compare. Make a place-value chart like the one on the first page of this letter if needed. Circle the greater decimal.

- Challenge! After you have finished the activity, you should now have four sets of decimal numbers with the greater decimal circled. Can you determine the greatest decimal of those four decimals?

SOAP
3.17 oz

LOTION
8.5 oz

# Explore Comparing and Rounding Decimals

You already know how to compare and round whole numbers. In this lesson, you will use place-value understanding to compare and round decimals. Use what you know to try to solve the problem below.

> **Grace chooses one red and one blue button from her button collection. The blue button is 1.2 centimeters wide and the red button is 1.08 centimeters wide. Which button is wider?**

## Learning Targets

- Compare two decimals to thousandths based on meanings of the digits in each place, using >, =, and < symbols to record the results of comparisons.
- Use place value understanding to round decimals to any place.

**SMP** 1, 2, 3, 4, 5, 6, 7

## 🧰 Math Toolkit

- base-ten blocks ✐
- base-ten grid paper
- decimal grids
- thousandths decimal
- place-value charts
- number lines ✐

## TRY IT

## DISCUSS IT

**Ask your partner:** How did you get started?

**Tell your partner:** I started by . . .

# CONNECT IT

## ① LOOK BACK

Which button is wider? Use the *greater than* symbol (>) or the *less than* symbol (<) to write an **inequality** statement that compares the widths of the red and blue buttons Grace chose from her collection.

## ② LOOK AHEAD

You can use decimal comparisons to help you round decimals to a given place value. Rounding decimals is similar to rounding whole numbers.

**a.** A number line can be a useful tool for rounding. Place and label the numbers 1.3 and 1.8 on the number line below.

1
1.0

1.5

2
2.0

**b.** What is 1.3 rounded to the nearest whole number? Explain how you know.

**c.** What is 1.8 rounded to the nearest whole number? Explain how you know.

**d.** What is 1.5 rounded to the nearest whole number? Explain how you know.

## ③ REFLECT

How is rounding decimals like rounding whole numbers?

# Prepare for Comparing and Rounding Decimals

1  Think about what you know about comparing numbers. Fill in each box. Use words, numbers, and pictures. Show as many ideas as you can.

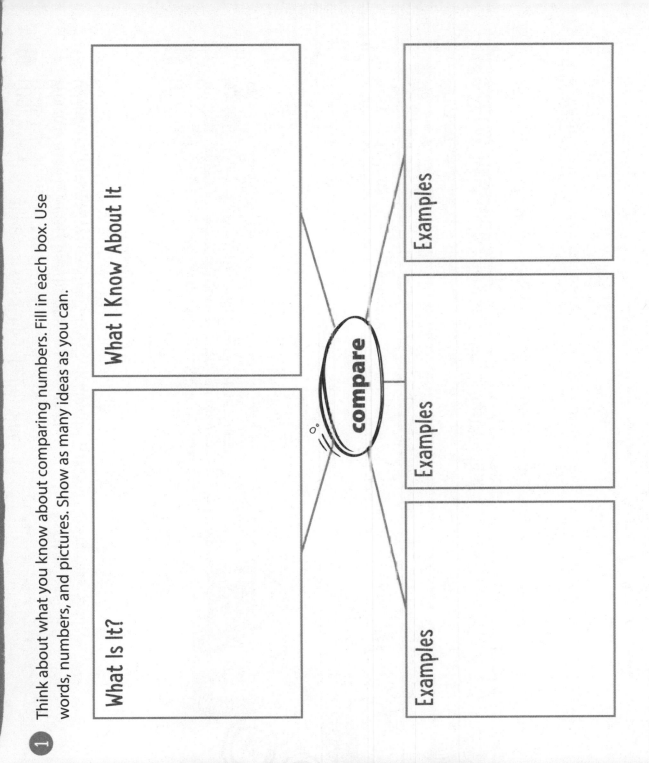

What Is It?

What I Know About It

compare

Examples

Examples

Examples

Examples

2  Lyle says that 0.89 > 1.23 because 8 tenths is greater than 2 tenths. Is he right? Explain.

3  Solve the problem. Show your work.

**Maha has two colors of modeling clay. She has
1.05 kilograms of blue modeling clay and
1.3 kilograms of orange modeling clay. Which
color of modeling clay does Maha have more of?**

4  Check your answer. Show your work.

*Solution* .................................................

# Develop Comparing Decimals

Read and try to solve the problem below.

**Gary and Melissa compare the distances they bike each morning to get to school.**

- **Gary bikes 3.275 kilometers.**

- **Melissa bikes 3.24 kilometers.**

**Who bikes farther to get to school?**

## TRY IT

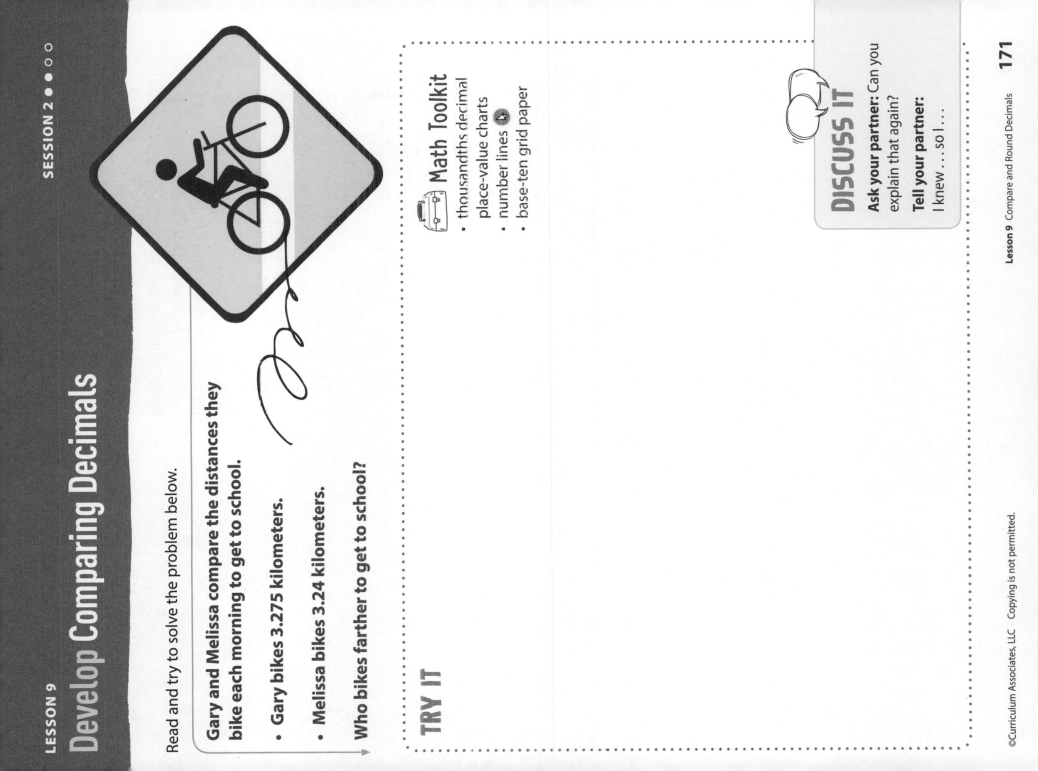

### Math Toolkit
- thousandths decimal place-value charts
- number lines
- base-ten grid paper

---

## DISCUSS IT

**Ask your partner:** Can you explain that again?

**Tell your partner:** I knew . . . so I . . . .

Explore different ways to understand comparing decimals.

> **Gary and Melissa compare the distances they bike each morning to get to school.**
>
> - **Gary bikes 3.275 kilometers.**
> - **Melissa bikes 3.24 kilometers.**

← **Who bikes farther to get to school?**

## MODEL IT
**Express the two distances as mixed numbers with like denominators.**

Gary: $3.275 = 3\frac{275}{1,000}$

Melissa: $3.24 = 3\frac{24}{100}$

$$= 3\frac{240}{1,000}$$

You can now compare $3\frac{275}{1,000}$ to $3\frac{240}{1,000}$.

## MODEL IT
**Write the distances in a place-value chart.**

| | Ones | . | Tenths | Hundredths | Thousandths |
|---|---|---|---|---|---|
| **Gary** | 3 | . | 2 | 7 | 5 |
| **Melissa** | 3 | . | 2 | 4 | 0 |

Gary bikes 3,275 thousandths kilometers to get to school.
Melissa bikes 3,240 thousandths kilometers to get to school.

You can use the chart to compare place values starting with the ones.

## CONNECT IT

**Now you will use the problem from the previous page to help you understand how to compare decimals.**

1 Both **Model Its** change the way the fractional part or decimal part of 3.24 is represented. What is the same about how the denominator of the fraction and the place value of the decimal change?

2 What is the same about how the numerator of the fraction and the digits to the right of the decimal point change?

3 How does rewriting the fractional part or decimal part of 3.24 make it easier to compare 3.24 to 3.275?

4 Write an inequality statement using the symbol > to compare the distances Gary and Melissa bike. Who bikes farther to school?

5 Look at the place-value chart in the second **Model It**. What is the greatest place value for which the numbers 3.275 and 3.24 have different digits? ...............

How can you use this place value to show that Gary bikes farther?

6 **REFLECT**

Look back at your **Try It**, strategies by classmates, and **Model Its**. Which models or strategies do you like best for comparing decimals? Explain.

........................................................................

........................................................................

........................................................................

## APPLY IT

**Use what you just learned to solve these problems.**

**7** Brayden and Kayla measured the width of their kitchen tables. Brayden's table is 1.46 meters wide. Kayla's table is 1.62 meters wide. Whose table is the widest? Show your work.

*Solution* ..................................................

**8** Heather's rabbit has a mass of 2.190 kilograms. Jelani's rabbit has a mass of 2.195 kilograms. Write an inequality statement comparing the masses of the rabbits. Whose rabbit has the greater mass? Show your work.

*Solution* ..................................................

**9** Select all the decimals that are greater than 715.148 and also less than 715.35.

Ⓐ 715.340

Ⓑ 715.4

Ⓒ 714.156

Ⓓ 715.075

Ⓔ 715.28

# Practice Comparing Decimals

**Study the Example comparing decimals rewritten as mixed numbers. Then solve problems 1–6.**

### EXAMPLE

Package A has a mass of 1.401 kilograms. Package B has a mass of 1.29 kilograms. Write an inequality statement comparing the masses of the packages.

Express the masses as mixed numbers with like denominators. Then compare.

$1.401 = 1\frac{401}{1,000}$        $1.29 = 1\frac{29}{100} = 1\frac{290}{1,000}$

$1\frac{401}{1,000}$ is greater than $1\frac{290}{1,000}$.

So, $1.401 > 1.29$. The mass of Package A is greater than the mass of Package B.

---

1 Complete the steps to write an inequality statement comparing 2.087 and 2.15.

$2.087 = 2\dfrac{\boxed{\phantom{000}}}{\boxed{\phantom{000}}}$          $2.15 = 2\dfrac{15}{\boxed{\phantom{000}}} = 2\dfrac{\boxed{\phantom{000}}}{1,000}$

$2\dfrac{\boxed{\phantom{000}}}{\boxed{\phantom{000}}}$ is ............ than $2\dfrac{\boxed{\phantom{000}}}{\boxed{\phantom{000}}}$.

$2.087 \boxed{\phantom{0}} 2.15$

2 Which statements show correct reasoning about the decimals 0.4 and 0.06?

Ⓐ $0.4 > 0.06$ because $\frac{40}{100} > \frac{6}{100}$.

Ⓑ $0.4 > 0.06$ because 4 tenths is greater than 6 hundredths.

Ⓒ $0.4 < 0.06$ because $\frac{4}{100} < \frac{6}{10}$.

Ⓓ $0.4 < 0.06$ because 6 hundredths is greater than 4 tenths.

Ⓔ $0.06 > 0.4$ because $\frac{6}{10} > \frac{4}{10}$.

## 3 Write a number from the box to make each statement true.

a. 0.07 = ...............

b. 0.07 > ...............

c. 0.07 < ...............

| 0.007 | 0.070 | 0.072 |
|---|---|---|
| 0.068 | 0.608 | |

## 4 Compare 5.269 and 5.038.

a. Write 5.269 and 5.038 as mixed numbers.

$5.269 = 5\dfrac{\boxed{\phantom{00}}}{1,000}$   $5.038 = 5\dfrac{\boxed{\phantom{00}}}{\boxed{\phantom{00}}}$

b. Compare 5.269 and 5.038 using >, =, or <.

## 5 Penelope has two kittens. Dot weighs 3.83 pounds, and Dash weighs 3.805 pounds. Which kitten weighs more?

Fill in the place-value chart with the weights of the two kittens. Then explain how you can use the chart to solve the problem.

| Ones | . | Tenths | Hundredths | Thousandths |
|---|---|---|---|---|
| 3 | . | | | |
| 3 | . | | | |

## 6 Daslyn has a piece of rope 2.085 meters long and another piece 2.63 meters long. Which piece can she cut to make a piece that is 2.5 meters long? Explain.

# Develop Rounding Decimals

Read and try to solve the problem below.

**Tyson runs in a race at a track meet. One stopwatch shows his time as 11.25 seconds. Another stopwatch shows his time as 11.245 seconds. Round each time to the nearest tenth of a second.**

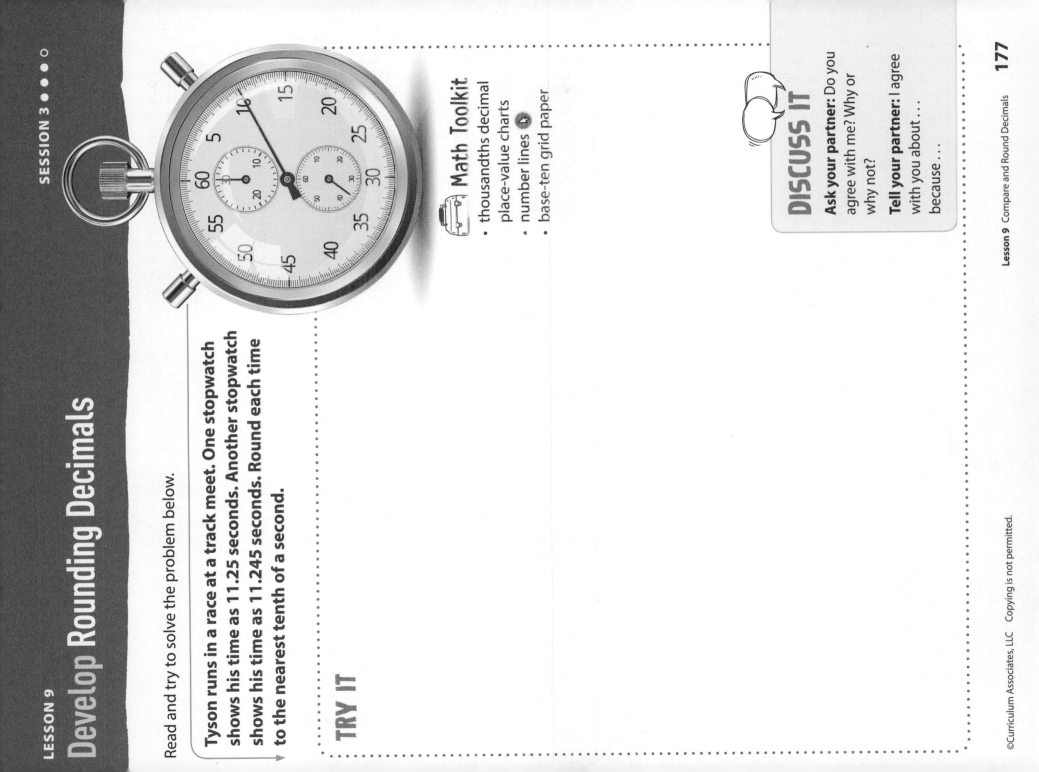

## Math Toolkit
- thousandths decimal place-value charts
- number lines
- base-ten grid paper

## TRY IT

## DISCUSS IT

**Ask your partner:** Do you agree with me? Why or why not?

**Tell your partner:** I agree with you about.... because....

Explore ways to understand rounding decimals.

> Tyson runs in a race at a track meet. One stopwatch shows his time as 11.25 seconds. Another stopwatch shows his time as 11.245 seconds. Round each time to the nearest tenth of a second.

## PICTURE IT

You can place each number on a number line to see its relationship to nearby tenths.

11.2        11.25        11.3

11.25 is exactly halfway between 11.2 and 11.3.

11.2        11.24   11.25        11.3
                    11.245

You can locate 11.245 between 11.24 and 11.25. 11.245 is less than halfway between 11.2 and 11.3.

## MODEL IT

You can use a place-value chart to compare a decimal to nearby tenths.

| Tens | Ones | . | Tenths | Hundredths |
|------|------|---|--------|------------|
| 1 | 1 | . | 2 | 0 |
| 1 | 1 | . | 2 | 5 |
| 1 | 1 | . | 3 | 0 |

25 hundredths is halfway between 20 hundredths and 30 hundredths.

When you are rounding to the nearest tenth, you do not need to look at the thousandths place.

| Tens | Ones | . | Tenths | Hundredths | Thousandths |
|------|------|---|--------|------------|-------------|
| 1 | 1 | . | 2 | 0 | 0 |
| 1 | 1 | . | 2 | 4 | 5 |
| 1 | 1 | . | 3 | 0 | 0 |

24 hundredths is closer to 20 hundredths than it is to 30 hundredths.

## CONNECT IT

**Now you will use the problem from the previous page to help you understand how to round decimals.**

1 Look at **Picture It** and **Model It**. Why do the number lines and place-value charts start at 11.2 and end at 11.3?

2 How do you know 11.25 is located at the halfway point between 11.2 and 11.3?

3 What are 11.25 and 11.245 rounded to the nearest tenth? Use the number line to support your answers.

4 How do the place-value charts help you see that 11.245 is closer to 11.2 than to 11.3?

5 If you are rounding to the nearest tenth, what place value do you look at to decide how to round the number? .............................

6 Explain how you would round a decimal to the nearest hundredth.

7 **REFLECT**

Look back at your **Try It**, strategies by classmates, **Picture It** and **Model It**. Which models or strategies do you like best for rounding decimals? Explain.

....................................................................................................................

....................................................................................................................

# APPLY IT

**Use what you just learned to solve these problems.**

**8** Belinda paid $108.34 for groceries. Rounded to the nearest dollar, how much did Belinda pay for groceries? Show your work.

*Solution* ........................................................................

**9** A dropper holds 0.817 milliliter of fluid. What is this amount rounded to the nearest hundredth? Show your work.

*Solution* ........................................................................

**10** Which decimals have been rounded correctly to the nearest tenth?

Ⓐ 7.834 rounded to 7.83

Ⓑ 10.056 rounded to 10.1

Ⓒ 0.651 rounded to 0.65

Ⓓ 203.209 rounded to 203.2

Ⓔ 115.007 rounded to 120.10

# Practice Rounding Decimals

**Study the Example showing how to round a decimal by plotting it on a number line. Then solve problems 1–4.**

## EXAMPLE

Chiara runs 0.446 kilometer in one lap around the track. What is this distance rounded to the nearest hundredth?

Place **0.446** on a number line to see its relationship to nearby hundredths.

**0.446**

0.44          0.445          0.45

0.446 is between 0.44 and 0.45, and closer to 0.45.

The distance rounded to the nearest hundredth is 0.45 kilometer.

1 Use a number line and a place-value chart to round the distance 0.446 kilometer to the nearest tenth.

**a.** Is 0.446 located to the right or the left of 0.45 on the number line below? Explain how you know. Then place a point on the number line to show the approximate location of 0.446.

0.40          0.45          0.50

**b.** Write the two tenths closest to 0.446 in the place-value chart.

| Ones | . | Tenths | Hundredths | Thousandths |
|------|---|--------|------------|-------------|
| 0 | . | 4 | 4 | 6 |
|  | . |  |  |  |
|  | . |  |  |  |

**c.** What is 0.446 kilometer rounded to the nearest tenth? ................

**2** Aubra and Tony are rounding the number 1.65 to the nearest tenth. On a number line, they see 1.65 is exactly halfway between 1.6 and 1.7. Aubra says to round to the greater value, 1.7. Tony says that because 1.65 is in the middle, you can round to either value. Who is right? Explain.

**3** One gallon is equal to about 3.785 liters. What is this amount rounded to the nearest tenth? to the nearest hundredth? Show your work.

*Solution* ...........................................................................................................

**4** Look at problem 3. What is the greatest number of whole liters of water you could pour into a one-gallon container without it overflowing? Explain your answer.

# Refine Comparing and Rounding Decimals

**Complete the Example below. Then solve problems 1–8.**

## EXAMPLE

**Makayla's mass at birth was 3.747 kilograms.**
**Her brother John's mass at birth was 3.477 kilograms.**
**Whose mass at birth rounded to the nearest whole**
**kilogram was 4 kilograms?**

Look at how you could show your work using a number line.

```
        3.477        3.747
  ←────●───────────────●──────→
  3  3.1 3.2 3.3 3.4 3.5 3.6 3.7 3.8 3.9  4
```

The point representing Makayla's mass at birth is closer to 4
than to 3. The point representing John's mass at birth is closer
to 3 than to 4.

*Solution* ........................................................................

Rounding decimals is like
rounding whole numbers.

**PAIR/SHARE**
How do the masses at birth
compare?

## APPLY IT

**1** A grocery store charges to the nearest tenth of a pound for
tomatoes. Landon has 2.386 pounds of tomatoes. How many
pounds of tomatoes will the store charge Landon for? Show
your work.

How do you use place value
to round whole numbers
and decimals?

**PAIR/SHARE**
About how many whole
pounds of tomatoes did
Landon purchase?

*Solution* ........................................................................

**2** Ellie purchases 14.297 gallons of gas. Her friend Alivia purchases 14.209 gallons of gas. Write an inequality statement comparing the two gas purchases. Show your work.

How do I use place value to compare numbers?

**PAIR/SHARE**
How could you use rounding to compare the numbers?

......................................................................

**Solution** ....................................................................

**3** Which of the following comparisons is NOT true?

Ⓐ 42.300 = 42.3

Ⓑ 5.020 < 5.20

Ⓒ 0.149 < 1.490

Ⓓ 108.308 > 108.4

Do you compare the number of digits or compare the place value of the digits?

Ava chose Ⓐ as the correct answer. How did she get that answer?

**PAIR/SHARE**
Does Ava's answer make sense?

**4** Malcolm rounds each weight shown below to the nearest hundredth of a pound.

2.456 pounds

2.457 pounds

2.454 pounds

2.459 pounds

Which weight does NOT round to 2.46 pounds?

Ⓐ 2.456 pounds

Ⓑ 2.457 pounds

Ⓒ 2.454 pounds

Ⓓ 2.459 pounds

**5** Which comparison is NOT true?

Ⓐ $1.78 < 1.92$

Ⓑ $1\frac{78}{100} < 1\frac{92}{100}$

Ⓒ $1 + \left(7 \times \frac{1}{10}\right) + \left(8 \times \frac{1}{100}\right) < 1 + \left(9 \times \frac{1}{10}\right) + \left(2 \times \frac{1}{100}\right)$

Ⓓ $1 + \frac{70}{10} + \frac{80}{100} < 1 + \frac{9}{10} + \frac{2}{100}$

**6** Tori and Alvin use a stopwatch to record the amount of time it takes a marble to roll down a ramp. Tori's marble takes 2.835 seconds, while Alvin's marble takes 2.845 seconds. Tell whether each sentence is *True* or *False*.

| | True | False |
|---|---|---|
| Rounded to the nearest tenth, both times are the same. | Ⓐ | Ⓑ |
| Rounded to the nearest hundredth, both times are the same. | Ⓒ | Ⓓ |
| Both times are closer to 2.8 than 2.9. | Ⓔ | Ⓕ |
| Both times are more than halfway between 2.84 and 2.85. | Ⓖ | Ⓗ |
| Tori's marble was faster. | Ⓘ | Ⓙ |

**7** The weights of four packages of meat are shown below.

| Package A | 1.748 pounds |
| Package B | 1.645 pounds |
| Package C | 1.754 pounds |
| Package D | 1.532 pounds |

**Part A** Each package is priced by how much it weighs to the nearest tenth of a pound. Order the packages from greatest to least weight. Show your work.

**Part B** Explain how the order would change if you rounded the weights to the nearest hundredth.

**Solution** ·······································································

**8** MATH JOURNAL

Round 23.546 to the nearest tenth and nearest hundredth. Explain your thinking.

 **SELF CHECK** Go back to the Unit 2 Opener and see what you can check off.

# Add Decimals

## Dear Family,

**This week your child is learning to add decimals.**

The strategies you use to add whole numbers can also be used to add decimals. You might use place-value understanding, decimal models, or number properties that allow you to break apart numbers and add numbers in different orders.

For example, you can add 4.38 and 0.6 by lining the numbers up by place value.

| Ones | . | Tenths | Hundredths |
|------|---|--------|------------|
| 4 | . | 3 | 8 |
| + 0 | . | 6 | 0 |
| 4 | . | 9 | 8 |

> 6 tenths is the same as 60 hundredths!

So, 4.38 + 0.6 = 4.98.

You can also use concrete models, such as decimal grids, to add **4.38** and **0.6**. Each grid of 100 squares represents one whole.

4    + **0.38**    + **0.6**    = 4.98

Invite your child to share what he or she knows about adding decimals by doing the following activity together.

# ACTIVITY ADDING DECIMALS

**Do this activity with your child to add decimals.**

Work with your child to make up and solve real-world problems involving addition of decimals.

***Materials*** calculator (optional)

- Take turns finding or making up some stories with decimal numbers. Include a decimal addition problem for the other person to solve.

- First, try to solve the problems with paper and pencil. Then check your answers with a calculator.

- Here are some examples of problems you might solve:

1. Gavin caught two fish on a camping trip. The masses of the fish are 12.25 kilograms and 7.4 kilograms. What is the total mass of the fish Gavin caught?

2. Angelique jumped forward 1.83 meters. Then she jumped forward another 1.72 meters. What is the total distance Angelique jumped?

- Be on the lookout for other real-world examples of adding decimals. For example, a grocery receipt shows decimal addition. Challenge your child to estimate the sum, then look at the receipt to check.

***Answers:*** **1.** 19.65 kilograms; **2.** 3.55 meters

# Explore Adding Decimals

You know how to add whole numbers by adding the values of digits with the same place value. Now you will learn to add decimals. Use what you know to try to solve the problem below.

> **Sabrina and Christie are running in a relay. Sabrina runs 100 meters in 13.6 seconds. Christie runs the same distance in 12.2 seconds. What is their total time?**

## Learning Target

- Add, subtract, multiply, and divide decimals to hundredths, using concrete models or drawings and strategies based on place value, properties of operations, and/or the relationship between addition and subtraction; relate the strategy to a written method and explain the reasoning used.

SMP 1, 2, 3, 4, 5, 6, 7

## Math Toolkit

- base-ten blocks
- base-ten grid paper
- decimal grids
- number lines
- thousandths decimal place-value charts

## TRY IT

## DISCUSS IT

**Ask your partner:** How did you get started?

**Tell your partner:** I started by . . .

# CONNECT IT

## 1 LOOK BACK

Explain how you can find Sabrina and Christie's total time.

..................................................................................................

..................................................................................................

## 2 LOOK AHEAD

You can add decimals in different ways, just like you can add whole numbers in different ways. Think about the problem 32.14 + 17.5.

**a.** Write the problem in the place-value chart below and find the sum.

| Tens | Ones | . | Tenths | Hundredths |
|------|------|---|--------|------------|
|      |      | . |        |            |
| +    |      | . |        |            |
|      |      | . |        |            |

How did the place-value chart help you add?

..................................................................................................

**b.** Use expanded form to break apart each addend by place value.

Break apart 32.14:                    Break apart 17.5:

..................................................................................................

Find the sum 32.14 + 17.5 by adding the parts in any order.

..................................................................................................

## 3 REFLECT

How is adding decimals like adding whole numbers?

..................................................................................................

..................................................................................................

..................................................................................................

# Prepare for Adding Decimals

1   Think about what you know about breaking apart numbers with addition. Fill in each box. Use words, numbers, and pictures. Show as many ideas as you can.

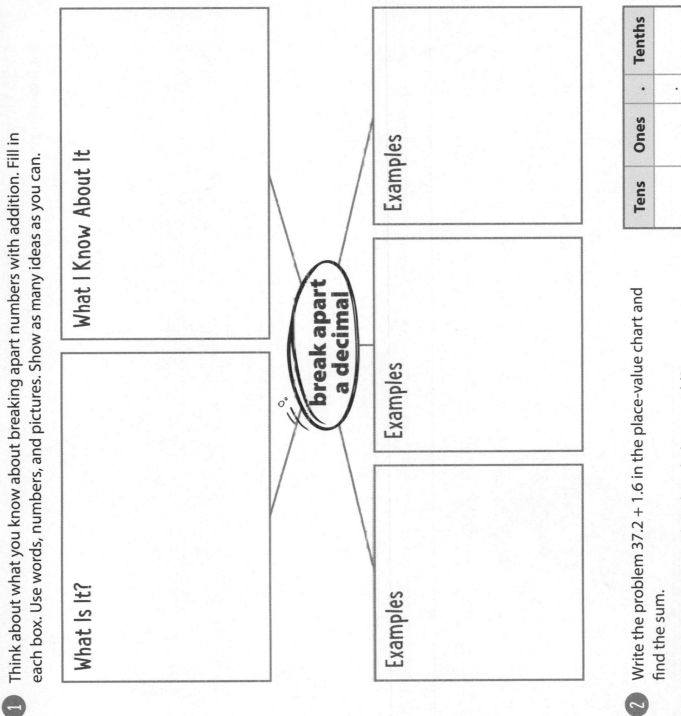

What Is It?

What I Know About It

break apart a decimal

Examples

Examples

Examples

2   Write the problem 37.2 + 1.6 in the place-value chart and find the sum.

How did the place-value chart help you add?

| Tens | Ones | . | Tenths |
|------|------|---|--------|
|      |      | . |        |
|      |      | . |        |
| +    |      | . |        |
|      |      |   |        |

3   Solve the problem. Show your work.

**Manny and Soo went mountain biking. They biked 15.36 kilometers on the red trail and then rode 13.5 kilometers on the blue trail. What was the total distance they biked?**

4   Check your answer. Show your work.

# Develop Adding Decimals

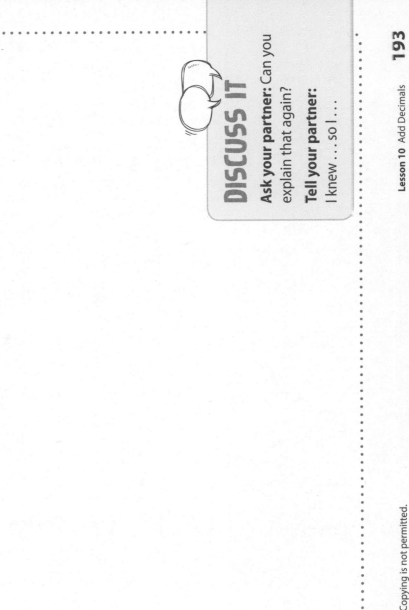

Read and try to solve the problem below.

From his home, Tim rides the bus 3.82 miles. Then he walks 0.4 mile from the bus stop to school. How many miles does Tim travel from home to school?

## TRY IT

## Math Toolkit
- base-ten blocks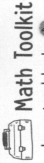
- base-ten grid paper
- decimal grids
- number lines
- thousandths decimal place-value charts

## DISCUSS IT

**Ask your partner:** Can you explain that again?

**Tell your partner:** I knew . . . so I . . . .

Explore different ways to understand adding decimals.

> From his home, Tim rides the bus 3.82 miles. Then
> he walks 0.4 mile from the bus stop to school. How
> many miles does Tim travel from home to school?

## PICTURE IT

You can picture adding two decimals on a number line.

**3.82**

+0.1    +0.1    +0.1    +0.1

3.8    3.9    4.0    4.1    4.2    4.3

Starting at 3.82, you can make 4 jumps of 0.1 to the right to show the sum of
3.82 and 0.4.

## MODEL IT

You can use a place-value chart to help you understand how to add decimals.

| | Ones | • | Tenths | Hundredths |
|---|---|---|---|---|
| **Bus ride** | 3 | . | 8 | 2 |
| **Bus stop to school** | 0 | . | 4 | 0 |

$\frac{4}{10}$ is equivalent to $\frac{40}{100}$, so
you can write a 0 in the
hundredths column.

The sum is 3 ones + 12 tenths + 2 hundredths.

# CONNECT IT

**Now you will use the problem from the previous page to help you understand how to add decimals.**

**1** How can you use the number line in **Picture It** to figure out how many miles Tim travels from home to school?

..................................................................

**2** Look at **Model It**. What is another way to express 12 tenths? ..................

What is another way to express the sum? ..................................

What is this sum in decimal form? ..................

**3** You can add the decimals without a place-value chart by stacking them vertically. Why do you align the 8 in 3.82 with the 4 in 0.40?

$$\begin{array}{r} 3.82 \\ +\ 0.40 \\ \hline \end{array}$$

**4** The addition problem to the right is partially completed. Explain why there is a 1 above the ones place. Then complete the sum.

$$\begin{array}{r} \overset{1}{\phantom{0}}3.82 \\ +\ 0.40 \\ \hline \boxed{\phantom{0}}.22 \end{array}$$

**5** Explain how to add decimals.

**6** REFLECT

Look back at your **Try It**, strategies by classmates, and **Picture It** and **Model It**. Which models or strategies do you like best for adding decimals? Explain.

..................................................................
..................................................................
..................................................................
..................................................................

## APPLY IT

### Use what you just learned to solve these problems.

**7** Yana makes a trail mix with 6.25 ounces of dried fruit and 1.8 ounces of sunflower seeds. How many ounces of trail mix does Yana make? Show your work.

*Solution* ......................................................................................................

**8** What is the value of the expression 2.25 + 63.05 + 0.6? First, estimate the sum. Then find an exact answer. Show your work.

*Solution* ......................................................................................................

**9** Jorge spends $42.75 on a new jacket and $88.30 on a pair of running shoes. How much money does he spend in all? Show your work.

*Solution* ......................................................................................................

# Practice Adding Decimals

**Study the Example showing decimal addition using a place-value chart. Then solve problems 1–5.**

## EXAMPLE

Alana walks 3.45 miles before lunch and 5.18 miles after lunch. How many miles does she walk in all?

| Ones | . | Tenths | Hundredths |
|------|---|--------|------------|
| 3 | . | 4 | 5 |
| 5 | . | 1 | 8 |

3 ones + 5 ones = 8 ones
4 tenths + 1 tenth = 5 tenths
5 hundredths + 8 hundredths = 13 hundredths

Sum = 8 ones + **5 tenths** + **13 hundredths**
   = 8 ones + **6 tenths** + **3 hundredths**

Alana walks 8.63 miles in all.

1 Look at the Example. Suppose Alana walks 6.6 miles the next day. Complete the place-value chart and steps to find the number of miles she walks in two days.

| Ones | . | Tenths | Hundredths |
|------|---|--------|------------|
| 8 | . | 6 | 3 |
| | . | 6 | |

Sum = 14 ones + ............ tenths + ............ hundredths

   = ............ ones + 2 tenths + 3 hundredths

   = ............ ten + ............ ones + ............ tenths + ............ hundredths

Alana walks ............ miles in two days.

2  You can also add decimals by writing the problem vertically, lining up the decimal points to keep track of place values.

The problem to the right is partially completed. Explain why there is a 1 above the tenths place.

$$\begin{array}{r} \overset{1}{\phantom{0}}14.52 \\ +\ 22.29 \\ \hline 1 \end{array}$$

3  Find the sum for the addition problem in problem 2.
Tell whether each statement about it is *True* or *False*.

|  | True | False |
|---|---|---|
| It is more than 36. | Ⓐ | Ⓑ |
| It is closer to 37 than to 36. | Ⓒ | Ⓓ |
| It is 36.71. | Ⓔ | Ⓕ |
| It is 36.81. | Ⓖ | Ⓗ |

4  The size 4 soccer ball Sean's team uses should have a mass of no more than 0.37 kilogram and no less than 0.31 kilogram. A soccer bag has two balls in it. What is the greatest mass they could have together? The least? Show your work.

5  Look at problem 4. Will the mass of three soccer balls be more than 1 kilogram? Explain.

**Solution**

# Refine Adding Decimals

**Complete the Example below. Then solve problems 1–9.**

## EXAMPLE

**Diana has two beads on her bracelet. The length of the red bead is 0.68 centimeter, and the length of the yellow bead is 1.22 centimeters. What is the total length of the two beads on Diana's bracelet?**

Look at how you could show your work using decimal grids.

$1 + 0.22 + 0.08 + 0.6 = 1.90$

*Solution* ........................................................

The student used decimal grids to show the addends. How could you show the addends using base-ten blocks?

PAIR/SHARE
Does it matter in what order you add the decimals?

## APPLY IT

**1** A U.S. quarter has a mass of 5.67 grams. A penny has a mass of 2.5 grams. What is the total mass of the two coins? Show your work.

How many hundredths are equivalent to 5 tenths?

**PAIR/SHARE**
How do you know what operation to use to solve this problem?

*Solution* ........................................................

**2** Kenton is shopping for clothes during a special event. He pays $24.99 for a pair of jeans and $5.25 for a clearance-priced shirt. He also pays $10 for a belt. How much does Kenton pay for his clothes? Show your work.

This problem takes more than one step to solve.

**PAIR/SHARE**
Explain how to check if your answer is reasonable.

**3** What is 11.54 + 1.25 + 0.16?

Ⓐ 25.64

Ⓑ 12.96

Ⓒ 12.95

Ⓓ 12.85

Chloe chose Ⓓ as the correct answer. How did she get that answer?

**Solution**

You can break apart the numbers by place value to add them.

**PAIR/SHARE**
How could Chloe check her answer?

**4** Randy rides his bike 1.23 miles to school. After school, he rides 0.9 mile to the library and another 1.05 miles to a park. How many miles does Randy ride his bike in all?

**5** Rafael runs the first half of a race in 23.08 seconds and the second half of the race in 27.92 seconds. What is Rafael's total time for the race?

Ⓐ 50 seconds

Ⓑ 50.72 seconds

Ⓒ 51 seconds

Ⓓ 51.9 seconds

**6** Choose all of the expressions that represent the sum 11.66 + 3.5.

Ⓐ $12 + \frac{1}{100}$

Ⓑ 1 ten + 5 ones + 1 tenth + 6 hundredths

Ⓒ twelve and one hundredth

Ⓓ 14.71

Ⓔ fifteen and sixteen hundredths

**7** Find the sum $2.32 + 1.7 + 0.09$. Show your work.

*Solution* ...........................................................................................................................

**8** The sum of three decimal numbers is 6. Exactly one of the numbers is less than 1.
What could the numbers be? Show your work.

*Solution* ...........................................................................................................................

**9** MATH JOURNAL

Write an addition problem involving two decimal numbers. At least one decimal
must include hundredths. Then explain how to solve your problem.

 SELF CHECK  Go back to the Unit 2 Opener and see what you can check off.

# Subtract Decimals

## Dear Family,
**This week your child is learning to subtract decimals.**

Your child can use what he or she knows about subtracting whole numbers to subtract decimals.

Strategies for subtraction include place-value understanding, drawing decimal models or number lines, using number properties that allow you to break apart numbers, and using the relationship between addition and subtraction.

For example, you can subtract 0.32 from 3.48 by lining up numbers by place value.

| Ones | . | Tenths | Hundredths |
|------|---|--------|------------|
| 3 | . | 4 | 8 |
| 0 | . | 3 | 2 |
| 3 | . | 1 | 6 |

(− on the left of the second and third rows)

You can also subtract 0.32 from 3.48 on a number line by breaking apart 0.32 into 0.3 and 0.02 and subtracting In parts.

On the number line below, the tick marks are 0.02 (2 hundredths) of a unit apart, so each hop of 5 tick marks represents subtracting 0.1. Starting at **3.48**, you can subtract 0.1 three times and then subtract 0.02. So, **3.48 − 0.32 = 3.16.**

Invite your child to share what he or she knows about subtracting decimals by doing the following activity together.

## ACTIVITY SUBTRACTING DECIMALS

**Do this activity with your child to subtract decimals.**

*Materials* calculator (optional)

Work with your child to make up and solve real-world problems involving subtraction of decimals.

• Take turns finding or making up some stories with decimal numbers. Include a decimal subtraction problem for the other person to solve.

• First, try to solve the problems with paper and pencil. Then check your answers with a calculator.

• Here are some examples:

1. A large fish measured 284.56 centimeters long. At one time, the world's longest goldfish was 47.4 centimeters long. What is the difference in length between the two fish?

2. A dog jumped 1.13 meters, and its human owner jumped 1.21 meters. How much further did the owner jump than the dog?

• Be on the lookout for other real-world examples of subtracting decimals. For example, a grocery receipt shows decimal subtraction when coupons are used to reduce the price of certain items. Challenge your child to estimate how much you saved on groceries by using coupons, and look at the receipt to check.

*Answers:* **1.** 237.16 centimeters; **2.** 0.08 meters

# Explore Subtracting Decimals

## Learning Target

- Add, subtract, multiply, and divide decimals to hundredths, using concrete models or drawings and strategies based on place value, properties of operations, and/or the relationship between addition and subtraction; relate the strategy to a written method and explain the reasoning used.

SMP 1, 2, 3, 4, 5, 6, 7

You have learned how to add decimals by adding the values of the digits with the same place values. Now you will learn how to subtract decimals. Use what you know to try to solve the problem below.

**The mass of a female hummingbird is 4.5 grams. The mass of a male hummingbird is 3.2 grams. What is the difference between the masses of the female and male hummingbirds?**

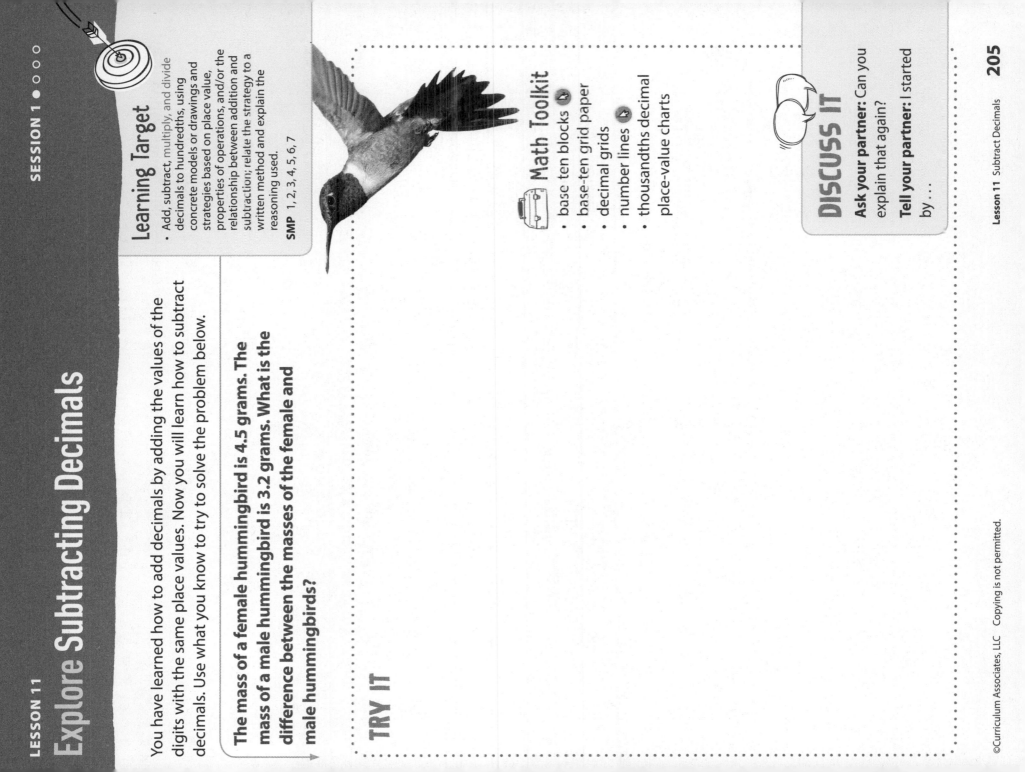

## Math Toolkit
- base ten blocks
- base-ten grid paper
- decimal grids
- number lines
- thousandths decimal place-value charts

## TRY IT

## DISCUSS IT

**Ask your partner:** Can you explain that again?

**Tell your partner:** I started by . . .

# CONNECT IT

## 1 LOOK BACK

Explain how you can find the difference between the masses of the female and male hummingbirds.

........................................................................

........................................................................

## 2 LOOK AHEAD

You can subtract decimals in different ways just like you can subtract whole numbers in different ways. Think about the problem **2.98 − 2.56**.

**a.** Write the problem in the place-value chart.

| Ones | • | Tenths | Hundredths |
|------|---|--------|------------|
|      | • |        |            |
|      | • |        |            |
| —    |   |        |            |

**b.** Subtract within each place. Write the difference.

**c.** You can also find the difference using a number line and an adding on strategy.

2.5    2.6    2.7    2.8    2.9    3.0

**2.56**    **2.98**

$$2.98 - 2.56 = 0.04 + 0.3 + 0.08 = \text{..................}$$

## 3 REFLECT

How is subtracting decimals like subtracting whole numbers?

........................................................................

........................................................................

# Prepare for Subtracting Decimals

1   Think about what you know about addition and subtraction. Fill in each box. Use
    words, numbers, and pictures. Show as many ideas as you can.

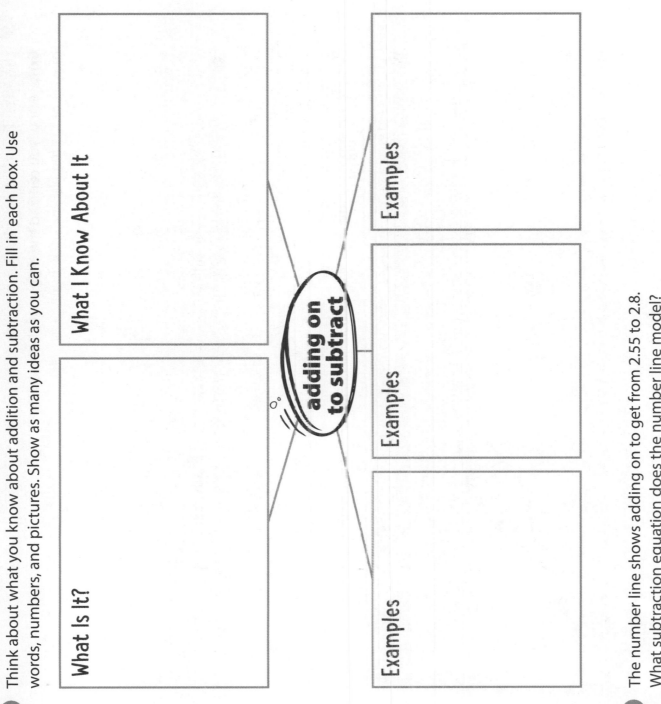

**What Is It?**

**What I Know About It**

adding on
to subtract

**Examples**

**Examples**

**Examples**

2   The number line shows adding on to get from 2.55 to 2.8.
    What subtraction equation does the number line model?

+0.05

+0.2

2.5    2.55    2.6    2.7    2.8

*Equation* ........................................................

**3** Solve the problem. Show your work.

**Tamara caught a fish that weighs 5.6 pounds. Victoria caught a fish that weighs 3.4 pounds. What is the difference between the weights of the fish?**

**4** Check your answer. Show your work.

# Develop Subtracting Decimals to Hundredths

Read and try to solve the problem below.

> Marty eats 2.05 ounces of cheese from a 4.6-ounce block of cheddar cheese. How many ounces of cheddar cheese are left?

## TRY IT

**Math Toolkit**
- base-ten blocks
- base-ten grid paper
- decimal grids
- number lines
- thousandths decimal place-value charts

©Curriculum Associates, LLC   Copying is not permitted.

---

## DISCUSS IT

**Ask your partner:** How did you get started?

**Tell your partner:** The strategy I used to find the answer was . . .

Explore different ways to understand subtracting decimals.

> Marty eats 2.05 ounces of cheese from a 4.6-ounce block of cheddar cheese. How many ounces of cheddar cheese are left?

## PICTURE IT

**You can subtract decimals using base-ten models.**

Model 4 wholes and 6 tenths.

6 tenths = 60 hundredths

Cross out 2 wholes and 5 hundredths.

## MODEL IT

**You can subtract decimals using a place-value chart.**

Using a place-value chart helps you make sure the place values are lined up correctly.

| | Ones | • | Tenths | Hundredths |
|---|---|---|---|---|
| **Original amount** | 4 | . | 6 | 0 |
| **Amount ate** | 2 | . | 0 | 5 |

$\frac{6}{10}$ is equivalent to $\frac{60}{100}$, so you can write a 0 in the hundredths column.

# CONNECT IT

**Now you will use the problem from the previous page to help you understand how to subtract decimals.**

**1** Look at the base-ten models in **Picture It**. Explain why parts of the models are crossed out.

.................................................................

**2** According to **Picture It**, how many ounces of cheese are left?

.................................................................

**3** Look at the place-value chart in **Model It**. You can subtract the decimals without a place-value chart by stacking them vertically. Line up the decimal points to keep track of place values.

$$\begin{array}{r} 4.60 \\ -\ 2.05 \\ \hline \end{array}$$

Explain why you cannot subtract the 5 from the 6 when finding the difference.

.................................................................

**4** Another way to express 6 tenths is ................ tenths + 10 hundredths.

So you can rewrite the problem as shown at the right.

Complete the subtraction. There are ................ ounces of cheese left.

$$\begin{array}{r} \overset{5}{4}.\overset{10}{6}0 \\ -\ 2.05 \\ \hline \boxed{\phantom{000}} \end{array}$$

**5** Explain how to subtract two decimals.

.................................................................

# REFLECT

**6** Look back at your **Try It**, strategies by classmates, and **Picture It** and **Model It**. Which models or strategies do you like best for subtracting decimals? Explain.

.................................................................

.................................................................

.................................................................

## APPLY IT

**Use what you just learned to solve these problems.**

**7** Anya has $3.07 in her change purse. She spends $1.15 on snacks at the vending machine. How much money does Anya have left? Show your work.

*Solution* ..........................................................

**8** Destiny is sending a box to a friend. The box weighs 23.5 pounds. Destiny removes a 4.47-pound book to decrease the shipping cost. What is the new weight of the box? Show your work.

*Solution* ..........................................................

**9** What is 241.3 − 81.55?

Ⓐ 150.85

Ⓑ 169.75

Ⓒ 159.85

Ⓓ 159.75

# Practice Subtracting Decimals to Hundredths

**Study the Example showing decimal subtraction using a place-value chart. Then solve problems 1–5.**

## EXAMPLE

Last year, Jeff ran the 40-yard dash in 5.8 seconds. This year, he ran it in 5.48 seconds. How much faster did he run this year than last year?

Use a place-value chart to write this year's and last year's times. Regroup as needed to subtract.

| | Ones | . | Tenths | Hundredths |
|---|---|---|---|---|
| **Last year's time** **is the same as** | 5 5 | . . | 8 7 | 0 10 |
| **This year's time** | 5 | . | 4 | 8 |

**5 ones − 5 ones = 0 ones**
**7 tenths − 4 tenths = 3 tenths**
**10 hundredths − 8 hundredths = 2 hundredths**

Difference − 0 ones + 3 tenths + 2 hundredths

Jeff ran 0.32 second faster this year than last year.

**1** Look at the Example. Rob ran the 40-yard dash in 4.95 seconds this year. Complete the place-value chart and steps to find how much faster Rob ran than Jeff.

| | Ones | . | Tenths | Hundredths |
|---|---|---|---|---|
| **Jeff's time** *is the same as* | 5 4 | . . | 4 | 8 |
| **Rob's time** | 4 | . | 9 | 5 |

_____ ones − 4 ones = _____ ones

_____ tenths − 9 tenths = _____ tenths

_____ hundredths − 5 hundredths = _____ hundredths

Difference = 0 ones + _____ tenths + _____ hundredths

Rob ran _____ second faster than Jeff.

2  Find the difference for the subtraction problem shown at the right.

The difference is _____.

$$\begin{array}{r} \overset{2\ 11}{7.\cancel{3}\cancel{1}} \\ -\ 5.24 \\ \hline \end{array}$$

3  Show how to find the difference 3.31 — 1.24 using base-ten blocks.
Show your work using quick-draw models.

**Solution** ....................................................................................................................

4  A cold piece of metal is placed into a cup of hot water. This causes the temperature of the water to fall 5.25°C. The original temperature of the water was 62.4°C. What is the new temperature?

Ⓐ 57.25°C

Ⓑ 57.15°C

Ⓒ 10.10°C

Ⓓ 10.9°C

5  Haley's anole lizard has a tail that is 7.25 centimeters long.
Caleb's anole lizard has a tail that is 6.17 centimeters long.
An anole lizard's tail is half the length of the lizard. How much longer is Haley's lizard than Caleb's lizard? Show your work.

**Solution** ....................................................................................................................

# Develop Adding On to Subtract

Read and try to solve the problem below.

**Galen can reach up to a height of 1.87 meters while standing flat on the ground. His father can reach a height of 2.56 meters. How much higher than Galen can Galen's father reach? Use addition to help solve the problem.**

## TRY IT

**Math Toolkit**
- base-ten blocks
- base-ten grid paper
- decimal grids
- number lines
- thousandths decimal place-value charts

## DISCUSS IT

**Ask your partner:** Why did you choose that strategy?

**Tell your partner:** A model I used was . . . It helped me . . .

Explore ways to understand using the relationship between addition and subtraction to subtract decimals.

Galen can reach up to a height of 1.87 meters while standing flat on the ground. His father can reach a height of 2.56 meters. How much higher than Galen can Galen's father reach? Use addition to help solve the problem.

## PICTURE IT

You can draw a bar model to understand the problem.

Use the bar model to write equations that represent the problem.

Subtraction equation: $2.56 - 1.87 = d$

Related addition equation: $1.87 + d = 2.56$

## MODEL IT

You can use a number line to model adding on to find a difference.

Start at **1.87** on the number line and add on to get to **2.56**.

Find the numbers that you add to get to an easier number.

**1.87** + **0.03** = 1.90 ← Add on **3 hundredths** to get to the next tenth.

1.90 + **0.1** = 2.00 ← Add on **1 tenth** to get to the next whole number.

2.00 + **0.56** = 2.56 ← Add on **56 hundredths** to get to the total, 2.56.

## CONNECT IT

**Now you will use the problem from the previous page to understand how to use the relationship between addition and subtraction to subtract decimals.**

1. Look at the bar model and the addition and subtraction equations in **Picture It.** What does the letter *d* represent?

   What do the numbers 2.56 and 1.87 represent?

2. Look at the number line in **Model It.** Why does the number line start at 1.87?

3. How can you use the jump numbers above the number line to find the value of *d*? ........

4. How much higher can Galen's father reach? ........

5. How can addition help you subtract decimals?

6. **REFLECT**

   Look back at your **Try It**, strategies by classmates, and **Picture It** and **Model It.** Which models or strategies do you like best for using addition to help you subtract decimals? Explain.

   ........................................................

   ........................................................

   ........................................................

## APPLY IT

**Use what you just learned to solve these problems.**

**6** At a swim meet, Quinn's time for the 50-meter freestyle event was 39.3 seconds. His sister, Darby, swam the same event in 38.85 seconds. How much faster did Darby swim 50 meters than Quinn? Show your work.

*Solution* ....................................................................

**7** Tamika has two guinea pigs for pets. Smokey weighs 39.73 ounces and Tito weighs 42.25 ounces. How much more does Tito weigh than Smokey? Show how to solve the problem by adding on.

*Solution* ....................................................................

**8** Which equation can you use to find 55.15 − 47.29?

Ⓐ $47.29 + n = 55.15$

Ⓑ $55.15 + n = 47.29$

Ⓒ $n = 47.29 + 55.15$

Ⓓ $47.29 = (55.1 + 0.5) - n$

# Practice Adding On to Subtract

**Study the Example showing how to use adding on to find a difference. Then solve problems 1–5.**

## EXAMPLE

The distance around a baseball is about 23.5 centimeters.
The distance around a tennis ball is about 20.98 centimeters.
How many centimeters greater is the distance around a baseball than the distance around a tennis ball?

Let $d$ be the difference in distances, in centimeters.

$23.5 - d = 20.98$ is the same as $20.98 + d = 23.5$.

Use adding on to find $d$. Start at **20.98**.

$20.98 + 0.02 = 21$ ⟵ Add on **0.02** to get to the next whole number.

$21 + 2 = 23$ ⟵ Add on **2** to get to the whole number closest to **23.5**.

$23 + 0.5 = 23.5$ ⟵ Add on **0.5** to get to **23.5**.

$d = 2$ ones + 5 tenths + 2 hundredths = **2.52**

The distance around a baseball is 2.52 centimeters greater than the distance around a tennis ball.

---

**1** Complete the bar model for $n = 11.75 - 9.30$.
Write a related addition equation.

**2** Complete the missing numbers above the jump arrows to show the parts that were added on to find $11.75 - 9.30$. Then add to find the difference.

*Solution* ......................................................

**3** A pitcher has 17.6 fluid ounces of iced tea in it. Erin pours 12.06 fluid ounces of tea into a glass to drink. How many fluid ounces of tea remain in the pitcher? Show how to solve the problem by adding on.

*Solution* .............................................................................................................................

**4** Use pictures, numbers, or words to explain how you can use the adding on strategy to find the difference $120.45 - 116.9$. What is the difference?

*Solution* .............................................................................................................................

**5** Two friends have large dogs. Tamika has a Great Dane that has a mass of 53.63 kilograms. Omar has a St. Bernard that has a mass of 78.3 kilograms. What is the difference, $d$, between the masses of the dogs?

**a.** Complete the bar model for the problem.

$d$

**b.** Write an equation that shows how adding on can be used to find the value of $d$. Then use the equation to solve the problem.

*Solution* .............................................................................................................................

# Refine Subtracting Decimals

**Complete the Example below. Then solve problems 1–8.**

## EXAMPLE

**A bowl has 16.5 ounces of mixed nuts. There are 8.25 ounces of peanuts, 5.3 ounces of almonds, and the rest are cashews. How many ounces of cashews are in the bowl of mixed nuts?**

Look at how you could show your work using equations.

Let $c$ = ounces of cashews.

$$8.25 + 5.3 + c = 16.5$$

$$
\begin{array}{r}
8.25 \\
+ 5.30 \\
\hline
13.55
\end{array}
\qquad
\begin{array}{r}
{\scriptstyle 5\ 14\ 10} \\
1\cancel{6}.\cancel{5}\cancel{0} \\
- 13.55 \\
\hline
2.95
\end{array}
$$

$$8.25 + 5.30 + 2.95 = 16.50$$

**Solution** ........................................

What operations are used to solve the problem?

## APPLY IT

1  On average, outdoor cats live 3.18 years and indoor cats live 16.7 years. How much longer does an average indoor cat live than an average outdoor cat? Show your work.

How many hundredths are equivalent to 7 tenths?

**Solution** ........................................

**2** Ling pays $2.12 for a gallon of milk and $7.79 for a 64-ounce jar of peanut butter. She uses a coupon to get $1.25 off the price of the peanut butter. How much does Ling pay for the milk and peanut butter? Show your work.

This problem takes more than one step to solve.

**3** Three boxes of cereal have masses of 379.4 grams, 424.25 grams, and 379.37 grams. What is the difference between the masses of the box of cereal with the greatest mass and the box of cereal with the least mass?

Ⓐ 44.15 grams

Ⓑ 44.85 grams

Ⓒ 44.88 grams

Ⓓ 45.12 grams

Cambria chose Ⓓ as the correct answer. How did she get that answer?

**Solution**

**4** What is the value of the expression 13.25 − 11.4?

Ⓐ 12.11

Ⓑ 2.85

Ⓒ 2.25

Ⓓ 1.85

**5** Which equations can be used to represent the bar model?

| 14.74 |
|---|

| 5.30 | |
|---|---|

$n$

Ⓐ $n = 5.30 - 14.74$

Ⓑ $14.74 = 5.3 + n$

Ⓒ $14.74 - n = 5.3$

Ⓓ $5.3 = n + 14.74$

Ⓔ $n = 14.74 + 5.3$

**6** Two boxes of books have a total mass of 35.1 kilograms. If one of the boxes of books has a mass of 22.08 kilograms, what is the mass of the other box? Show your work.

**Solution**

**7** Choose all the models or expressions that represent the difference 3.7 − 1.02.

Ⓐ

Ⓑ
2.5  2.6  2.7  2.8  2.9  3.0  3.1  3.2  3.3  3.4  3.5  3.6  3.7

Ⓒ 2 ones + 6 tenths + 8 hundredths

Ⓓ
2.5  2.6  2.7  2.8  2.9  3.0  3.1  3.2  3.3  3.4  3.5  3.6  3.7

Ⓔ

**8** MATH JOURNAL

Show how to find 2.62 − 1.91. Explain the strategy you chose.

☑ **SELF CHECK** Go back to the Unit 2 Opener and see what you can check off.

# Add Fractions

## Dear Family,

**This week your child is learning to add fractions with unlike denominators.**

Here is how a model can show fraction addition, such as $1\frac{3}{5} + \frac{1}{3}$.

$1\frac{3}{5}$     $+$     $\frac{1}{3}$

> The denominators, 5 and 3, tell how many equal parts are in the whole. 5 and 3 are **unlike denominators.**

The parts of the whole are different sizes, thirds and fifths. You cannot add different-size parts. You need to divide the model to show equal-size parts, fifteenths.

$1\frac{3}{5} = 1\frac{9}{15}$     $+$     $\frac{1}{3} = \frac{5}{15}$

> The denominator, 15, tells that there are 15 equal parts in the whole. So, 15 and 15 are **like denominators.**

Then add. $1\frac{3}{5} + \frac{1}{3} = 1\frac{9}{15} + \frac{5}{15} = 1\frac{14}{15}$

Some other ways your child can think about adding fractions are to use a number line model or to use multiplication to replace the given fractions with equivalent fractions that have the same denominator.

Invite your child to share what he or she knows about adding fractions by doing the following activity together.

# ACTIVITY ADDING FRACTIONS

**Do this activity with your child to add fractions.**

Work together with your child to solve real-world problems about adding fractions.

- Suppose you want to make some healthy snacks and you have $\frac{7}{8}$ cup of cream cheese and $\frac{3}{4}$ cup raisins.

- Look at the two recipes below. Add fractions to decide if there is enough cream cheese and raisins to make both recipes.

Recipe

## Recipe for Creamed Crackers

**Ingredients:**
12 crackers (any variety)

$\frac{1}{2}$ cup cream cheese

$\frac{1}{4}$ cup raisins

**Directions:**
Spread cream cheese evenly on crackers.

Sprinkle with raisins.

Recipe

## Recipe for Celery Logs

**Ingredients:**
6 two-inch pieces of celery

$\frac{1}{3}$ cup cream cheese

$\frac{1}{8}$ cup raisins

**Directions:**
Spread cream cheese evenly on celery.

Sprinkle with raisins.

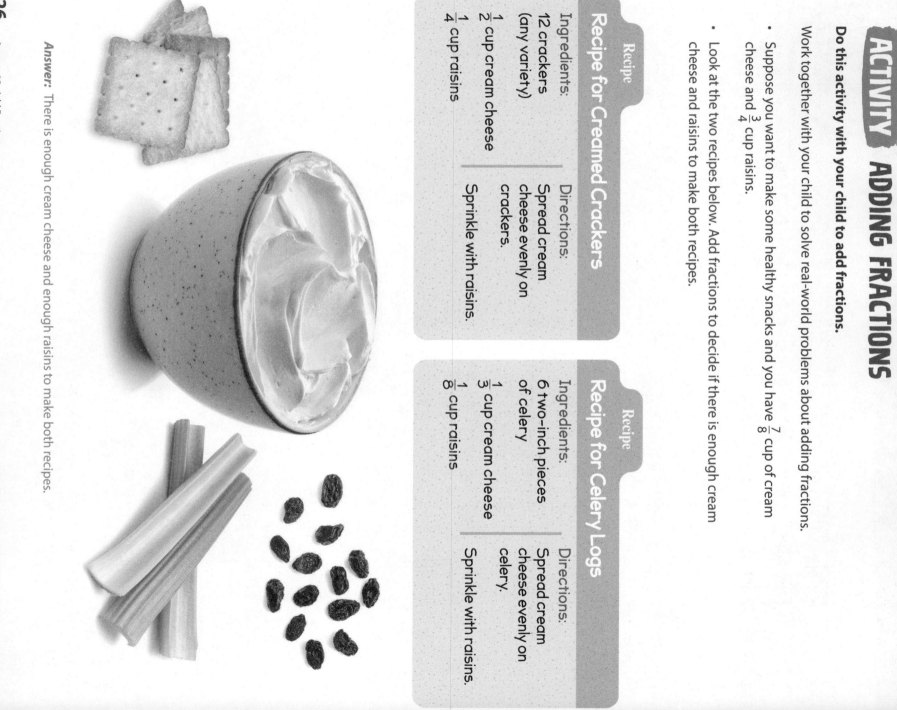

***Answer:*** There is enough cream cheese and enough raisins to make both recipes.

# Explore Adding Fractions

## Learning Target

- Add and subtract fractions with unlike denominators (including mixed numbers) by replacing given fractions with equivalent fractions in such a way as to produce an equivalent sum or difference of fractions with like denominators.

SMP 1, 2, 3, 4, 5, 6, 7

You know how to add fractions with like denominators. Now you will learn how to add fractions with unlike denominators. Use what you know to try to solve the problem below.

→ Emiliano needs $\frac{1}{2}$ stick of butter to make corn bread. He also needs $\frac{1}{4}$ stick of butter to make apple muffins. What fraction of a stick of butter does he need in all?

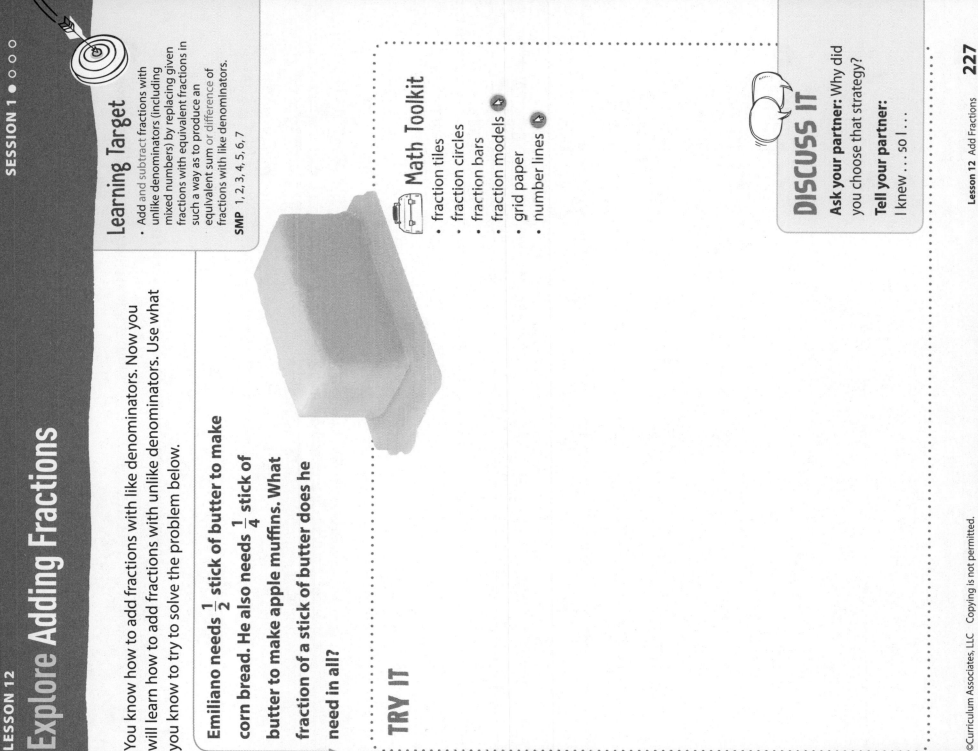

## Math Toolkit
- fraction tiles
- fraction circles
- fraction bars
- fraction models
- grid paper
- number lines

## TRY IT

## DISCUSS IT

**Ask your partner:** Why did you choose that strategy?

**Tell your partner:** I knew . . . so I . . . .

# CONNECT IT

## 1 LOOK BACK

Explain how you found how much butter Emiliano needs.

.......................................................................................

## 2 LOOK AHEAD

Before adding fractions, the fractions must have the same-size parts of a whole. You can use what you know about multiples and equivalent fractions to find a common denominator for fractions that have unlike denominators.

**a.** Use the fractions $\frac{1}{2}$ and $\frac{1}{3}$. Write the next four multiples of each denominator. Then circle the multiple that 2 and 3 have in common.

**Multiples of 2:** 2, ............, ............, ............, ............

**Multiples of 3:** 3, ............, ............, ............, ............

**b.** Complete the models and equations to show equivalent fractions for $\frac{1}{2}$ and $\frac{1}{3}$ using the common multiple as the common denominator.

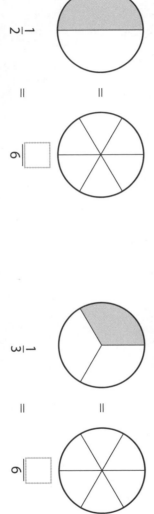

$\frac{1}{2}$ = $\frac{\boxed{\phantom{0}}}{6}$

$\frac{1}{3}$ = $\frac{\boxed{\phantom{0}}}{6}$

**c.** Use the equivalent fractions to add.

$$\frac{1}{2} + \frac{1}{3} = \frac{\boxed{\phantom{0}}}{6} + \frac{\boxed{\phantom{0}}}{6} = \frac{\boxed{\phantom{0}}}{6}$$

## 3 REFLECT

What equivalent fractions could you write to add $\frac{1}{2}$ and $\frac{2}{3}$? Explain.

.......................................................................................

# Prepare for Adding Fractions

1   Think about what you know about equivalent fractions. Fill in each box. Use words, numbers, and pictures. Show as many ideas as you can.

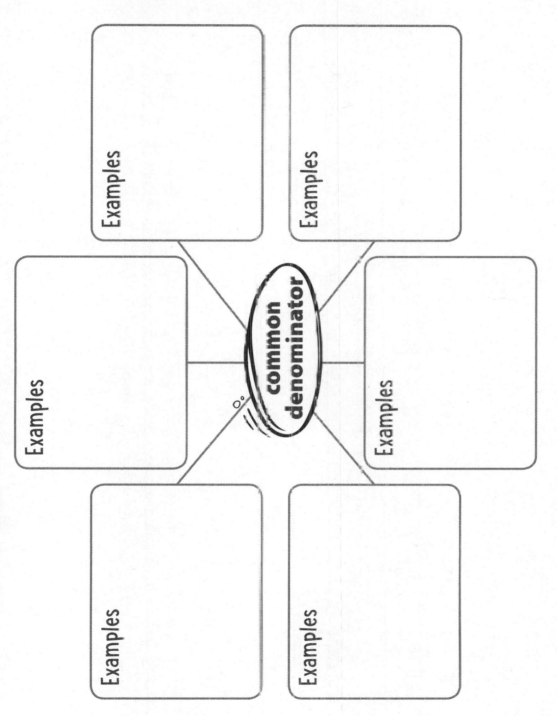

Examples

Examples

Examples

Examples

Examples

Examples

common denominator

2   How can you find a common denominator for $\frac{1}{3}$ and $\frac{1}{5}$?

3   Solve the problem. Show your work.

**Naeem needs $\frac{1}{4}$ cup of milk to make a carrot cake. He also needs $\frac{1}{8}$ cup of milk to make the icing for the cake. What fraction of a cup of milk does Naeem need in all?**

*Solution* ...................................................................................................................

4   Check your answer. Show your work.

# Develop Adding Fractions with Unlike Denominators

Read and try to solve the problem below.

Maggie paddles her kayak $\frac{1}{2}$ mile to an island.
Then she paddles $\frac{4}{5}$ mile to a beach. How far
does Maggie paddle her kayak in all?

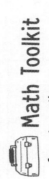

## TRY IT

**Math Toolkit**
- fraction tiles
- fraction circles
- fractions bars
- fraction models
- grid paper
- number lines

## DISCUSS IT

**Ask your partner:** Do you agree with me? Why or why not?

**Tell your partner:** I disagree with this part because . . .

Explore different ways to understand adding fractions with unlike denominators.

> Maggie paddles her kayak $\frac{1}{2}$ mile to an island.
> Then she paddles $\frac{4}{5}$ mile to a beach. How far does
> Maggie paddle her kayak in all?

## PICTURE IT

**You can picture the fractions in the problem using fraction bars.**

The fraction bars are divided into halves and fifths.

Island
$\frac{1}{2}$ mile

Beach
$\frac{4}{5}$ mile

Both fraction bars need to be divided into same-size parts.

Island
$\frac{5}{10}$ mile

Beach
$\frac{8}{10}$ mile

Now you can add equivalent fractions.

## MODEL IT

**You can model the problem with an equation.**

Replace the fractions $\frac{1}{2}$ and $\frac{4}{5}$ with equivalent fractions with a common denominator.

$$\frac{1}{2} = \frac{1 \times 5}{2 \times 5} = \frac{5}{10} \text{ and}$$

$$\frac{4}{5} = \frac{4 \times 2}{5 \times 2} = \frac{8}{10}$$

So, $\frac{1}{2} + \frac{4}{5} = \frac{5}{10} + \frac{8}{10}$.

## CONNECT IT

**Now you will use the problem from the previous page to help you understand how to add any two fractions with unlike denominators.**

**1** Explain why both fraction bars in **Picture It** are divided into 10 equal pieces.

**2** Write the total distance Maggie paddles as a fraction. _____ miles

Write the total distance Maggie paddles as a mixed number. _____ miles

**3** Look at the denominators in **Model It**. What do you notice about the relationship between the original denominators, 2 and 5, and the common denominator, 10?

**4** Is 10 the only common denominator for 2 and 5? Justify your answer.

**5** Explain how to add two fractions with unlike denominators.

**6** **REFLECT**

Look back at your **Try It**, strategies by classmates, and **Picture It** and **Model It**. Which models or strategies do you like best for adding fractions with unlike denominators? Explain.

.................................................................................................................

.................................................................................................................

.................................................................................................................

## APPLY IT

**Use what you just learned to solve these problems.**

**7** Hank practices $\frac{5}{8}$ of the words on his spelling list on Monday. He practices another $\frac{1}{4}$ of his list on Tuesday. What fraction of his spelling list has Hank practiced so far? Show your work.

**8** What is the sum of $\frac{7}{6}$ and $\frac{5}{8}$? Show your work.

*Solution* .........................................................................................

**9** What is the value of the expression $\frac{2}{3} + \frac{5}{12}$?

Ⓐ $\frac{7}{36}$

Ⓑ $\frac{7}{15}$

Ⓒ $\frac{13}{12}$

Ⓓ $\frac{38}{36}$

*Solution* .........................................................................................

# Practice Adding Fractions with Unlike Denominators

**Study the Example showing one way to add fractions with unlike denominators.
Then solve problems 1–4.**

## EXAMPLE

What is $\frac{3}{4} + \frac{1}{6}$?

To add fractions, the size of the parts must be the same. Write each addend as an equivalent fraction with a common denominator.

Identify 12 as a common multiple of the denominators 4 and 6. Divide the models into 12 equal parts.

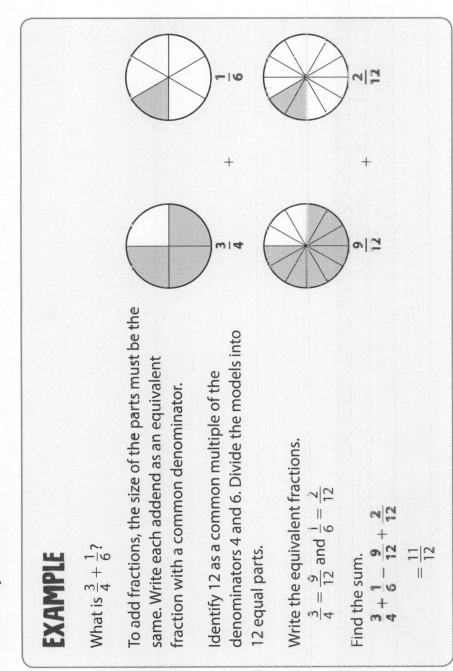

Write the equivalent fractions.

$$\frac{3}{4} = \frac{9}{12} \text{ and } \frac{1}{6} = \frac{2}{12}$$

Find the sum.

$$\frac{3}{4} + \frac{1}{6} = \frac{9}{12} + \frac{2}{12}$$
$$= \frac{11}{12}$$

1  The Example uses 12 as the common multiple of 4 and 6.

   **a.** Name a different common multiple of 4 and 6.

   **b.** If you used the common multiple from part a as the common denominator, how would the models in the Example be different? How would they be the same?

   **c.** Use the common multiple from part a as the common denominator to write equivalent fractions for $\frac{3}{4}$ and $\frac{1}{6}$.

   $\frac{3}{4} = $ ................    $\frac{1}{6} = $ ................

**2** Find a common denominator for each pair of fractions. Then use multiplication to write each fraction as an equivalent fraction with the common denominator.

**a.** $\frac{1}{8}$ and $\frac{1}{2}$    common denominator ..............

$$\frac{1 \times \boxed{\phantom{0}}}{8 \times \boxed{\phantom{0}}} = \frac{\boxed{\phantom{0}}}{\boxed{\phantom{0}}} \qquad \frac{1 \times \boxed{\phantom{0}}}{2 \times \boxed{\phantom{0}}} = \frac{\boxed{\phantom{0}}}{\boxed{\phantom{0}}}$$

**b.** $\frac{1}{8}$ and $\frac{9}{5}$    common denominator ..............

$$\frac{1 \times \boxed{\phantom{0}}}{8 \times \boxed{\phantom{0}}} = \frac{\boxed{\phantom{0}}}{\boxed{\phantom{0}}} \qquad \frac{9 \times \boxed{\phantom{0}}}{5 \times \boxed{\phantom{0}}} = \frac{\boxed{\phantom{0}}}{\boxed{\phantom{0}}}$$

**c.** $\frac{1}{8}$ and $\frac{11}{6}$    common denominator ..............

$$\frac{1 \times \boxed{\phantom{0}}}{8 \times \boxed{\phantom{0}}} = \frac{\boxed{\phantom{0}}}{\boxed{\phantom{0}}} \qquad \frac{11 \times \boxed{\phantom{0}}}{6 \times \boxed{\phantom{0}}} = \frac{\boxed{\phantom{0}}}{\boxed{\phantom{0}}}$$

**3** Show how to find the sum of $\frac{5}{6}$ and $\frac{1}{9}$ using the fraction bars below.

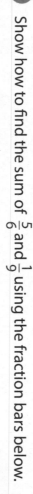

Write an equation for the sum.

**4** Glenn swims $\frac{2}{3}$ mile on Monday, $\frac{3}{4}$ mile on Wednesday, and $\frac{5}{6}$ mile on Friday. What is the total distance Glenn swims on those three days? Show your work.

**Solution** ...............................................................................................................

# Develop Adding with Mixed Numbers

Read and try to solve the problem below.

Jenna spent $1\frac{2}{3}$ hours mowing the back yard. After taking a break, she spent $\frac{3}{4}$ hour mowing the front yard. How many hours did she spend mowing the whole yard?

## TRY IT

**Math Toolkit**
- fraction tiles
- fraction circles
- fractions bars
- fraction models
- grid paper
- number lines

**DISCUSS IT**

**Ask your partner:** Can you explain that again?

**Tell your partner:** I do not understand how . . . .

Explore different ways to understand adding with mixed numbers.

**Jenna spent $1\frac{2}{3}$ hours mowing the back yard. After taking a break, she spent $\frac{3}{4}$ hour mowing the front yard. How many hours did she spend mowing the whole yard?**

## PICTURE IT

**You can picture the fractions in the problem using models.**

The shaded parts represent time spent on the back yard, $1\frac{2}{3}$ **hours,** and the front yard, $\frac{3}{4}$ **hour.**

$1\frac{2}{3}$ **hours**       +       $\frac{3}{4}$ **hours**

The sections need to be divided into same-size parts to add. Use dashed lines to divide the fraction models into 12 equal parts.

$\frac{8}{12}$ **hours**       +       $\frac{9}{12}$ **hours**

## MODEL IT

**You can use a number line to add fractions.**

The number line is divided first into thirds and then into twelfths, with a point at $1\frac{2}{3}$.

Start at $1\frac{2}{3}$ and jump right a total of $\frac{9}{12}$.

$\frac{1}{4} = \frac{3}{12}$, so $3\frac{3}{4} = \frac{3}{12} + \frac{3}{12} + \frac{3}{12}$.

$\frac{3}{12} + \frac{3}{12} + \frac{3}{12} = \frac{9}{12}$

## CONNECT IT

**Now you will use the problem from the previous page to help you understand how to add with mixed numbers.**

**1** Look at the models on the previous page. What is a common denominator of $1\frac{2}{3}$ and $\frac{3}{4}$? ............

**2** You can find this common denominator without a model. Write a multiplication equation that shows how the denominators 3 and 4 are related to 12.

..............

**3** Use this common denominator to find equivalent fractions for $1\frac{2}{3}$ and $\frac{3}{4}$.

$$1\frac{2}{3} + \frac{3}{4} = 1\frac{\square}{12} + \frac{\square}{12}$$

Then write the sum as a mixed number.

$$= 1\frac{\square}{12}$$

**4** The fractional part of the mixed number in problem 3 is more than 1. How could you rewrite the mixed number so that its fractional part is less than 1?

How many hours did Jenna spend mowing the whole yard? ........................

**5** Explain how to add with mixed numbers.

..........................

**6** REFLECT

Look back at your **Try It**, strategies by classmates, and **Picture It** and **Model It**. Which models or strategies do you like best for adding with mixed numbers? Explain.

............................

............................

# APPLY IT

## Use what you just learned to solve these problems.

**7** What is the sum $1\frac{1}{6} + 2\frac{3}{8}$? Show your work.

*Solution* ....................

**8** Cameron has $4\frac{3}{4}$ pounds of raspberries, $2\frac{1}{8}$ pounds of blueberries, and $\frac{1}{2}$ pound of blackberries to make a fruit salad. How many pounds of fruit does Cameron have in all? Show your work.

*Solution* ....................

**9** What is the value of the expression $5\frac{3}{5} + 4\frac{1}{15}$? Show your work.

*Solution* ....................

# Practice Adding with Mixed Numbers

**Study the Example showing how to add with mixed numbers. Then solve problems 1–4.**

## EXAMPLE

What is $1\frac{2}{3} + 1\frac{1}{2}$?

To add mixed numbers, the fractional parts must be the same size.

Replace the given fractions with equivalent fractions that have the denominator 6.

$1\frac{2}{3}$   +   $1\frac{1}{2}$

$1\frac{4}{6}$   +   $1\frac{3}{6}$

Find the sum. $1\frac{2}{3} + 1\frac{1}{2} = 1\frac{4}{6} + 1\frac{3}{6}$

$$= 2\frac{7}{6}$$

Rewrite the mixed number so that the fractional part is less than 1.

$$2\frac{7}{6} = 2 + \frac{7}{6} = 2 + 1\frac{1}{6}$$

$$= 3\frac{1}{6}$$

1   Draw a model to show how you can use equivalent fractions to find the sum $2\frac{1}{6} + 3\frac{1}{4}$. Show your work.

*Solution* ................................................................

**2** One way to find a common denominator is by multiplying the denominators of the two fractions together and using the product as the common denominator.

Use this method to find a common denominator for each pair of fractions. Write the equivalent fractions.

**a.** $1\frac{3}{5} = 1\frac{\boxed{\phantom{0}}}{20}$  $1\frac{3}{4} = 1\frac{\boxed{\phantom{0}}}{20}$

**b.** $2\frac{1}{2} = $ ............  $\frac{4}{5} = $ ............

**c.** $\frac{3}{8} = $ ............  $\frac{1}{6} = $ ............

**3** Show how to add $2\frac{1}{2} + \frac{4}{5}$ using the number line below.

Write an equation to represent the problem.

**4** Maya is packing her backpack for a hike. In one pocket, she puts in a $\frac{1}{2}$-pound bag of trail mix, a water bottle weighing $2\frac{1}{8}$ pounds, and a flashlight weighing $\frac{1}{4}$ pound. How much weight do these three items add to her backpack? Show your work.

*Solution* ......................................................................

# Refine Adding Fractions

**Complete the Example below. Then solve problems 1–8.**

## EXAMPLE

**What is $\frac{11}{8} + \frac{5}{6}$?**

Look at how you could show your work using equations.

24 is a multiple of 8 and 6.

$$\frac{11 \times 3}{8 \times 3} = \frac{33}{24} \text{ and } \frac{5 \times 4}{6 \times 4} = \frac{20}{24}$$

$$\frac{33}{24} + \frac{20}{24} = \frac{53}{24}$$

$$\frac{53}{24} = \frac{24}{24} + \frac{24}{24} + \frac{5}{24} = 1 + 1 + \frac{5}{24} = 2\frac{5}{24}$$

*Solution* ....................

The student found a common denominator before adding.

**PAIR/SHARE**
How would the solution method be different if you first wrote $\frac{11}{8}$ as $1\frac{3}{8}$?

## APPLY IT

1 What Is $\frac{3}{5} + \frac{13}{15}$? Show your work.

How can you use an estimate to check if your answer is reasonable?

**PAIR/SHARE**
Explain why you chose the type of model you did to solve this problem.

*Solution* ....................

**2** Michael rides his bike $2\frac{2}{3}$ miles on Saturday. He rides another $1\frac{5}{6}$ miles on Sunday. How many miles did Michael ride his bike on both days combined? Show your work.

............................................................

**Solution** ............................................................

**3** Sasha needs $\frac{3}{4}$ cup of flour to make a batch of muffins and $1\frac{2}{3}$ cups of flour to make a loaf of bread. How many cups of flour does Sasha need to make both a batch of muffins and a loaf of bread?

Ⓐ $\frac{17}{12}$

Ⓑ $\frac{8}{7}$

Ⓒ $1\frac{5}{7}$

Ⓓ $2\frac{5}{12}$

Nicola chose Ⓐ as the correct answer. How did she get that answer?

**4** The model below represents the expression $1\frac{5}{8} + 2\frac{1}{3}$.

Which of the following could NOT be represented by the model?

Ⓐ $1 + 2 + \frac{6}{10}$

Ⓑ $1\frac{15}{24} + 2\frac{8}{24}$

Ⓒ $1 + 2 + \frac{23}{24}$

Ⓓ $\frac{39}{24} + \frac{56}{24}$

**5** Sam has $5\frac{1}{2}$ yards of rope. He needs an additional $3\frac{5}{6}$ yards for a project. What is the total length of rope Sam needs for his project? Show your work.

**Solution**

**6** Which two fractions below can be added using the denominator 18?

| $\frac{1}{4}$ | $\frac{5}{6}$ | $\frac{7}{12}$ | $\frac{1}{8}$ | $\frac{4}{9}$ |

**Solution**

**7** Lucy is making a smoothie by following the recipe below.

Recipe

## Sunshine Smoothie

$1\frac{1}{3}$ cups banana

$\frac{1}{2}$ cup yogurt

1 cup strawberries

$\frac{3}{4}$ cup orange juice

Place ingredients in blender.

Blend until smooth.

Explain whether the recipe will make enough for Lucy and 3 friends to each have at least 1 cup of smoothie. If it does not make enough, explain how to change the recipe to make enough.

**8** **MATH JOURNAL**

Lin says that $\frac{5}{7} + \frac{3}{2}$ is $\frac{31}{14}$. Carlos says the sum is $\frac{8}{9}$. Who is right? Explain your answer.

 **SELF CHECK** Go back to the Unit 2 Opener and see what you can check off.

# Subtract Fractions

## Dear Family,

## This week your child is learning to subtract fractions with unlike denominators.

Your child might see a problem like this:

*Hailey needs $2\frac{1}{4}$ cups of almond milk for a recipe. She has $\frac{1}{2}$ cup. How much more almond milk does Hailey need?*

One way to model subtracting $\frac{1}{2}$ from $2\frac{1}{4}$ is with a number line.

Start at the point $2\frac{1}{4}$.

> Each whole on the number line is divided into 4 equal parts.

0    1    2  $2\frac{1}{4}$    3

To subtract $\frac{1}{2}$, you need to find a common denominator with the fraction in $2\frac{1}{4}$. The number 4 is a multiple of 2 and 4, so 4 is a common denominator.

Because $\frac{1}{2}$ is equivalent to $\frac{2}{4}$, you can start at $2\frac{1}{4}$ and jump back (left) $\frac{2}{4}$.

> Each jump back is $\frac{1}{4}$.

0    $1\frac{3}{4}$    2  $2\frac{1}{4}$    3

The number line shows that $2\frac{1}{4} - \frac{1}{2} = 1\frac{3}{4}$. Hailey needs $1\frac{3}{4}$ cups of almond milk.

Some other ways your child can think about subtracting fractions include using fraction bars or using multiplication to replace the given fractions with equivalent fractions that have the same denominator.

Invite your child to share what he or she knows about subtracting fractions by doing the following activity together.

# ACTIVITY SUBTRACTING FRACTIONS

**Do this activity with your child to subtract fractions.**

*Materials* ruler, yardstick, or measuring tape, and a variety of household objects

Work with your child to compare the lengths or heights of various objects around your home.

- Find two objects and measure their lengths. Measure the length of one object to the nearest $\frac{1}{2}$ inch and the length of the second object to the nearest $\frac{1}{8}$ or $\frac{1}{16}$ inch.

    *Examples:* lengths of fork and spoon, lengths of hand and foot

- Determine how much longer one object is than the other.

- Continue to practice adding fractions by finding the combined length of two or more objects and then comparing the combined length to another length.

- Find the combined length of your hand and foot. Next, find the combined length of a family member's hand and foot. Then find the difference between the two combined lengths.

Look for other real-world examples of subtracting fractions with your child.

# Explore Subtracting Fractions

In the previous lesson, you learned about adding fractions. Now you will learn about subtracting fractions. Use what you know to try to solve the problem below.

**Paul has a $\frac{3}{4}$-inch long bolt.**

**He buys a bolt that is $\frac{1}{8}$ inch longer and a bolt that is $\frac{1}{8}$ inch shorter than the $\frac{3}{4}$-inch bolt. What are the lengths of the two bolts he buys?**

## Learning Target

- Add and subtract fractions with unlike denominators (including mixed numbers) by replacing given fractions with equivalent fractions in such a way as to produce an equivalent sum or difference of fractions with like denominators.

**SMP** 1, 2, 3, 4, 5, 6, 7

## TRY IT

🧰 **Math Toolkit**
- fraction tiles
- fraction circles
- fraction bars
- fraction models 🖐
- grid paper
- number lines 🖐

## DISCUSS IT

**Ask your partner:** Can you explain that again?

**Tell your partner:** I started by . . .

## CONNECT IT

### 1 LOOK BACK

Explain how to find the lengths of the two bolts Paul buys.

....................................................................................................

....................................................................................................

### 2 LOOK AHEAD

Just like with adding fractions, you must find a common denominator to subtract fractions with unlike denominators.

**a.** Write the first four multiples of each denominator, such as $\frac{3}{4} - \frac{1}{3}$. Then circle the common multiple to find a common denominator.

Multiples of 4: ..............., ..............., ..............., ...............

Multiples of 3: ..............., ..............., ..............., ...............

**b.** Complete the models and equations to show the equivalent fractions for $\frac{3}{4}$ and $\frac{1}{3}$ using the common multiple as the common denominator.

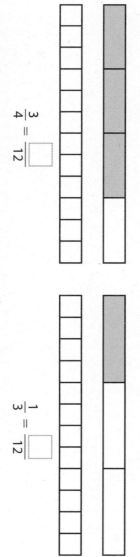

$$\frac{3}{4} = \frac{\square}{12}$$

$$\frac{1}{3} = \frac{\square}{12}$$

**c.** Use the equivalent fractions to subtract.

$$\frac{3}{4} - \frac{1}{3} = \frac{\square}{12} - \frac{\square}{12} = \frac{\square}{12}$$

### 3 REFLECT

How is subtracting fractions like adding fractions?

....................................................................................................

....................................................................................................

# Prepare for Subtracting Fractions

1  Think about what you know about fractions. Fill in each box. Use words, numbers, and pictures. Show as many ideas as you can.

| In My Own Words | My Illustrations |
|---|---|
| | |

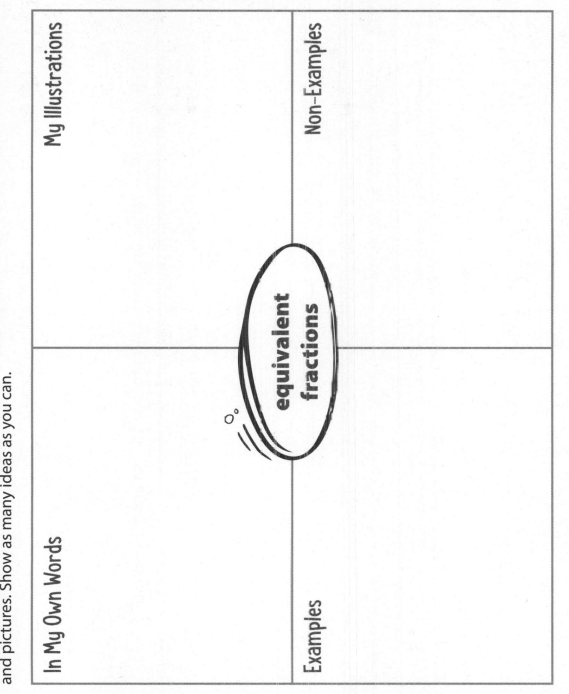

equivalent fractions

| Examples | Non-Examples |
|---|---|
| | |

2  Jackie says that the fraction $\frac{7}{8}$ is equivalent to $\frac{3}{4}$. Is she right? Explain.

**3** Solve the problem. Show your work.

**Solange has a nut that is $\frac{5}{8}$ inch wide. She buys a nut that is $1\frac{1}{4}$ inch wider and a nut that is $\frac{1}{4}$ inch narrower than the $\frac{5}{8}$-inch nut. What are the widths of the two nuts she buys?**

**Solution** ..................................................................................

**4** Check your answer. Show your work.

# Develop Subtracting Fractions with Unlike Denominators

Read and try to solve the problem below.

**Gavin has $\frac{2}{3}$ pint of water left in his water bottle.**

**He drinks $\frac{1}{2}$ pint. How much water is left in the bottle now?**

## TRY IT

🧰 **Math Toolkit**
- fraction tiles
- fraction circles
- fraction bars
- fraction models ▲
- grid paper
- number lines ▲

---

## DISCUSS IT

**Ask your partner:** How did you get started?

**Tell your partner:** I am not sure how to find the answer because . . .

Explore different ways to understand subtracting fractions with unlike denominators.

> **Gavin has $\frac{2}{3}$ pint of water left in his water bottle. He drinks $\frac{1}{2}$ pint.**
> **How much water is left in the bottle now?**

## PICTURE IT

**You can use a picture to model subtracting fractions.**

The water bottle is marked to show that
it has $\frac{2}{3}$ pint of water in it. Gavin drinks
$\frac{1}{2}$ pint of water.

Use equivalent fractions to find a
common denominator.

$$\frac{2}{3} = \frac{4}{6}$$

$$\frac{1}{2} = \frac{3}{6}$$

Now the water bottle is marked to show
sixths. You can subtract $\frac{3}{6}$ from $\frac{4}{6}$.

## MODEL IT

**You can use a number line to model subtracting fractions.**

The number line below is divided into sixths, the common denominator.

Start at $\frac{4}{6}$ and jump left $\frac{3}{6}$. ($\frac{3}{6}$ is three $\frac{1}{6}$ units on the number line.)

# CONNECT IT

**Now you will use the problem from the previous page to help you understand how to use equivalent fractions to subtract.**

**1** Look at **Picture It** and **Model It** from the previous page. Why is $\frac{1}{2}$ rewritten as $\frac{3}{6}$? Why is $\frac{2}{3}$ rewritten as $\frac{4}{6}$?

**2** Why are sixths chosen as a common denominator?

**3** Use sixths as a common denominator. Write an equation to show the difference of $\frac{2}{3}$ and $\frac{1}{2}$.

**4** How much water is left in the bottle?

**5** Could you have subtracted with a different common denominator? Provide an example.

**6** Explain how to subtract two fractions with unlike denominators.

**7 REFLECT**

Look back at your **Try It**, strategies by classmates, and **Picture It** and **Model It**. Which models or strategies do you like best for subtracting fractions with unlike denominators? Explain.

# APPLY IT

**Use what you just learned to solve these problems.**

**8** What is $\frac{7}{8} - \frac{1}{6}$? Show your work.

**Solution** ....................................................................................

**9** Emily's shelf is $\frac{3}{4}$ foot wide. Her clock is $\frac{2}{3}$ foot wide.

How much wider is her shelf than her clock? Show your work.

**Solution** ....................................................................................

**10** What is the value of the expression $\frac{9}{10} - \frac{3}{5}$? Show your work.

**Solution** ....................................................................................

# Practice Subtracting Fractions with Unlike Denominators

**Study the Example showing one way to subtract fractions with unlike denominators. Then solve problems 1–5.**

## EXAMPLE

Felicia lives $\frac{4}{5}$ mile from school and $\frac{3}{10}$ mile from the soccer field. How much closer does she live to the soccer field than to school?

You can show $\frac{4}{5} - \frac{3}{10}$ using a number line. Use a common multiple to find the common denominator.

Rewrite the fractions as needed. $\frac{4}{5} = \frac{8}{10}$

Show the difference between the distance from school, $\frac{8}{10}$ mile, and the distance from the soccer field, $\frac{3}{10}$ mile, on a number line.

Felicia lives $\frac{5}{10}$, or $\frac{1}{2}$, mile closer to the soccer field than to school.

1 How could you count back on a number line to find the difference between $\frac{4}{5}$ and $\frac{5}{10}$? Show your work.

The difference is ................

2 Eric added up on a number line to find $\frac{4}{5} - \frac{5}{10}$. Use equivalent fractions and an addition equation to show how Eric found the difference.

**3** What is the difference between $\frac{5}{6}$ and $\frac{1}{4}$? Show your work.

**4**

$\frac{5}{6} - \frac{1}{4} =$ ................

Show how you can use the visual model to subtract $\frac{3}{4} - \frac{5}{8}$.

$\frac{3}{4} - \frac{5}{8} =$ ................

**5** James sleeps $\frac{3}{8}$ of each day. He spends $\frac{1}{3}$ of each day at work.
What fraction of his day is he not sleeping or working?
Show your work.

**Solution** ............................................................................

# Develop Subtracting with Mixed Numbers

Read and try to solve the problem below.

> **On Saturday, Chloe spent 3 $\frac{1}{4}$ hours at the park with her family. Then she spent 1 $\frac{2}{3}$ hours riding her bike. How much longer did Chloe spend at the park than riding her bike?**
>
> **Give your answer as a number of hours.**

## TRY IT

**Math Toolkit**
- fraction tiles
- fraction circles
- fraction bars
- fraction models
- grid paper
- number lines

---

## DISCUSS IT

**Ask your partner:** Why did you choose that strategy?

**Tell your partner:** A model I used was . . . It helped me . . .

Explore different ways to understand subtracting with mixed numbers.

**On Saturday, Chloe spent $3\frac{1}{4}$ hours at the park with her family. Then she spent $1\frac{2}{3}$ hours riding her bike. How much longer did Chloe spend at the park than riding her bike?**

**Give your answer as a number of hours.**

## PICTURE IT

**You can use fraction bars to picture subtracting with mixed numbers.**

Chloe spent $3\frac{1}{4}$ hours at the park. To subtract $1\frac{2}{3}$ hours, find a common denominator.

Hours spent at the park: $3\frac{1}{4} = 3\frac{3}{12}$    Hours spent riding her bike: $1\frac{2}{3} = 1\frac{8}{12}$

Model $3\frac{3}{12}$.

You need **more twelfths** to subtract $1\frac{8}{12}$.

$$3\frac{3}{12} = 2\frac{15}{12}$$

## MODEL IT

**You can use equations to subtract mixed numbers.**

You can regroup one whole and break apart the mixed numbers to find $3\frac{3}{12} - 1\frac{8}{12}$.

3 wholes and $\frac{3}{12}$ is the same as 2 wholes and $\frac{15}{12}$.

$$2 - 1 = 1 \text{ and } \frac{15}{12} - \frac{8}{12} = \frac{7}{12}$$

## CONNECT IT

**Now you will use the problem from the previous page to help you understand how to subtract mixed numbers with regrouping.**

1 Look at the first set of fraction bars in **Picture It**. Why is the last bar split into 12 pieces instead of 4 pieces?

2 Now look at the second set of fraction bars in **Picture It**. Explain why $3\frac{3}{12}$ is now shown as $2\frac{15}{12}$.

3 Look at **Model It**. How does the regrouping of $3\frac{3}{12}$ as $2\frac{15}{12}$ help you find how much longer Chloe spent at the park than riding her bike?

4 How much longer did Chloe spend at the park than riding her bike? ........... hour(s)

5 Show how you can use addition to check your answer.

6 Do you always need to regroup when you subtract mixed numbers with unlike denominators? Explain.

7 **REFLECT**

Look back at your **Try It**, strategies by classmates, and **Picture It** and **Model It**. Which models or strategies do you like best for subtracting mixed numbers? Explain.

..................................................................................................................

..................................................................................................................

## APPLY IT

### Use what you just learned to solve these problems.

**8** What is $7\frac{3}{5} - \frac{9}{10}$? Show your work.

*Solution* ..........................................................................................................

**9** What is the difference between $2\frac{5}{8}$ and $1\frac{1}{4}$? Show your work.

*Solution* ..........................................................................................................

**10** Charlie is practicing the long jump. His first jump is a distance of $16\frac{5}{6}$ feet. His second jump is a distance of $18\frac{2}{3}$ feet. How much longer is Charlie's second jump?

Ⓐ $1\frac{1}{6}$ feet

Ⓑ $1\frac{5}{6}$ feet

Ⓒ $2\frac{1}{6}$ feet

Ⓓ $2\frac{5}{6}$ feet

# Practice Subtracting with Mixed Numbers

**Study the Example showing how to subtract mixed numbers. Then solve problems 1–5.**

## EXAMPLE

What is the difference between $3\frac{3}{8}$ and $1\frac{3}{4}$?

You can show $3\frac{3}{8} - 1\frac{3}{4}$ using fraction bars.

Rewrite the mixed numbers using common denominators. $3\frac{3}{8} - 1\frac{6}{8}$

Model $3\frac{3}{8}$. Divide the last fraction bar into eighths.

Divide one more fraction bars into eighths so there are enough eighths to subtract.

$\frac{6}{8}$

1

Find the difference: $2\frac{11}{8} - 1\frac{6}{8} = 1\frac{5}{8}$.

1 Now use the fraction bars to find $3\frac{3}{8} - 1\frac{1}{4}$. Show your work.

$3\frac{3}{8} - 1\frac{1}{4} =$ _____

2 What is $6\frac{5}{6} - 4\frac{1}{3}$? Show your work.

*Solution* _____

**3** Sometimes it is helpful to rewrite mixed numbers in a form that includes a fraction greater than 1. Use the number line to write the missing numbers.

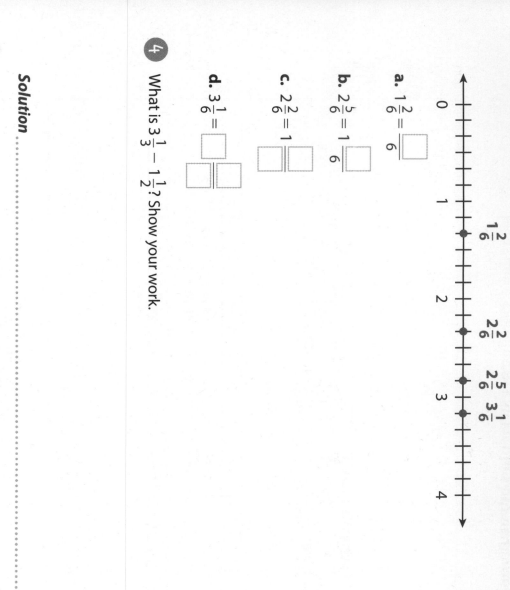

a. $1\frac{2}{6} = \frac{\Box}{6}$

b. $2\frac{5}{6} = 1\frac{\Box}{6}$

c. $2\frac{2}{6} = 1\frac{\Box}{\Box}$

d. $3\frac{1}{6} = \frac{\Box}{\Box}$

**4** What is $3\frac{1}{3} - 1\frac{1}{2}$? Show your work.

*Solution* .................................................................................................................

**5** Emil's backpack weighs $6\frac{3}{8}$ pounds. He removes a book that weighs $\frac{3}{4}$ pound. Then he removes a book that weighs $\frac{1}{2}$ pound. How much does Emil's backpack weigh now? Show your work.

*Solution* .................................................................................................................

# Refine Subtracting Fractions

**Study the Example below. Then solve problems 1–8.**

## EXAMPLE

**The first chapter of Henry's book is $5\frac{2}{3}$ pages long. The second chapter is $8\frac{2}{5}$ pages long. How much longer is the second chapter than the first chapter?**

Look at how you could show your work using equations.

$5\frac{2}{3} - 5 + \left(\frac{2 \times 5}{3 \times 5}\right) - 5\frac{10}{15}$

$8\frac{2}{5} - 8 + \left(\frac{2 \times 3}{5 \times 3}\right) - 8\frac{6}{15} - \left(7 + \frac{15}{15}\right) + \frac{6}{15} - 7\frac{21}{15}$

$\begin{array}{r} 7\frac{21}{15} \\ - 5\frac{10}{15} \\ \hline 2\frac{11}{15} \end{array}$

After finding a common denominator, the student used a vertical format to subtract.

**Solution**

## APPLY IT

**1** What is $5\frac{4}{5} - 1\frac{9}{10}$? Show your work.

**Solution**

**2** What number do you add to $\frac{3}{4}$ to get $\frac{5}{6}$? Show your work.

What common multiple of 6 and 4 can you use as a common denominator?

**Solution** ..........................................................................

*PAIR/SHARE*

Explain why you chose the model you did to solve this problem.

**3** Cara's bathroom floor has an area of $3\frac{2}{3}$ square yards. She lays down a rug that has an area of $1\frac{1}{4}$ square yards. What area of her floor is NOT covered by the rug?

Ⓐ 2 square yard

Ⓑ $2\frac{1}{12}$ square yards

Ⓒ $2\frac{5}{12}$ square yards

Ⓓ $2\frac{3}{7}$ square yards

Jordan chose Ⓓ as the correct answer. How did he get that answer?

*PAIR/SHARE*

What equivalent mixed number could you subtract?

*PAIR/SHARE*

Does a denominator of 7 make sense?

Quack!
Quack!

**4** What is the value of the expression $\frac{3}{5} - \frac{1}{3}$?

Ⓐ $\frac{2}{2}$

Ⓑ $\frac{4}{15}$

Ⓒ $\frac{2}{5}$

Ⓓ $\frac{6}{15}$

**5** Mackenzie's footprint is $\frac{7}{12}$ foot long. Her dad's footprint is $1\frac{1}{6}$ feet long.

Can the equation be used to find how much longer Mackenzie's dad's footprint is than Mackenzie's?

|  | Yes | No |
|---|---|---|
| $1\frac{2}{12} - \frac{7}{12} = ?$ | Ⓐ | Ⓑ |
| $\frac{7}{12} + 1\frac{1}{6} = ?$ | Ⓒ | Ⓓ |
| $1\frac{1}{6} - \frac{2}{3} = ?$ | Ⓔ | Ⓕ |
| $\frac{14}{12} - \frac{7}{12} = ?$ | Ⓖ | Ⓗ |

**6** The sum of $4\frac{1}{2}$ and what number is $12\frac{5}{7}$? Show your work.

**Solution** ...........................................................................................................

**7** Carter has an older sister and a younger brother.

**Part A** Carter's sister is $17\frac{1}{3}$ years old. Carter is $2\frac{1}{2}$ years younger than his sister.
What is Carter's age in years? Show your work.

*Solution* ................................................................

**Part B** Carter's brother is $5\frac{3}{4}$ years younger than their sister. How much older is
Carter than his brother? Show your work.

*Solution* ................................................................

**8** MATH JOURNAL

Find the difference between $1\frac{2}{5}$ and $\frac{9}{10}$. Explain how you solved the problem.

.............................................................................

✓ **SELF CHECK**  Go back to the Unit 2 Opener and see what you can check off.

# Add and Subtract in Word Problems

## Dear Family,

**This week your child is learning to add and subtract fractions and decimals in word problems.**

Your child is also learning to estimate the answer in order to check whether an answer is reasonable or not. He or she might see a problem like this:

*Paul used $\frac{5}{8}$ cup of milk to make muffins and $\frac{1}{3}$ cup of milk to make nut bread.*

*How much milk did Paul use to make muffins and nut bread?*

To solve the problem, add the fractions $\frac{5}{8}$ and $\frac{1}{3}$.

It can be helpful to show the fractions on number lines.

To estimate the sum, you can use a benchmark fraction for each fraction in the problem. Here, $\frac{1}{2}$ is a good benchmark fraction to use.

$\frac{5}{8}$ is close to $\frac{1}{2}$ and $\frac{1}{3}$ is close to $\frac{1}{2}$. Since $\frac{1}{2} + \frac{1}{2} = 1$, an estimate of $\frac{5}{8} + \frac{1}{3}$ is about 1.

Now add the fractions $\frac{5}{8} + \frac{1}{3}$. The fractions need to have equal-size parts, so write equivalent fractions with like denominators. Then add.

$\frac{5}{8} = \frac{15}{24}$   $\frac{1}{3} = \frac{8}{24}$

$\frac{15}{24} + \frac{8}{24} = \frac{23}{24}$

Is a sum of $\frac{23}{24}$ a reasonable answer? Check the sum against the estimate you made.

The estimate is about 1, and $\frac{23}{24}$ is about 1, so the sum is reasonable.

Invite your child to share what he or she knows about adding and subtracting fractions in word problems by doing the following activity together.

## ACTIVITY  ADDING AND SUBTRACTING FRACTIONS IN WORD PROBLEMS

**Do this activity with your child to add and subtract in word problems.**

Work together with your child to identify some real-world situations when you might use fractions, such as when you are cooking, building, or gardening.

• Here are some examples in which you might add and subtract fractions:

A recipe for soup calls for $2\frac{1}{3}$ cups of water and $1\frac{3}{8}$ cups of milk.

One piece of wood is $4\frac{1}{2}$ feet long and another piece is $2\frac{2}{3}$ feet long.

A string used for tomato plants is $3\frac{3}{4}$ feet long. Another string is $2\frac{1}{3}$ feet long.

Choose one of the examples above. Add the mixed numbers in that example. Work together to first make an estimate of the sum. Check your answer against the estimate to make sure your answer is reasonable.

# Explore Adding and Subtracting in Word Problems

Now that you can add and subtract fractions with different denominators, you can use this skill to solve word problems. Use what you know to try to solve the problem below.

Aleena has a 1-gallon watering can that is full of water. She uses $\frac{3}{8}$ gallon to water her roses and $\frac{1}{3}$ gallon to water her geraniums. How much water did Aleena use to water both the roses and geraniums?

## Learning Target

- Solve word problems involving addition and subtraction of fractions referring to the same whole, including cases of unlike denominators, e.g., by using visual fraction models or equations to represent the problem. Use benchmark fractions and number sense of fractions to estimate mentally and assess the reasonableness of answers.

SMP 1, 2, 3, 4, 5, 6

## Math Toolkit
- fraction tiles
- fraction circles
- fraction bars
- fraction models
- grid paper
- number lines

## TRY IT

## DISCUSS IT

**Ask your partner:** How did you get started?

**Tell your partner:** I knew . . . so I . . . .

# CONNECT IT

## 1 LOOK BACK

Explain how you found how much water Aleena used to water both the roses and the geraniums.

## 2 LOOK AHEAD

A benchmark fraction is a common fraction that you can easily compare to other fractions. The number line below shows the location of some benchmark fractions between 0 and 2. You can use these fractions to estimate sums and differences.

$$0 \quad \frac{1}{4} \quad \frac{1}{2} \quad \frac{3}{4} \quad 1 \quad 1\frac{1}{4} \quad 1\frac{1}{2} \quad 1\frac{3}{4} \quad 2$$

a. Between which two benchmark fractions is $\frac{3}{8}$? How do you know?

b. Between which two benchmark fractions is $\frac{1}{3}$? How do you know?

c. Use your answers from parts a and b above to find a low estimate for the sum $\frac{3}{8} + \frac{1}{3}$ and a high estimate for the sum $\frac{3}{8} + \frac{1}{3}$. Explain your reasoning.

## 3 REFLECT

The actual sum of any two fractions will be somewhere between a low estimate and a high estimate for the sum. How does the actual sum you found in problem 1 compare to your low estimate and high estimate for the sum?

# Prepare for Adding and Subtracting in Word Problems

**1** Think about what you know about benchmark fractions. Fill in each box. Use words, numbers, and pictures. Show as many ideas as you can.

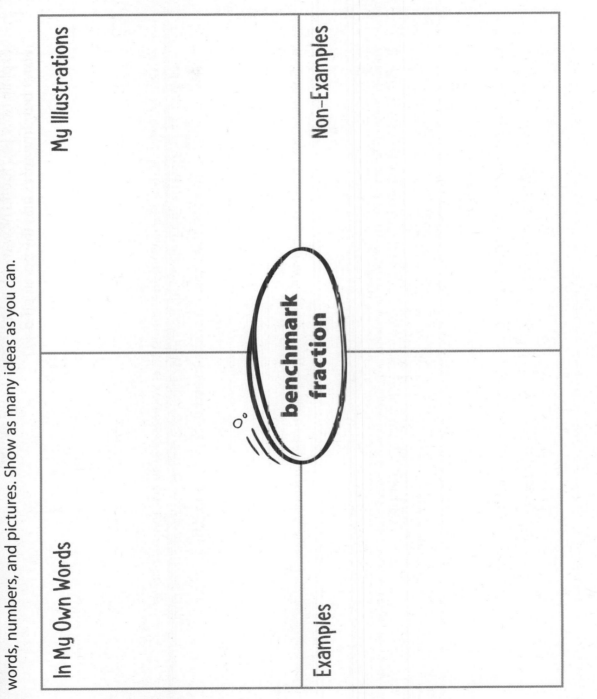

| In My Own Words | My Illustrations |
|---|---|
| | |

benchmark fraction

| Examples | Non-Examples |
|---|---|
| | |

**2** Between which two benchmark fractions is $\frac{5}{8}$? How do you know?

0    $\frac{1}{4}$    $\frac{1}{2}$    $\frac{3}{4}$    1    $1\frac{1}{4}$    $1\frac{1}{2}$    $1\frac{3}{4}$    2

③ Solve the problem. Show your work.

**Hai has a 1-gallon jug of water. He drinks $\frac{1}{8}$ gallon of water before lunch and $\frac{2}{3}$ gallon of water after lunch. How much water did Hai drink all day?**

④ Check your answer. Show your work.

**Solution** ...............................................................................

# Develop Estimating in Word Problems with Fractions

Read and try to solve the problem below.

Frankie purchases a $3\frac{1}{2}$-pound bag of chicken.

He uses $1\frac{1}{3}$ pounds of chicken for fajitas.

How many pounds of chicken does Frankie

have left? Estimate and solve. Tell if your

answer is reasonable.

## TRY IT

### Math Toolkit
- fraction tiles
- fraction circles
- fraction bars
- fraction models
- grid paper
- number lines

## DISCUSS IT

**Ask your partner:** Do you agree with me? Why or why not?

**Tell your partner:** I disagree with this part because ....

Explore different ways to understand estimating with fractions.

**Frankie purchases a $3\frac{1}{2}$-pound bag of chicken. He uses $1\frac{1}{3}$ pounds of chicken for fajitas. How many pounds of chicken does Frankie have left?**

**Estimate and solve. Tell if your answer is reasonable.**

## MODEL IT

**You can use a number line to find benchmark fractions to estimate.**

$3\frac{1}{2}$ is already a benchmark fraction you can use to estimate.

You can find a benchmark fraction close to $1\frac{1}{3}$ to help you estimate the difference.

## MODEL IT

**You can model the problem with a number line.**

Since $2 \times 3 = 6$, the fractions in the problem, $3\frac{1}{2}$ and $1\frac{1}{3}$, can be rewritten using a common denominator of 6. $3\frac{1}{2} = 3\frac{3}{6}$, and $1\frac{1}{3} = 1\frac{2}{6}$.

The number line below is divided into sixths. It shows starting with a total of $3\frac{1}{2}$ pounds and then making two jumps to the left for the $1\frac{1}{3}$ pounds of chicken used.

You can rewrite $3\frac{1}{2} - 1\frac{1}{3}$ as $3\frac{3}{6} - 1\frac{2}{6}$.

# CONNECT IT

**Now you will use the problem from the previous page to help you understand how to use estimation with adding and subtracting fractions.**

**1** Look at the first **Model It**. Identify the closest half on each side of $1\frac{1}{3}$.

$1\frac{1}{3}$ is greater than ............. and less than ..............

Why are halves a good choice for benchmark fractions for $1\frac{1}{3}$?

**2** Use one of the benchmark fractions for $1\frac{1}{3}$ that you found in problem 1 to estimate how many pounds of chicken Frankie has left. Write a subtraction equation to show your estimated difference.

**3** Use the common denominator found in the second **Model It** to find the actual difference. How many pounds of chicken does Frankie have left?

**4** Is the actual difference greater than or less than your estimate in problem 2? Why?

**5** Explain how you can check if a fraction sum or difference is reasonable.

**6** REFLECT

Look back at your **Try It**, strategies by classmates, and **Model Its**. Which models or strategies do you like best for estimating with fractions? Explain.

...........................................................................................................

...........................................................................................................

...........................................................................................................

## APPLY IT

**Use what you just learned to solve these problems.**

**7** Tim's bean sprout grew $3\frac{3}{8}$ inches. Teegan's bean sprout grew $2\frac{3}{4}$ inches.
How many more inches did Tim's bean sprout grow than Teegan's?
Estimate to tell if your solution is reasonable. Show your work.

Tim's bean sprout grew ..................................... more than
Teegan's bean sprout.

**8** Samantha likes to run at least 5 miles each day. She plans a new course: from home
to the park is $1\frac{1}{3}$ miles, from the park to the library is $2\frac{2}{5}$ miles, and from the park
to home is $\frac{2}{3}$ mile. Will Samantha run at least 5 miles on this new course?

Use only estimation to decide. Then explain if you are confident in your estimate or
if you need to find an actual sum. Show your work.

Samantha ..................... run at least 5 miles.

# Practice Estimating in Word Problems with Fractions

**Study the Example showing how to estimate a sum using benchmark fractions. Then solve problems 1–5.**

## EXAMPLE

David grew $1\frac{3}{4}$ inches last year and $1\frac{5}{8}$ inches this year. Estimate how much he grew in the two years.

You can estimate $1\frac{3}{4} + 1\frac{5}{8}$ using benchmark fractions. The number line below shows common fractions used as benchmark fractions to estimate sums and differences.

$1\frac{3}{4}$ is one of the benchmark fractions. $1\frac{5}{8}$ Is a little greater than $1\frac{1}{2}$. Estimate using $1\frac{1}{2}$.

$$1\frac{3}{4} + 1\frac{1}{2} = 1\frac{3}{4} + 1\frac{2}{4} = 2\frac{5}{4}, \text{ or } 3\frac{1}{4}.$$

The sum is a little greater than $3\frac{1}{4}$, so David grew a little more than $3\frac{1}{4}$ inches.

① Look at the Example. Shade the fraction bars below to show that $1\frac{5}{8}$ is a little greater than $1\frac{1}{2}$.

$1\frac{5}{8}$

$1\frac{1}{2}$

② Find the actual sum $1\frac{3}{4} + 1\frac{5}{8}$ to determine how much David grew in two years. Use the estimate to explain how you know your answer is reasonable. Show your work.

**Solution** ..........................................................................................................

**Irene makes $4\frac{2}{3}$ cups of pancake batter. She splits the batter into 2 bowls. She mixes blueberries into $2\frac{1}{4}$ cups of batter and walnuts into the rest of the batter.**

③ Estimate how much of the batter has walnuts in it. Explain your estimate.

④ Find the actual amount of batter that has walnuts in it.
Explain how you know your answer is reasonable. Show your work.

**Solution** ......

⑤ Irene makes a second batch of $3\frac{1}{4}$ cups of pancake batter. She wants to know how much more batter she made in the first batch. She estimates that the difference between the sizes of the two batches is $2\frac{1}{12}$ cups. Explain why this estimate is *not* reasonable.

# Develop Using Estimation with Decimals

Read and try to solve the problem below.

**Scott is conducting a science experiment. He has 3.74 liters of Liquid A and 3.65 liters of Liquid B. He pours both liquids into a container.**

**How much liquid is in the container? Estimate and solve. Tell if your answer is reasonable.**

## TRY IT

**Math Toolkit**
- base-ten blocks
- base-ten grid paper
- decimal grids
- number lines
- thousandths decimal place-value charts

## DISCUSS IT

**Ask your partner:** Can you explain that again?

**Tell your partner:** I agree with you about . . . because . . .

Explore different ways to understand estimating with decimals.

**Scott is conducting a science experiment. He has 3.74 liters of Liquid A and 3.65 liters of Liquid B. He pours both liquids into a container.**

**How much liquid is in the container? Estimate and solve. Tell if your answer is reasonable.**

## PICTURE IT

**You can picture an estimate of the problem using decimal grids.**

Both 3.74 liters and 3.65 liters are about 4 liters.

3.74

3.65

An estimate of the sum is 4 + 4.

The actual sum can be found by finding 3.74 + 3.65.

## MODEL IT

**You can use a number line to help estimate.**

3.74 and 3.65 are both between 3.5 and 4.

3    3.5    3.65  3.74    4

An estimate of the sum is 3.5 + 3.5.

The actual sum can be found by finding 3.74 + 3.65.

## CONNECT IT

**Now you will use the problem from the previous page to help you understand how to estimate with decimals.**

1 Look at **Picture It**. Why is 4 a good number to use for each addend in an estimated sum?

2 Is the actual sum of the measures of Liquids A and B in **Picture It** less than or greater than the estimated sum? Why?

3 Look at **Model It**. Why is 3.5 a good number to use for each addend in an estimated sum?

4 Is the actual sum of the measures of Liquids A and B in **Model It** less than or greater than the estimated sum? Why?

5 Explain how you can check if a decimal sum or difference is reasonable.

## REFLECT

Look back at your **Try It**, strategies by classmates, and **Picture It** and **Model It**. Which models or strategies do you like best for estimating with decimals? Explain.

# APPLY IT

**Use what you just learned to solve these problems.**

**7** Sean has 12.6 meters of garden netting. He needs 15.85 meters to enclose his garden. How many more meters of netting does Sean need to buy? Estimate to tell if your solution is reasonable. Show your work.

Sean needs ............... meters more of garden netting.

**8** Erika wants at least 6 kilograms of apples for a recipe. She picks a 2.56-kilogram bag of red apples, a 1.18-kilogram bag of green apples, and a 2.79-kilogram bag of yellow apples. Does Erika need to pick more apples?

Use estimation only to decide. Then explain if you are confident in your estimate or if you need to find an actual sum. Show your work.

Erika ............... to pick more apples.

**9** Vinh is having lunch at a café. He has $15 in his pocket and has already ordered a sandwich for $8.57 and a drink for $2.34. Vinh also wants to buy a side salad for $5.25. Does he have enough money? Estimate or find an exact answer to solve. Show your work.

Vinh ............... enough money.

# Practice Using Estimation with Decimals

**Study the Example showing how to estimate a difference using decimal grids. Then solve problems 1–4.**

## EXAMPLE

Kamala has 2.73 liters of lemonade. She wants to have about 5.5 liters for her party. About how much more lemonade does Kamala need?

One way to estimate is to round to the nearest tenth. **5.5** is given to the nearest tenth. **2.73** is about **2.7**.

Kamala needs about 2.8 liters more of lemonade.

1 Look at the Example. Does this situation require an exact answer, or is the estimate enough? Explain.

2 Suppose Kamala wants to have exactly 5.5 liters of lemonade for her party. How much more lemonade does she need? Show your work.

Kamala needs ................ liters more of lemonade.

**3** Ryan and Sarah are looking at cell phone plans. They could share a group plan that costs $119.95 per month, or they could each pay for an individual plan that costs $62.77 per month.

**a.** Estimate which choice would cost less for Ryan and Sarah. Explain why.

**b.** How much money could they save per month by paying for the choice that costs less instead of the choice that costs more? Show your work.

Ryan and Sarah can save ................................. by choosing a(n) ................. plan.

**4** Chris wants to make at least 4.5 pounds, but no more than 5 pounds, of berry salad. He finds a carton of raspberries that weighs 1.83 pounds, a carton of blueberries that weighs 1.5 pounds, a carton of blackberries that weighs 1.72 pounds, and a carton of strawberries that weighs 1.29 pounds. If Chris wants to use three different types of berries, what is one combination of cartons he could buy? Explain. Show your work.

**Solution** .......................................................................................

...............................................................................................

...............................................................................................

...............................................................................................

# Refine Adding and Subtracting in Word Problems

Complete the Example below. Then solve problems 1–7.

## EXAMPLE

**Steven buys a movie ticket for $14.75 and then buys some snacks for the movie. He spends a total of $19.23. About how much did Steven spend on snacks?**

Look at how you could show your work using a number line.

**Solution** ................................................................

The student rounded to the nearest tenth to estimate the answer.

**PAIR/SHARE**
How do you know if the amount spent on snacks will be more or less than $4?

## APPLY IT

1 Parker mixes $3\frac{1}{2}$ ounces of blue paint with $1\frac{2}{5}$ ounces of yellow paint to make green paint for the leaves of a tree. How many ounces of green paint did Parker make?

Estimate and then compute. Explain how you know your result is reasonable. Show your work.

**PAIR/SHARE**
Will there be a little more than $4\frac{1}{2}$ ounces or a little less than $4\frac{1}{2}$ ounces of green paint?

**Solution** ................................................................

**PAIR/SHARE**
Was your estimate more than or less than the actual answer? By how much?

② Jaime's football has a mass of 0.435 kilograms. His football helmet has a mass of 2.57 kilograms. Estimate how much more the mass of the helmet is than the mass of the football. Explain your estimate. Show your work.

I could think about rounding to the nearest half or whole kilogram, instead of to the nearest tenth or hundredth.

③ Which is a reasonable estimate for the difference $5\frac{1}{2} - 3\frac{5}{9}$?

Ⓐ between $\frac{1}{2}$ and 1

Ⓑ between 1 and $1\frac{1}{2}$

Ⓒ between $1\frac{1}{2}$ and 2

Ⓓ between 2 and $2\frac{1}{2}$

Elise chose Ⓓ as the correct answer. How did she get that answer?

*Solution*

**4** William compares monthly rainfall amounts for the summer months using the table below.

| Month | Monthly Rainfall |
|---|---|
| June | $3\frac{3}{16}$ inches |
| July | $3\frac{3}{4}$ inches |
| August | $3\frac{1}{2}$ inches |

Which estimate is closest to the actual difference between the rainfall amounts for June and July?

Ⓐ $\frac{1}{4}$ inch

Ⓑ $\frac{1}{2}$ inch

Ⓒ 1 inch

Ⓓ $1\frac{1}{2}$ inches

**5** Carter is at the school store. He wants to buy a pack of notebooks that costs $4.79, a calculator that costs $33.54, and a tablet case that costs $12.67. About how much money does Carter plan to spend at the school store? Will the actual cost be more or less than your estimate? Explain. Show your work.

**Solution**

**6** A certain liquid boils at 175.62°F. The liquid is currently at 68.8°F. Jimmy says that the temperature needs to rise by about 125°F to boil.

**Part A** Without finding the actual difference, explain why Jimmy's estimate is or is not reasonable.

**Part B** Find the actual amount the temperature must rise for the liquid to boil. Show your work.

*Solution* ........................................................................................................

**7** **MATH JOURNAL**

Ramona has $4\frac{1}{5}$ gallons of red paint. She knows she needs at least $12\frac{3}{4}$ gallons to paint her whole house. Use benchmark fractions to explain about how much more paint Ramona needs.

☑ **SELF CHECK** Go back to the Unit 2 Opener and see what you can check off.

Lesson 14   Add and Subtract in Word Problems

# Self Reflection

## In this unit you learned to . . .

| Skill | Lesson |
|---|---|
| Recognize that a digit in one place represents 10 times as much as it represents in the place to its right and $\frac{1}{10}$ of what it represents in the place to its left. | 6 |
| Use patterns to understand multiplying and dividing whole numbers and decimals. | 7 |
| Read and write decimals in different forms, for example: $80.63 = (8 \times 10) + (6 \times \frac{1}{10}) + (3 \times \frac{1}{100})$. | 8 |
| Compare decimals, for example: $3.47 > 3.096$. | 9 |
| Round decimals, for example: 6.274 rounded to the nearest tenth is 6.3. | 9 |
| Add and subtract decimals, for example: $20.08 + 5.15 = 25.23$. | 10, 11 |
| Add and subtract fractions with unlike denominators, for example: $\frac{3}{5} + \frac{1}{4} = \frac{17}{20}$. | 12, 13 |
| Estimate sums and differences of fractions or decimals. | 14 |

## Think about what you have learned.

**Use words, numbers, and drawings.**

**1** Three examples of what I learned are . . .

**2** The hardest thing I learned to do is . . . . . . . . . . . . . . . . . . . . . . because . . .

**3** I could use more practice with . . .

# Use Decimals and Fractions

## Study an Example Problem and Solution

**Read this problem involving decimals. Then look at Alex's solution to this problem.**

### Dog Collars

Alex is organizing a pet fair. Money from the fair will be donated to the local pet shelter. Alex's friend Bella will have a booth at the fair. Here is Bella's sign.

> **Adorable Dog Collars**
>
> Small ............................. $10.75
> Medium .......................... $12.00
> Large ............................. $13.25

Supplies to make a small collar cost $1.60. Bella estimates that the supplies for each size collar cost $0.40 more than the next smaller size. Bella hopes to make at least $225 for the pet shelter by selling collars.

- Find how much Bella makes on each collar after paying for supplies.

- Show a way to make at least $225 by selling collars.

- Include at least 5 collars of each size in your plan.

**Read the sample solution on the next page. Then look at the checklist below. Find and mark parts of the solution that match the checklist.**

☑ **PROBLEM-SOLVING CHECKLIST**

- ☐ Tell what is known.
- ☐ Tell what the problem is asking.
- ☐ Show all your work.
- ☐ Show that the solution works.

**a. Circle** something that is known.

**b. Underline** something that you need to find.

**c. Draw a box around** what you do to solve the problem.

**d. Put a checkmark** next to the part that shows the solution works.

# ALEX'S SOLUTION

Hi, I'm Alex. Here's how I solved this problem.

- **I know the selling price** of each collar. **I need to find the cost** to make each size collar and subtract it from the price.

| Size | Price | Cost of Supplies | Donation Amount |
|------|-------|------------------|-----------------|
| Small | $10.75 | $1.60 | $9.15 |
| Medium | $12.00 | $1.60 + $0.40 = $2.00 | $10.00 |
| Large | $13.25 | $2.00 + $0.40 = $2.40 | $10.85 |

I used a table to organize my information.

- **I'll round the donation amounts so that I can estimate.** I can multiply each rounded amount by 5 since I have to include at least 5 of each size collar.

$9.15 → $9 and $9 × 5 = $45

$10.00 → $10 and $10 × 5 = $50

$10.85 → $11 and $11 × 5 = $55

$45 + $50 + $55 = $150

By rounding and estimating first, I avoid some computing with decimals.

- **I can see** that I need about $75 more to get to $225. I can try to make about $25 with each of the three collar sizes.

$9 × 3 = $27    $10 × 3 = $30    $11 × 3 = $33

- **Now I can find the actual amounts from 5 + 3 small collars, 5 + 3 medium collars, and 5 + 3 large collars.**

- Since I want to sell 8 of each size collar, I can add together the donation amount from 1 of each size, then multiply by 8.

$9.15 + $10.00 + $10.85 = $30.00

$30 × 8 = $240

If Bella sells 8 of each size collar, she will be able to donate $240.

The solution works because it includes at least 5 collars of each size and it makes more than $225 for the shelter.

This is my final answer.

# Try Another Approach

**There are many ways to solve problems. Think about how you might solve the Dog Collars problem in a different way.**

## Dog Collars

Alex is organizing a pet fair. Money from the fair will be donated to the local pet shelter. Alex's friend Bella will have a booth at the fair. Here is Bella's sign.

Supplies to make a small collar cost $1.60. Bella estimates that the supplies for each size collar cost $0.40 more than the next smaller size. Bella hopes to make at least $225 for the pet shelter by selling collars.

- Find how much Bella makes on each collar after paying for supplies.

- Show a way to make at least $225 by selling collars.

- Include at least 5 collars of each size in your plan.

### Adorable Dog Collars

Small.........................$10.75

Medium....................$12.00

Large .......................$13.25

## PLAN IT

**Answer these questions to help you start thinking about a plan.**

**A.** How can you use estimation to help find a solution?

**B.** How can you use Alex's solution to plan how to find a different solution?

## SOLVE IT

**Find a different solution for the Dog Collars problem. Show all your work on a separate sheet of paper.**

You may want to use the Problem-Solving Tips to get started.

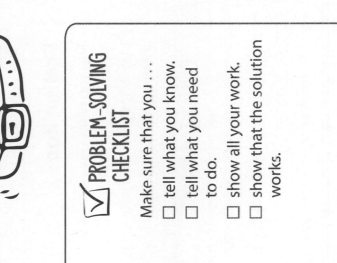

### PROBLEM-SOLVING TIPS

● **Models** You might want to use . . .

· number lines.

· tables.

● **Word Bank**

| | | |
|---|---|---|
| round | multiply | greater than |
| estimate | product | decimal |

● **Sentence Starters**

· I can round _____

· If I multiply _____

---

☑ PROBLEM-SOLVING CHECKLIST

Make sure that you . . . .

☐ tell what you know.

☐ tell what you need to do.

☐ show all your work.

☐ show that the solution works.

---

## REFLECT

**Use Mathematical Practices** As you work through the problem, discuss these questions with a partner.

· **Use Models** How can you use division to help find a solution?

· **Reason Mathematically** What strategies can you use to solve this problem?

# Discuss Models and Strategies

**Read the problem. Write a solution on a separate sheet of paper. Remember, there can be lots of ways to solve a problem!**

## Petting Zoo

The zoo where Alex works has agreed to bring some animals to the pet fair. Guests can pay to feed and play with the animals. Alex has to decide which animals to bring and how much food they will need.

### Petting Zoo Notes

- Include 2 or 3 different kinds of animals.

- Include more than 6 but fewer than 9 animals.

- Have enough food to feed each animal a day's worth of food.

Alex reads the keeper's notes to find about how much an average animal eats in a day.

How much food should Alex bring to the pet fair?

### Keeper's Notes
**About Feeding Animals**

**Rabbit:** $\frac{1}{8}$ pound of pellets and $\frac{1}{4}$ pound of vegetables.

**Goat:** $4\frac{1}{2}$ pounds of hay and $2\frac{1}{4}$ pounds of grains.

**Small Pig:** $5\frac{1}{2}$ pounds of food (mix of grains and vegetables, at least one pound of each food).

**Calf:** 10 pounds of hay and $4\frac{1}{2}$ pounds of grains

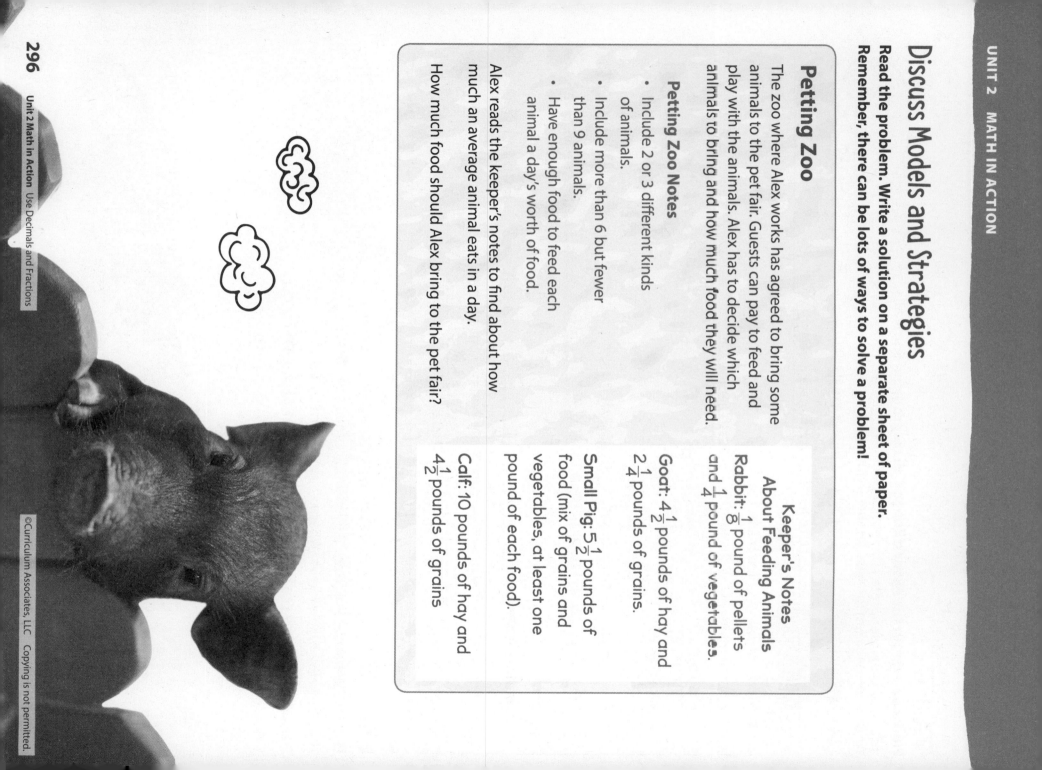

# PLAN IT AND SOLVE IT

**Find a solution to the Petting Zoo problem.**

Write a detailed plan for Alex. Be sure to include:

- which animals and how many of each to bring to the pet fair.
- a list of the food she will need to feed all the animals for one day, including amounts of each kind of food.
- reasons for the choices you made.

You may want to use the Problem-Solving Tips to get started.

⌐ PROBLEM-SOLVING TIPS

● **Questions**
  - How does the size of the animal affect your choice?
  - Which animals eat some of the same kind of food?

● **Sentence Starters**
  - I would bring _____
  - Alex needs about _____

☑ PROBLEM-SOLVING CHECKLIST

Make sure that you . . .
- ☐ tell what you know.
- ☐ tell what you need to do.
- ☐ show all your work.
- ☐ show that the solution works.

# REFLECT

**Use Mathematical Practices** As you work through the problem, discuss these questions with a partner.

- **Make Sense of Problems** What will you do first? Why?
- **Make an Argument** How can you justify the choices you made?

# Persevere On Your Own

**Read the problems. Write a solution on a separate sheet of paper.**

## Barely Used

Alex's friend Brandi has a collection of used books, CDs, and DVDs that people have given her. She will sell them at a booth at the pet fair. Brandi thinks she can sell enough items to make more than a $100 donation to the pet shelter. Look at Brandi's prices.

- Paperback Books $0.95
- Hardcover Books $3.37
- DVDs $3.25
- CDs $1.95

What items can Brandi sell to make more than $100?

## SOLVE IT

**Find a combination of items that Brandi needs to sell to meet her goal.**

- Include some of all four items.

- For each item, tell how many Brandi needs to sell and how much money she will make.

- Give the total amount Brandi will make selling all the items on your list.

- Explain why this total works.

## REFLECT

**Use Mathematical Practices**  After you complete the task, choose one of these questions to discuss with a partner.

- **Use Models**  What equations or expressions did you use to find your solution?

- **Persevere**  What were all of the steps you took to find a solution?

## Ring Toss

In a ring toss game, a player throws rings until four rings land around pegs. To find the score, add blue fractions (top row of pegs) and then subtract red fractions (bottom two rows). To win, the player's score must be at least 1, but no more than $1\frac{1}{4}$.

A player's first ring lands around the blue $\frac{3}{4}$ peg in the top row.

Where can the other three rings land so the player wins?

## SOLVE IT

**Tell a combination of three pegs that will let the player win.**

• Tell which three pegs the rings could land on.

• Explain your choices.

• Show why your solution works.

## REFLECT

**Use Mathematical Practices** After you complete the task, choose one of these questions to discuss with a partner.

• **Persevere** What are some different ways you could start your solution?

• **Make an Argument** How do you know the numbers you choose work?

**1** Which number is equivalent to 0.15 × 10³?

Ⓐ 0.015                    Ⓑ 0.15

Ⓒ 15                       Ⓓ 150

**2** The driving distance between Buffalo, NY, and Rochester, NY, is 117.456 kilometers. What is this distance rounded to the nearest tenth of a kilometer?

Ⓐ 117 kilometers           Ⓑ 117.5 kilometers

Ⓒ 117.46 kilometers        Ⓓ 120 kilometers

**3** Julie likes to ride her bike during summer vacation. In June, she rides her bike 104.78 miles. In July, she rides 129.53 miles. In August, she rides 61.05 miles. Which statements are true?

Ⓐ Julie rides 68.48 miles less in August than in July.

Ⓑ Julie rides a total of 295.36 miles during summer vacation.

Ⓒ Julie rides 43.73 miles more in June than in August.

Ⓓ Julie rides more miles in June than in July.

Ⓔ Rounded to the nearest tenth, Julie rides 129.6 miles in July.

**4** Decide if each equation is true. Choose *True* or *False* for each equation.

| | True | False |
|---|---|---|
| $3\frac{4}{5} + 6\frac{2}{10} = 10$ | Ⓐ | Ⓑ |
| $22\frac{7}{9} - 16\frac{1}{4} = 6\frac{19}{36}$ | Ⓒ | Ⓓ |
| $\frac{2}{3} - \frac{1}{6} = \frac{1}{3}$ | Ⓔ | Ⓕ |
| $6 + \frac{1}{5} = \frac{6}{5}$ | Ⓖ | Ⓗ |
| $\frac{1}{2} + \frac{1}{4} + \frac{2}{5} = \frac{4}{11}$ | Ⓘ | Ⓙ |

**5** The expression $(2 \times 10) + (6 \times 1) + (5 \times \frac{1}{10}) + (7 \times \frac{1}{100}) + (4 \times \frac{1}{1,000})$ shows a number written in expanded form. Use the expression to write the number in decimal form. Write your answer in the blank.

........................

**6** It snowed $5\frac{1}{2}$ inches in January and $4\frac{7}{8}$ inches in February. How many more inches did it snow in January than in February? Show your work.

*Solution* ...............................

**7** Choose >, <, or = to compare each pair of numbers.

| | > | < | = |
|---|---|---|---|
| 6.104 ☐ 6.106 | Ⓐ | Ⓑ | Ⓒ |
| 6.079 ☐ 5.793 | Ⓓ | Ⓔ | Ⓕ |
| 5.785 ☐ 5.793 | Ⓖ | Ⓗ | Ⓘ |
| 6.10 ☐ 6.1 | Ⓙ | Ⓚ | Ⓛ |

**8** Fill in the numbers missing from these patterns. Write your answers in the blanks.

Multiply by 10:     0.004, _____, 0.4, _____, 40, 400

Divide by 10:     700, _____, 7, 0.7, 0.07, _____

## Performance Task

**Answer the questions and show all your work on separate paper.**

You have a movie theater gift card worth $40, so you invite a friend to go to the movies with you. Your friend challenges you to spend the exact value of the gift card. Find at least one way to do so by choosing from the items listed below.

| Item | Price |
|------|-------|
| 2D Movie Ticket | $7.25 |
| 3D Movie Ticket | $8.50 |
| Small Popcorn | $3.25 |
| Medium Popcorn | $5.50 |
| Large Popcorn | $7.75 |
| Bottle of Water | $2.50 |
| 1 Ounce of Snack Mix | $0.50 |

### Checklist

Did you . . .

☐ organize your choices?

☐ check your calculations?

☐ use words and numbers to complete the task?

## REFLECT

**Use Mathematical Practices** After you complete the task, choose one of the following questions to answer.

- **Persevere** What strategies did you use? If a strategy did not work, what did you do?

- **Model** How did you use equations to solve this problem?

# Vocabulary

**Draw or write to show examples for each term. Then draw or write to show other math words in the unit.**

---

**base ten** a ten-digit number system in which the value of a digit depends on its place. The value of each place is 10 times the value of the place to the right and $\frac{1}{10}$ of the value of the place to the left.

**My Example**

---

**exponent** the number in a power that tells how many times to use the base as a factor in repeated multiplication.

**My Example**

---

**power of 10** a number that can be written as a product of tens. For example, 100 and 1,000 are powers of 10 because $100 = 10 \times 10$ and $1,000 = 10 \times 10 \times 10$.

**My Example**

---

**base (of a power)** in a power, the number that is used as a repeated factor.

**My Example**

---

**expanded form** a way to write a number to show the place value of each digit.

**My Example**

---

**inequality** a mathematical statement that uses an inequality symbol ($<$ or $>$) to show the relationship between expressions with different values.

**My Example**

---

**thousandths**  the parts formed when a
whole is divided into 1,000 equal parts.

**My Example**

**My Word:** _____

**My Example**

**My Word:** _____

**My Example**

**My Word:** _____

**My Example**

**My Word:** _____

**My Example**

**My Word:** _____

**My Example**

# Cumulative Practice

Name: _____

## Set 1: Compare Whole Numbers

**Write <, >, or = in each circle to compare the numbers.**

**1** 21,442 ◯ 214,420

**2** 372 ◯ 3,151

**3** 9,000 ◯ 8,999

**4** 201,253 ◯ 201,189

**5** 915,298 ◯ 915,298

**6** 55,000 ◯ 50,555

## Set 2: Round Whole Numbers

**Round each number to the nearest ten for problems 1–3.**

**1** 621,583 ............

**2** 77 ............

**3** 596 ............

**Round each number to the nearest hundred for problems 4–6.**

**4** 1,547 ............

**5** 45,951 ............

**6** 312,677 ............

**Round each number to the nearest thousand for problems 7–9.**

**7** 52,131 ............

**8** 98,912 ............

**9** 672 ............

**Round each number to the nearest ten thousand for problems 10–12.**

**10** 915,039 ............

**12** 81,987 ............

**13** 8,645 ............

## Set 3: Add and Subtract Whole Numbers

**Add or subtract. Show your work.**

**1**
```
  54,138
+ 24,231
```

**2**
```
  9,135
+ 5,897
```

**3**
```
  17,821
+  4,830
```

**4**
```
  98,568
- 32,421
```

**5**
```
  15,293
-  9,424
```

**6**
```
  9,295
- 8,931
```

# Set 4: Multiply and Divide in Word Problems

**Multiply or divide to solve the problems. Show your work.**

**1** In a soccer game, Lia takes 3 times as many shots as Talisha. Talisha takes 5 shots. How many shots does Lia take?

**2** Paul is 6 times as old as his brother. Paul is 12 years old. How old is his brother?

**3** Sujin babysat 20 hours this week. That is 4 times as long as she babysat last week. How long did she babysit last week?

# Set 5: Multi-Step Problems

**Write an equation with a variable and then solve the problem. Show your work.**

**1** Adult movie tickets cost $10 and child movie tickets cost $5. What is the cost, c, of 4 adult tickets and 6 child tickets?

**2** Connor makes 3 batches of muffins. Each batch has 12 muffins. Connor eats 2 muffins. What is m, the number of muffins Connor has left?

**3** Shanice has 5 days to read 30 pages of her history book and 15 pages of her science book. She plans to read an equal number of pages each day. What is p, the number of pages Shanice must read per day?

Name: _____

## Set 6: Multiply by One-Digit and Two-Digit Numbers

**Multiply. Show your work.**

**1** 2,241
    × 6

**2** 784
    × 9

**3** 4,291
    ×  3

**4** 28
    × 12

**5** 46
    × 62

**6** 83
    × 44

## Set 7: Divide Three-Digit and Four-Digit Numbers

**Divide. Show your work.**

**1** 203 ÷ 7

**2** 6,528 ÷ 8

**3** 6,349 ÷ 9

## Set 8: Compare Fractions and Decimals

**Write <, >, or = in each circle to compare the decimals for problems 1–3.**

**1** 0.2 ◯ 0.20

**2** 0.24 ◯ 0.3

**3** 0.84 ◯ 0.48

**Compare the fractions using <, > or = for problems 4–6.
Show your work.**

**4** $\frac{2}{5}$ and $\frac{5}{8}$

**5** $\frac{3}{4}$ and $\frac{2}{3}$

**6** $\frac{3}{5}$ and $\frac{60}{100}$

# Set 9: Add and Subtract Fractions

**Fill in the blanks to complete the equations for problems 1–3.**

**1** $\frac{5}{8} = \frac{2}{8} + \underline{\hspace{1cm}}$

**2** $\frac{9}{10} = \frac{3}{10} + \frac{2}{10} + \underline{\hspace{1cm}}$

**3** $\frac{3}{6} = \frac{1}{6} + \frac{1}{6} + \underline{\hspace{1cm}}$

**Add or subtract to solve problems 4 and 5. Show your work.**

**4** Dora has $\frac{5}{10}$ pint of strawberries and $\frac{2}{10}$ pint of raspberries. How many pints of berries does she have altogether?

**5** Andy and Javier need to clean their whole house. Andy cleans $\frac{2}{6}$ of the house and Javier cleans $\frac{3}{6}$ of the house. What fraction of the house is left to clean?

# Set 10: Relate Decimals and Fractions

**Write each decimal as a fraction with a denominator of 100 for problems 1–3.**

**1** 0.07 = \underline{\hspace{1cm}}

**2** 0.6 = \underline{\hspace{1cm}}

**3** 1.25 = \underline{\hspace{1cm}}

**Write each fraction as a decimal for problems 4–6.**

**4** $\frac{9}{10} =$ \underline{\hspace{1cm}}

**5** $\frac{75}{100} =$ \underline{\hspace{1cm}}

**6** $\frac{2}{100} =$ \underline{\hspace{1cm}}

# Set 11: Multiply Fractions by Whole Numbers

**Solve the problems. Show your work.**

**1** Tim has 5 bags of grapes. Each bag weighs $\frac{1}{2}$ pound. How many pounds of grapes does he have?

**2** Julieta reads for $\frac{3}{4}$ of an hour for 6 days in a row. How much time does she spent reading altogether?

# Cumulative Practice

Name: _____

## Set 1: Volume

**Fill in the blanks to solve the problems.**

A

**1** Look at Figure A and fill in the blanks below.

There are _____ layers and _____ unit cubes in each layer.

_____ × _____ cubes = _____ unit cubes

The volume of Figure A is _____ unit cubes.

**2** Jordan stacks 5 layers of 6 units cubes to fill a small box.

How many cubes are in the box?

What is the volume of Jordan's box?

**3** A prism has a volume of 60 cubic inches. It has 4 layers of unit cubes.
How many unit cubes are in each layer?

## Set 2: Find Volume Using Unit Cubes

**Fill in the blanks to solve problems 1 and 2.**

B

C

**1** Prism B is filled with unit cubes that have side length 1 centimeter.

There are _____ layers with _____ cubes in each layer.

_____ cubes + _____ cubes + _____ cubes = _____ cubes

The volume of Prism B is _____.

**2** Prism C is filled with unit cubes that have side length 1 inch.

There are _____ layers with _____ cubes in each layer.

_____ × _____ cubes = _____ cubes

The volume of Prism C is _____.

**3** A rectangular prism is 6 feet long, 2 feet wide, and 3 feet tall. What is the
volume of the rectangular prism? Show your work.

# Set 3: Volume of Right Rectangular Prisms

**Solve the problem.**

**1** Maria's box is 5 inches tall, 4 inches long, and 2 inches wide.

a. Label the picture of the box with its dimensions.

b. What is the volume of the box? Show your work.

in.

in.

in.

The volume of the box is ........................ .

# Set 4: Find Volume Using Formulas

**Use a formula to solve the problems. Show your work.**

**1** A rectangular prism has length 5 inches, width 3 inches, and height 7 inches. What is the volume of the prism?

**2** A rectangular prism has a base with an area of 20 square centimeters and a height of 3 centimeters. What is the volume of the prism?

**3** A rectangular prism has length 6 centimeters, width 8 centimeters, and height 10 centimeters. What is the volume of the prism?

Name: _____

# Set 5: Breaking Apart Figures to Find Volume

**For the figures in problems 1–2, all sides meet at right angles. Find the volume of each figure. Show your work.**

**1**

1 ft
9 ft
3 ft
12 ft
5 ft

**2**

4 in.
7 in.
11 in.
12 in.
8 in.

_____ cubic feet

_____ cubic inches

**For the figures in problems 3–4, all sides meet at right angles. Find the volume of each figure.**

**3**

12 cm
12 cm
8 cm
10 cm
4 cm

**4**

2 ft
4 ft
6 ft
6 ft
6 ft

Volume = _____

Volume = _____

## Set 6: Multiply Multi-Digit Numbers

**Find the product. Show your work.**

1
$$\begin{array}{r} 138 \\ \times\ 15 \\ \hline \end{array}$$

2
$$\begin{array}{r} 363 \\ \times\ 28 \\ \hline \end{array}$$

3
$$\begin{array}{r} 524 \\ \times\ 18 \\ \hline \end{array}$$

4
$$\begin{array}{r} 2,593 \\ \times\ \ \ \ 53 \\ \hline \end{array}$$

## Set 7: Divide Multi-Digit Numbers

**Fill in the blanks of the area model to find the quotient.**

1  $288 \div 24 = ?$

24 | 288 → 24

$288 \div 24 =$ ..............

2  $2,016 \div 36 = ?$

$2,016 \div 36 = ?$

36 | 2,016 → 36

$2,016 \div 36 =$ ..............

# Glossary/Glosario

| English | Español | Example/Ejemplo |
|---|---|---|
| | ## Aa | |
| **acute angle** an angle that measures more than 0° but less than 90°. | **ángulo agudo** ángulo que mide más de 0° pero menos de 90°. | |
| **acute triangle** a triangle that has three acute angles. | **triángulo acutángulo** triángulo que tiene tres ángulos agudos. | |
| **addend** a number being added. | **sumando** número que se suma. | $24 + 35 = 59$ <br> addends |
| **algorithm** a set of routine steps used to solve problems. | **algoritmo** conjunto de pasos que se siguen rutinariamente para resolver problemas. | 17 R 19 <br> 31)546 <br> −31 <br> 236 <br> −217 <br> 19 |
| AM the time from midnight until before noon. | **a. m.** el tiempo que transcurre desde la medianoche hasta el mediodía. | |
| **angle** a geometric shape formed by two rays, lines, or line segments that meet at a common point. | **ángulo** figura geométrica formada por dos semirrectas, rectas o segmentos de recta que se encuentran en un punto. | |

## English | Español | Example/Ejemplo

**area** the amount of space inside a closed two-dimensional figure. Area is measured in square units such as square centimeters.

**área** cantidad de espacio dentro de una figura bidimensional cerrada. El área se mide en unidades cuadradas, como los centímetros cuadrados.

Area = 4 square units

---

**array** a set of objects arranged in equal rows and equal columns.

**matriz** conjunto de objetos agrupados en filas y columnas iguales.

---

**associative property of addition** when the grouping of three or more addends is changed, the total does not change.

**propiedad asociativa de la suma** cambiar la agrupación de tres o más sumandos no cambia el total.

$(2 + 3) + 4 = 2 + (3 + 4)$

---

**associative property of multiplication** changing the grouping of three or more factors does not change the product.

**propiedad asociativa de la multiplicación** cambiar la agrupación de tres o más factores no cambia el producto.

$(2 \times 4) \times 3 = 2 \times (4 \times 3)$

---

**attribute** any characteristic of an object or shape, such as number of sides or angles, lengths of sides, or angle measures.

**atributo** característica de un objeto o una figura, como el número de lados o ángulos, la longitud de los lados o la medida de los ángulos.

attributes of a square:
• 4 square corners
• 4 sides of equal length

---

**axis** a horizontal or vertical number line that determines a coordinate plane. The plural form is *axes*.

**eje** recta numérica horizontal o vertical que determina un plano de coordenadas.

y-axis

x-axis

---

# Bb

**base (of a power)** in a power, the number that is used as a repeated factor.

**base (de una potencia)** en una potencia, el número que se usa como factor repetido.

$8^2$

| English | Español | Example/Ejemplo |
|---|---|---|
| **base (of a prism)** one side of a prism, usually considered to be the side shown as the bottom of the prism. In the volume formula $V = b \times h$, $b$ represents the area of the base of the prism. | **base (de un prisma)** lado de un prisma (por lo general, el lado inferior). En la fórmula de volumen $V = b \times a$, $b$ representa el área de la base del prisma. | base |
| **base ten** a ten-digit number system in which the value of a digit depends on its place. The value of each place is 10 times the value of the place to the right and $\frac{1}{10}$ of the value of the place to the left. | **base diez** sistema numérico en el que el valor de un dígito depende de su valor posicional. El valor de cada posición es 10 veces el valor de la posición que está a la derecha y $\frac{1}{10}$ del valor de la posición que está a la izquierda. | |
| **benchmark fraction** a common fraction that you might compare other fractions to. | **fracción de referencia** fracción común que se puede comparar con otras fracciones. | $\frac{1}{4}, \frac{1}{2}, \frac{2}{3},$ and $\frac{3}{4}$ are often used as benchmark fractions. |

## Cc

| English | Español | Example/Ejemplo |
|---|---|---|
| **capacity** the amount a container can hold. Capacity can be measured in the same units as liquid volume. | **capacidad** cantidad que cabe en un recipiente. La capacidad se mide en las mismas unidades que el volumen líquido. | capacity of 2 liters |
| **category** a collection of objects grouped together based on attributes they have in common. | **categoría** grupo de objetos clasificados según atributos que tienen en común. | Quadrilaterals — category; Parallelograms; Rectangles; Squares — subcategory |
| **centimeter (cm)** a unit of length. There are 100 centimeters in 1 meter. | **centímetro (cm)** unidad de longitud. 100 centímetros equivalen a 1 metro. | Your little finger is about 1 **centimeter** (cm) across. |

| English | Español | Example/Ejemplo |
|---|---|---|
| **closed figure** a two-dimensional figure that begins and ends at the same point. | **figura cerrada** figura bidimensional que comienza y termina en el mismo punto. | Closed figure<br>Open figure |
| **column** a vertical line of objects or numbers, such as in an array or table. | **columna** línea vertical de objetos, como las de una matriz o una tabla. | |
| **common denominator** a number that is a common multiple of the denominators of two or more fractions. | **denominadores communes** número que es común múltiplo de los denominadores de dos o más fracciones. | $2 \times 3 = 6$, so 6 is a common denominator for $3\frac{1}{2}$ and $1\frac{1}{3}$. |
| **commutative property of addition** changing the order of addends does not change the total. | **propiedad conmutativa de la suma** cambiar el orden de los sumandos no cambia el total. | $3 + 4 = 4 + 3$ |
| **commutative property of multiplication** changing the order of the factors does not change the product. | **propiedad conmutativa de la multiplicación** cambiar el orden de los factores no cambia el producto. | $3 \times 2 = 2 \times 3$ |
| **compare** to decide if numbers, amounts, or sizes are *greater than*, *less than*, or *equal to* each other. | **comparar** determinar si un número, una cantidad o un tamaño es *mayor que*, *menor que* o *igual a* otro número, otra cantidad u otro tamaño. | $3.37 > 3.096$ |
| **compose** to make by combining parts. You can put together numbers to make a greater number or shapes to make a new shape. | **componer** combinar partes para formar algo. Se pueden combinar números para formar un número mayor o figuras para formar otra figura. | The three 50° angles compose the larger angle. |
| **composite number** a number that has more than one pair of factors. | **número compuesto** número que tiene más de un par de factores. | 16 is a composite number. |

| English | Español | Example/Ejemplo |
|---|---|---|
| **convert** to write an equivalent measurement using a different unit. | **convertir** expresar una medida equivalente en una unidad diferente. | 5 feet = 60 inches |
| **coordinate plane** a two-dimensional space formed by two perpendicular number lines called *axes*. | **plano de coordenadas** espacio bidimensional formado por dos rectas numéricas perpendiculares llamadas *ejes*. | **Coordinate Plane**<br> |
| **corresponding terms** terms that have the same position in two related patterns. For example, the second term in one pattern and the second term in a related pattern are corresponding terms. | **términos correspondientes** términos que tienen la misma posición en dos patrones relacionados. Por ejemplo, el segundo término de un patrón y el segundo término de un patrón relacionado son términos correspondientes. | Pattern A: 6, **9**, 12, 15, 18<br>Pattern B: 12, **18**, 24, 30, 36 |
| **cubic unit** the volume of a unit cube. | **unidad cúbica** el volumen de un cubo con aristas de 1 unidad de longitud. | 1 unit / 1 unit / 1 unit |
| **cup (c)** a unit of liquid volume in the customary system. 4 cups is equal to 1 quart. | **taza (tz)** unidad de volumen líquido del sistema usual. 4 tazas equivalen a 1 cuarto. | cup |

| English | Español | Example/Ejemplo |
|---|---|---|

**Dd**

**customary system** the measurement system commonly used in the United States that measures length in inches, feet, yards, and miles; liquid volume in cups, pints, quarts, and gallons; and weight in ounces and pounds.

**sistema usual** sistema de medición comúnmente usado en Estados Unidos. La longitud se mide en pulgadas, pies, yardas, y millas; el volumen líquido, en tazas, pintas, cuartos, y galones; y el peso, en onzas y libras.

| Length |
|---|
| 1 foot = 12 inches |
| 1 yard = 3 feet |
| 1 mile = 5,280 feet |

| Weight |
|---|
| 1 pound = 16 ounces |

| Liquid Volume |
|---|
| 1 quart = 2 pints |
| 1 quart = 4 cups |
| 1 gallon = 4 quarts |

**data** a set of collected information. Often numerical information such as a list of measurements.

**datos** conjunto de información reunida. A menudo es información numérica, tal como una lista de mediciones.

earthworm lengths (in inches):
$4\frac{1}{2}, 5, 5, 5\frac{1}{4}, 5\frac{1}{4}, 6, 6\frac{1}{4}$

**decimal** a number containing a decimal point that separates a whole from fractional place values (tenths, hundredths, thousandths, and so on).

**número decimal** número que contiene un punto decimal que separa la posición de las unidades de las posiciones fraccionarias (décimas, centésimas, milésimas, etc.).

1.293

**decimal point** the dot used in a decimal that separates the ones place from the tenths place.

**punto decimal** punto que se usa en un número decimal para separar la posición de las unidades de la posición de las décimas.

1.65
→ decimal point

**decompose** to break into parts. You can break apart numbers and shapes.

**descomponer** separar en partes. Se pueden separar en partes números y figuras.

$\frac{3}{8} = \frac{1}{8} + \frac{1}{8} + \frac{1}{8}$

**degree (°)** a unit of measure for angles. There are 360° in a circle.

**grado (°)** unidad de medida para ángulos. Hay 360° en un círculo.

There are 360° in a circle.

| English | Español | Example/Ejemplo |
|---|---|---|
| **denominator** the number below the line in a fraction that tells the number of equal parts in the whole. | **denominador** número que está debajo de la línea de una fracción. Dice cuántas partes iguales hay en el entero. | $\dfrac{2}{3}$ |
| **difference** the result of subtraction. | **diferencia** el resultado de la resta. | $\begin{array}{r} 16.75 \\ -\,15.70 \\ \hline \mathbf{1.05} \end{array}$ |
| **digit** a symbol used to write numbers. | **dígito** símbolo que se usa para escribir números. | The digits are 0, 1, 2, 3, 4, 5, 6, 7, 8, and 9. |
| **dimension** length in one direction. A figure may have one, two, or three dimensions. | **dimension** longitud en una dirección. Una figura puede tener una, dos o tres dimensiones. | 5 in. 2 in. 3 in. |
| **distribution** how spread out or how clustered pieces of data are. | **distribución** qué tan esparcidos o agrupados están los datos. | Most of the data are clustered between $\frac{1}{8}$ and $\frac{1}{2}$. <br> Tomato Weight (pounds) |
| **distributive property** when one of the factors of a product is written as a sum, multiplying each addend by the other factor before adding does not change the product. | **propiedad distributiva** cuando uno de los factores de un producto se escribe como suma, multiplicar cada sumando por el otro factor antes de sumar no cambia el producto. | $2 \times (3 + 6) = (2 \times 3) + (2 \times 6)$ |
| **divide** to separate into equal groups and find the number in each group or the number of groups. | **divisor** separar en grupos iguales y hallar cuántos hay en cada grupo o el número de grupos. | $2{,}850 \div 38 = 75$ |
| **dividend** the number that is divided by another number. | **dividendo** el número que se divide por otro número. | $15 \div 3 = 5$ |

| English | Español | Example/Ejemplo |
|---|---|---|

**division** an operation used to separate a number of items into equal-sized groups.

**división** operación que se usa para separar una cantidad de objetos en grupos iguales.

**Division**

$$12 \div 3 = 4$$

total number → number in
of groups → each group

**divisor** the number by which another number is divided.

**divisor** el número por el que se divide otro número.

$15 \div 3 = 5$

## Ee

**edge** a line segment where two faces meet in a three-dimensional shape.

**arista** segmento de recta donde se encuentran dos caras de una figura tridimensional.

edge

**elapsed time** the amount of time that has passed between a start time and an end time.

**tiempo transcurrido** tiempo que ha pasado entre el momento de inicio y el fin.

The elapsed time from 2:00 PM to 3:00 PM is 1 hour.

**equal** having the same value, same size, or same amount.

**igual** que tiene el mismo valor, el mismo tamaño o la misma cantidad.

$25 + 15 = 40$
$25 + 15$ **is equal to** 40.

**equal sign (=)** a symbol that means *is the same value as.*

**signo de igual (=)** símbolo que significa *tiene el mismo valor que.*

$12 + 4 = 16$

**equation** a mathematical statement that uses an equal sign (=) to show that two expressions have the same value.

**ecuación** enunciado matemático que tiene un signo de igual (=) para mostrar que dos expresiones tienen el mismo valor.

$25 - 15 = 10$

**equilateral triangle** a triangle that has all three sides the same length.

**triángulo equilátero** triángulo que tiene los tres lados de igual longitud.

8 in. 8 in.
8 in.

| English | Español | Example/Ejemplo |
|---|---|---|
| **equivalent fractions** two or more different fractions that name the same part of a whole or the same point on a number line. | **fracciones equivalentes** dos o más fracciones diferentes que nombran la misma parte de un entero y el mismo punto en una recta numérica. | $\frac{2}{4}$ = $\frac{1}{2}$ <br><br> $\frac{5}{10}$ = $\frac{1}{2}$ |
| **estimate (noun)** a close guess made using mathematical thinking. | **estimación** suposición aproximada que se hace usando el razonamiento matemático. | $28 + 21 = ?$ <br> $30 + 20 = 50$ <br> 50 is an estimate of the sum. |
| **estimate (verb)** to make a close guess based on mathematical thinking. | **estimar / hacer una estimación** hacer una suposición aproximada usando el razonamiento matemático. | $415 \div 20$ is about 21. |
| **evaluate** to find the value of an expression. | **evaluar** hallar el valor de una expresión. | The expression $48 \div (6 + 10)$ has a value of 3. |
| **even number** a whole number that always has 0, 2, 4, 6, or 8 in the ones place. An even number of objects can be put into pairs or into two equal groups without any leftovers. | **número par** número entero que siempre tiene 0, 2, 4, 6, o 8 en la posición de las unidades. Un número par de objetos puede agruparse en pares o en dos grupos iguales sin que queden sobrantes. | 20, 22, 24, 26, and 28 are even numbers. |
| **expanded form** a way to write a number to show the place value of each digit. | **forma desarrollada** manera de escribir un número para mostrar el valor posicional de cada dígito. | $34.56 = 30 + 4 + \frac{5}{10} + \frac{6}{100}$ |
| **exponent** the number in a power that tells how many times to use the base as a factor in repeated multiplication. | **exponente** el número de una potencia que dice cuántas veces debe multiplicarse la base. | $8^2$ |

| English | Español | Example/Ejemplo |
|---|---|---|

**expression** one or more numbers, unknown numbers, and/or operation symbols that represents a quantity.

**expresión** uno o más números, números desconocidos, o símbolos de operaciones que representan una cantidad.

$3 \times 4$ or $5 + b$

# Ff

**face** a flat surface of a solid shape.

**cara** superficie plana de una figura sólida.

face

**fact family** a group of related equations that use the same numbers, but in a different order, and two different operation symbols. A fact family can show the relationship between addition and subtraction or between multiplication and division.

**familia de datos** grupo de ecuaciones relacionadas que tienen los mismos números, ordenados de distinta manera, y dos símbolos de operaciones diferentes. Una familia de datos puede mostrar la relación que existe entre la multiplicación y la división.

$5 \times 4 = 20$
$4 \times 5 = 20$
$20 \div 4 = 5$
$20 \div 5 = 4$

**factor** a number that is multiplied.

**factor** número que se multiplica.

$4 \times 5 = 20$

factors

**factor pair** two numbers that are multiplied together to give a product.

**pares de factores** dos números que se multiplican para obtener un producto.

$4 \times 5 = 20$

factor pair

**factors of a number** whole numbers that multiply together to get the given number.

**factores de un número** números enteros que se multiplican para obtener el número dado.

$4 \times 5 = 20$
4 and 5 are factors of 20.

**foot (ft)** a unit of length in the customary system. There are 12 inches in 1 foot.

**pie (ft)** unidad de longitud del sistema usual. Un pie equivale a 12 pulgadas.

12 inches = 1 foot

| English | Español | Example/Ejemplo |
|---|---|---|
| **formula** a mathematical relationship that is expressed in the form of an equation. | **fórmula** relación matemática que se expresa en forma de ecuación. | $A = \ell \times w$ |

## Gg

| English | Español | Example/Ejemplo |
|---|---|---|
| **gallon (gal)** a unit of liquid volume in the customary system. There are 4 quarts in 1 gallon. | **galón (gal)** unidad de volumen líquido del sistema usual. 1 galón es igual a 4 cuartos. | 4 quarts = 1 gallon |
| **gram (g)** a unit of mass in the metric system. A paper clip has a mass of about 1 gram. There are 1,000 grams in 1 kilogram. | **gramo (g)** unidad de masa del sistema métrico. Un clip tiene una masa de aproximadamente 1 gramo. 1,000 gramos equivalen a 1 kilogramo. | 1,000 grams = 1 kilogram |
| **greater than symbol (>)** a symbol used to compare two numbers when the first is greater than the second. | **símbolo de mayor que (>)** símbolo que se usa para comparar dos números cuando el primero es mayor que el segundo. | 3.37 > 3.096 |
| **grouping symbols** a symbol, such as braces { }, brackets [ ], or parentheses ( ), used to group parts of an expression that should be evaluated before others. | **símbolos de agrupación** símbolos, tales como las llaves { }, los corchetes [ ], o los paréntesis ( ), que se usan para agrupar partes de una expresión que deben evaluarse antes que otras. | $3 + (5 \times 3) - 3 + 15$ $3 + \{5 \times 3\} = 3 + 15$ $3 + [5 \times 3] - 3 + 15$ |

## Hh

| English | Español | Example/Ejemplo |
|---|---|---|
| **hexagon** a polygon with exactly 6 sides and 6 angles. | **hexágono** polígono que tiene exactamente 6 lados y 6 ángulos. | |
| **hierarchy** a ranking of categories based on attributes. | **jerarquía** clasificación por categorías basada en atributos. | Quadrilaterals / Parallelograms / Rectangles / Squares |
| **hour (h)** a unit of time. There are 60 minutes in 1 hour. | **hora (h)** unidad de tiempo. 1 hora equivale a 60 minutos. | 60 minutes = 1 hour |

| English | Español | Example/Ejemplo |
|---|---|---|

**hundredths** the parts formed when a whole is divided into 100 equal parts.

**centésimos (fracciones)/ centésimas (decimales)** partes que se forman cuando un entero se divide en 100 partes iguales.

## Ii

**inch (in.)** a unit of length in the customary system. There are 12 inches in 1 foot.

**pulgada (pulg.)** unidad de longitud del sistema usual. 12 pulgadas equivalen a 1 pie.

The length of a quarter is about 1 **inch** (in.).

**inequality** a mathematical statement that uses an inequality symbol (< or >) to show the relationship between expressions with different values.

**desigualdad** enunciado matemático en el que se usa un signo de desigualdad (< o >) para mostrar que dos expresiones tienen valores diferentes.

3.275 > 3.240
3.240 < 3.275

**inverse operations** operations that undo each other. For example, addition and subtraction are inverse operations, and multiplication and division are inverse operations.

**operación inversa** operaciones que se anulan unas a otras. Por ejemplo, la suma y la resta son operaciones inversas, y la multiplicación y la división son operaciones inversas.

3,000 ÷ 10 = 300
300 × 10 = 3,000

**isosceles triangle** a triangle that has at least two sides the same length.

**triángulo isósceles** triángulo que tiene al menos dos lados de igual longitud.

8 in. / 8 in. / 6 in.

## Kk

**kilogram (kg)** a unit of mass in the metric system. There are 1,000 grams in 1 kilogram.

**kilogramo (kg)** unidad de masa del sistema métrico. 1 kilogramo equivale a 1,000 gramos.

1,000 grams = 1 kilogram

| English | Español | Example/Ejemplo |
|---------|---------|-----------------|
| **kilometer (km)** a unit of length in the metric system. There are 1,000 meters in 1 kilometer. | **kilómetro (km)** unidad de longitud del sistema métrico. 1 kilómetro equivale a 1,000 metros. | 1 kilometer = 1,000 meters |

## Ll

| English | Español | Example/Ejemplo |
|---------|---------|-----------------|
| **length** measurement that tells the distance from one point to another, or how long something is. | **longitud** medida que indica la distancia de un punto a otro, o cuán largo es un objeto. | length |
| **less than symbol (<)** a symbol used to compare two numbers when the first is less than the second. | **símbolo de menor que (<)** símbolo que se usa para comparar dos números cuando el primero es menor que el segundo. | 3.096 < 3.37 |
| **line** a straight row of points that goes on forever in both directions. | **recta** fila recta de puntos que continúa infinitamente en ambas direcciones. | |
| **line of symmetry** a line that divides a shape into two mirror images. | **eje de simetría** recta que divide una figura en dos imágenes reflejadas. | |
| **line plot** a data display that shows data as marks above a number line. | **diagrama de puntos** representación de datos en la cual se muestran los datos como marcas sobre una recta numérica. | **Sea Lion Lengths**<br><br>x<br>x x x x<br>x x x x x<br>48 49 50 51 52<br>**Inches** |
| **line segment** a straight row of points that starts at one point and ends at another point. | **segmento de recta** fila recta de puntos que comienza en un punto y termina en otro punto. | A ———— B |
| **liquid volume** the amount of space a liquid takes up. | **volumen líquido** cantidad de espacio que ocupa un líquido. | When you measure how much water is in a bucket, you measure liquid volume. |
| **liter (L)** a unit of liquid volume in the metric system. There are 1,000 milliliters in 1 liter. | **litro (l)** unidad de volumen líquido del sistema métrico. 1 litro equivale a 1,000 mililitros. | 1,000 milliliters = 1 liter |

| English | Español | Example/Ejemplo |
|---|---|---|

# Mm

**mass** the amount of matter in an object. Measuring the mass of an object is one way to measure how heavy it is. Units of mass include the gram and kilogram.

**masa** cantidad de materia que hay en un objeto. Medir la masa de un objeto es una manera de medir qué tan pesado es. El gramo y el kilogramo son unidades de masa.

The mass of a paper clip is about 1 gram.

**meter (m)** a unit of length in the metric system. There are 100 centimeters in 1 meter.

**metro (m)** unidad de longitud del sistema métrico. 1 metro es igual a 100 centímetros.

100 centimeters = 1 meter

**metric system** the measurement system that measures length based on meters, liquid volume based on liters, and mass based on grams.

**sistema métrico** sistema de medición. La longitud se mide en metros; el volumen líquido, en litros; y la masa, en gramos.

| Length |
|---|
| 1 kilometer = 1,000 meters |
| 1 meter = 100 centimeters |
| 1 meter = 1,000 millimeters |

| Mass |
|---|
| 1 kilogram = 1,000 grams |

| Volume |
|---|
| 1 liter = 1,000 milliliters |

**mile (mi)** a unit of length in the customary system. There are 5,280 feet in 1 mile.

**milla** unidad de longitud del sistema usual. 1 milla equivale a 5,280 pies.

5,280 feet = 1 mile

**milliliter (ml)** a unit of liquid volume in the metric system. There are 1,000 milliliters in 1 liter.

**mililitro (ml)** unidad de volumen líquido del sistema métrico. 1,000 mililitros equivalen a 1 litro.

1,000 milliliters = 1 liter

**millimeter (mm)** a unit of length in the metric system. There are 1,000 millimeters in 1 meter.

**milímetro (mm)** unidad de longitud del sistema métrico. 1,000 milímetros equivalen a 1 metro.

1,000 millimeters = 1 meter

| English | Español | Example/Ejemplo |
|---|---|---|
| **minute (min)** a unit of time. There are 60 minutes in 1 hour. | **minuto (min)** unidad de tiempo. 60 minutos equivalen a 1 hora. | 60 minutes = 1 hour |
| **mixed number** a number with a whole number part and a fractional part. | **número mixto** número con una parte entera y una parte fraccionaria. | $2\frac{3}{8}$ |
| **multiple** the product of a given number and any other whole number. | **múltiplo** producto de un número y cualquier otro número entero. | 4, 8, 12, 16, and so on, are multiples of 4. |
| **multiplication** an operation used to find the total number of items in a given number of equal-sized groups. See also *multiplicative comparison*. | **multiplicación** operación que se usa para hallar el número total de objetos en un número dado de grupos de igual tamaño. Ver también la *comparación multiplicativa*. | **Multiplication** $3 \times 4 = 12$ number ↑ number in ↑ total of groups each group |
| **multiplicative comparison** a comparison that tells how many times as many. | **comparación multiplicativa** comparación que dice cuántas veces una cantidad es otra cantidad. | $\frac{1}{2} \times 6 = 3$ tells that 3 is $\frac{1}{2}$ as many as 6, and that 3 is 6 times as many as $\frac{1}{2}$. |
| **multiply** to repeatedly add the same number a certain number of times. Used to find the total number of items in equal-sized groups. | **multiplicar** sumar el mismo número una y otra vez una cierta cantidad de veces. Se multiplica para hallar el número total de objetos que hay en grupos de igual tamaño. | 42 36 30 24 18 12 6 $7 \times 6 = 42$ |

# Nn

| | | |
|---|---|---|
| **numerator** the number above the line in a fraction that tells the number of equal parts that are being described. | **numerador** número que está encima de la línea de una fracción. Dice cuántas partes iguales se describen. | $\frac{2}{3}$ |

| English | Español | Example/Ejemplo |
|---|---|---|

# Oo

**obtuse angle** an angle that measures more than 90° but less than 180°.

**ángulo obtuso** ángulo que mide más de 90° pero menos de 180°.

**obtuse triangle** a triangle that has one obtuse angle.

**triángulo obtusángulo** triángulo que tiene un ángulo obtuso.

**odd number** a whole number that always has 1, 3, 5, 7, or 9 in the ones place. An odd number of objects cannot be put into pairs or into two equal groups without a leftover.

**número impar** número entero que siempre tiene el dígito 1, 3, 5, 7, o 9 en el lugar de las unidades. Los números impares no pueden ordenarse en pares o en dos grupos iguales sin sobrantes.

21, 23, 25, 27, and 29 are odd numbers.

**operation** a mathematical action such as addition, subtraction, multiplication, or division.

**operación** acción matemática como la suma, la resta, la multiplicación y la división.

$15 + 5 = 20$
$20 - 5 = 15$
$4 \times 6 = 24$
$24 \div 6 = 4$

**ordered pair** a pair of numbers, $(x, y)$, that describes the location of a point in the coordinate plane, where the x-coordinate gives the point's horizontal distance from the origin, and the y-coordinate gives the point's vertical distance from the origin.

**par ordenado** par de números, $(x, y)$, que describen la ubicación de un punto en el plano de coordenadas. La coordenada x indica la distancia horizontal del punto al origen, y la coordenada y indica la distancia vertical del punto al origen.

x-coordinate
$(x, y)$
y-coordinate

**origin** the point (0, 0) in the coordinate plane where the x-axis and y-axis intersect.

**origen** el punto (0, 0) en el plano de coordenadas, donde se intersecan el eje x y el eje y.

origin

| English | Español | Example/Ejemplo |
|---|---|---|
| **ounce (oz)** a unit of weight in the customary system. A slice of bread weighs about 1 ounce. There are 16 ounces in 1 pound. | **onza (oz)** unidad de peso del sistema usual. Una rebanada de pan pesa aproximadamente 1 onza. 16 onzas equivalen a 1 libra. | 16 ounces = 1 pound |

## Pp

| English | Español | Example/Ejemplo |
|---|---|---|
| **parallel lines** lines that are always the same distance apart and never cross. | **rectas paralelas** rectas que siempre están a la misma distancia y nunca se cruzan. | |
| **parallelogram** a quadrilateral with opposite sides parallel and equal in length. | **paralelogramo** cuadrilátero que tiene lados opuestos paralelos e iguales en longitud. | |
| **partial products** the products you get in each step of the partial-products strategy. You use place value to find partial products. | **productos parciales** los productos que se obtienen en cada paso de la estrategia de productos parciales. Se usa el valor posicional para hallar productos parciales. | The partial products for 124 × 3 are 3 × 100 or 300, 3 × 20 or 60, and 3 × 4 or 12. |
| **partial quotients** The quotients you get in each step of the partial-quotients strategy. You use place value to find partial quotients. | **cocientes parciales** los cocientes que se obtienen en cada paso de la estrategia de cocientes parciales. Se usa el valor posicional para hallar cocientes parciales. | The partial quotients for 2,124 ÷ 4 could be 2,000 ÷ 4 or 500, 100 ÷ 4 or 25, and 24 ÷ 4 or 6. |
| **partial sums** the sums you get in each step of the partial-sums strategy. You use place value to find partial sums. | **sumas parciales** las sumas que se obtienen en cada paso de la estrategia de sumas parciales. Se usa el valor posicional para hallar sumas parciales. | The partial sums for 124 + 234 are 100 + 200 or 300, 20 + 30 or 50, and 4 + 4 or 8. |
| **partial-products strategy** a strategy used to multiply multi-digit numbers. | **estrategia de productos parciales** estrategia que se usa para multiplicar números de varios dígitos. | 218<br>× 6<br>——<br>48 (6 × 8 ones)<br>60 (6 × 1 ten)<br>+ 1,200 (6 × 2 hundreds)<br>——<br>1,308 |

| English | Español | Example/Ejemplo |
|---|---|---|
| **partial-quotients strategy** a strategy used to divide multi-digit numbers. | **estrategia de cocientes parciales** estrategia que se usa para dividir números de varios dígitos. | 6<br>25<br>500<br>4)2,125<br>− 2,000<br>125<br>− 100<br>25<br>− 24<br>1<br><br>The partial quotients are 500, 25, and 6.<br>The quotient, 531, is the sum of the partial quotients. The remainder is 1. |
| **partial-sums strategy** a strategy used to add multi-digit numbers. | **estrategia de sumas parciales** estrategia que se usa para sumar números de varios dígitos. | Add the hundreds.    312<br>Add the tens.    +235<br>Add the ones.    500<br>   40<br>   + 7<br>   547 |
| **pattern** a series of numbers or shapes that follow a rule to repeat or change. See also *terms of a pattern.* | **patrón** serie de números o figuras que siguen una regla para repetirse o cambiar. Ver también *términos de un patrón.* | |
| **pentagon** a polygon with exactly 5 sides and 5 angles. | **pentágono** polígono con que tiene exactamente 5 lados y 5 ángulos. | |
| **perimeter** the distance around a two-dimensional shape. The perimeter is equal to the sum of the lengths of the sides. | **perímetro** longitud del contorno de una figura bidimensional. El perímetro es igual al total de las longitudes de los lados. | 40 yards<br>60 yards<br>60 yards<br>40 yards<br><br>The perimeter of the soccer field is 200 yards.<br>(60 yd + 40 yd + 60 yd + 40 yd) |

| English | Español | Example/Ejemplo |
|---|---|---|
| **period** a group of three places in a number, usually separated by commas. The first three periods are the ones period, the thousands period, and the millions period. | **período** grupo de tres valores posicionales de un número, generalmente separados por comas. Los primeros tres períodos son el período de las unidades, el período de los millares y el período de los millones. | 321,987<br>987 is the first period. |
| **perpendicular lines** two lines that meet to form a right angle, or a 90° angle. | **rectas perpendiculars** dos rectas que se unen para formar un ángulo recto, o un ángulo de 90°. | |
| **pint (pt)** a unit of liquid volume in the customary system. There are 2 cups in 1 pint. | **pinta (pt)** unidad de volumen líquido del sistema usual. 1 pinta equivale a 2 tazas. | 2 cups = 1 pint |
| **place value** the value of a digit based on its position in a number. | **valor posicional** valor de un dígito según su posición en un número. | The **2** in 3.52 is in the **hundredths** place and has a value of **2 hundredths** or **0.02**. |
| **plane figure** a two-dimensional figure, such as a circle, triangle, or rectangle. | **figura plana** figura bidimensional, como un círculo, triángulo o rectángulo. | |
| **PM** the time from noon until before midnight. | **p. m.** tiempo que transcurre desde el mediodía hasta la medianoche. | |
| **point** a single location in space. | **punto** ubicación única en el espacio. | *A*<br>• |
| **polygon** a two-dimensional closed figure made with three or more straight line segments that do not cross over each other. | **polígono** figura bidimensional cerrada formada que tiene tres o más segmentos de recta que no se cruzan. | |
| **pound (lb)** a unit of weight in the customary system. There are 16 ounces in 1 pound. | **libra (lb)** unidad de peso del sistema usual. 1 libra equivale a 16 onzas. | 16 ounces = 1 pound |

| English | Español | Example/Ejemplo |
|---|---|---|
| **power of 10** a number that can be written as a product of tens. | **potencia de 10** número que puede escribirse como producto de decenas. | 100 and 1,000 are powers of 10 because 100 = 10 × 10 and 1,000 = 10 × 10 × 10. |
| **prime number** a whole number greater than 1 whose only factors are 1 and itself. | **número primo** número entero mayor que 1 cuyos únicos factores son 1 y él mismo. | 2, 3, 5, 7, 11, 13, 17, 19 are prime numbers. |
| **product** the result of multiplication. | **producto** el resultado de la multiplicación. | 5 × 3 = 15 |
| **protractor** a tool used to measure angles. | **transportador** herramienta que se usa para medir ángulos. | |

## Qq

| English | Español | Example/Ejemplo |
|---|---|---|
| **quadrilateral** a polygon with exactly 4 sides and 4 angles. | **cuadrilátero** polígono que tiene exactamente 4 lados y 4 ángulos. | |
| **quart (qt)** a unit of liquid volume in the customary system. There are 4 cups in 1 quart. | **cuarto (ct)** unidad de volumen líquido del sistema usual. 1 cuarto equivale a 4 tazas. | 4 cups = 1 quart |
| **quotient** the result of division. | **cociente** el resultado de la división. | 15 ÷ 3 = 5 |

## Rr

| English | Español | Example/Ejemplo |
|---|---|---|
| **ray** a straight row of points that starts at one point and goes on forever in one direction. | **semirrecta** fila recta de puntos que comienza en un punto y continúa infinitamente en una dirección. | A •————→ B |
| **rectangular prism** a solid figure with 6 rectangular faces. | **prisma rectangular** figura sólida con seis caras rectangulares. | |

| English | Español | Example/Ejemplo |
|---------|---------|-----------------|
| **regroup** to compose or decompose tens, hundreds, thousands, and so forth. | **reagrupar** componer o descomponer decenas, centenas, millares, etc. | 10 tenths can be regrouped as 1 whole, or 1 tenth can be regrouped as 10 hundredths. |
| **remainder** the amount left over when one number does not divide another number a whole number of times. | **residuo** en la división, la cantidad que queda después de haber formado grupos iguales. | Remainder $17 \div 5 = 3\,R\,2$ |
| **rhombus** a quadrilateral with all sides the same length. | **rombo** cuadrilátero con todos los lados de la misma longitud. | |
| **right angle** an angle that looks like a square corner and measures 90°. | **ángulo recto** ángulo que parece la esquina de un cuadrado y mide 90°. | 90° |
| **right triangle** a triangle that has one right angle. | **triángulo rectángulo** triángulo con un ángulo recto. | 90° |
| **round** to find a number that is close in value to a given number by finding the nearest ten, hundred, or other place value. | **redondear** hallar un número que es cercano en valor al número dado hallando la decena, la centena o otro valor posicional más cercano. | 48 rounded to the nearest ten is 50. |
| **row** a horizontal line of objects or numbers, such as in an array or table. | **fila** línea horizontal de objetos o números, tal como las que aparecen en una matriz o una tabla. | |
| **rule** a procedure that is followed to go from one number or shape to the next in a pattern. | **regla** procedimiento que se sigue para ir de un número o una figura al número o la figura siguiente de un patrón. | 17, 22, 27, 32, 37, 42 rule: add 5 |

| English | Español | Example/Ejemplo |
|---|---|---|

## Ss

**scale (on a graph)** the value represented by the distance between one tick mark and the next on a number line.

**escala (en una gráfica)** el valor que representa la distancia entre una marca y la marca siguiente de una recta numérica.

Points Scored During the Game

**scalene triangle** a triangle that has no sides the same length.

**triángulo escaleno** triángulo que no tiene lados de igual longitud.

**scaling** resizing a quantity by multiplying by a factor.

**poner a escala** cambiar de tamaño una cantidad multiplicándola por un factor.

| Words | Symbols |
|---|---|
| **6 doubled** is 12. | $2 \times 6 = 12$ |
| **Half of 6** is 3. | $\frac{1}{2} \times 6 = 3$ |

stretching

shrinking

**second (s)** a unit of time. There are 60 seconds in 1 minute.

**segundo (s)** unidad de tiempo. Sesenta segundos equivalen a 1 minuto.

60 seconds = 1 minute

**side** a line segment that forms part of a two-dimensional shape.

**lado** segmento de recta que forma parte de una figura bidimensional.

side

**solid figure** a three-dimensional figure.

**figura sólida** figura tridimensional.

A rectangular prism is a solid figure.

| English | Español | Example/Ejemplo |
|---|---|---|
| **square** a quadrilateral with 4 square corners and 4 sides of equal length. | **cuadrado** cuadrilátero que tiene 4 esquinas cuadradas y 4 lados de igual longitud. | |
| **square unit** the area of a square with side lengths of 1 unit. | **unidad cuadrada** el área de un cuadrado que tiene lados de 1 unidad de longitud. | 1 unit  1 unit  1 unit  1 unit |
| **standard form** the way a number is written with numerals. | **forma estándar** manera de escribir un número usando dígitos. | The standard form of *twelve* is 12. |
| **subcategory** a category within a larger category. It shares all the same attributes as the larger category. | **subcategoría** categoría que está dentro de otra categoría. Tiene las mismas propiedades que la categoría más amplia. | Parallelograms are a subcategory of quadrilaterals. |
| **sum** the result of addition. | **suma** el resultado de la suma. | $34 + 25 = \mathbf{59}$ |
| **symbol** a character, such as a letter or question mark, that can be used to stand for an unknown number in an equation. | **símbolo** cualquier marca o dibujo, tal como una letra o un signo de interrogación, que puede usarse para representar un número desconocido en una ecuación. | $18 - ? = 9$ |

## Tt

| English | Español | Example/Ejemplo |
|---|---|---|
| **tenths** the parts formed when a whole is divided into 10 equal parts. | **décimos (fracciones)/ décimas (decimales)** partes que se forman cuando se divide un entero en 10 partes iguales. | |
| **terms** the numbers or shapes in a pattern. | **términos** los números o las figuras de un patrón. | 3, 9, 12, 15, 18, 21, 24 |

| English | Español | Example/Ejemplo |
|---|---|---|

**thousandths** the parts formed when a whole is divided into 1,000 equal parts.

**milésimas** partes que se forman cuando se divide un entero en 1,000 partes iguales.

$1 \div 1,000 = \frac{1}{1,000}$, or 0.001

---

**three-dimensional** solid, or having length, width, and height. For example, a cube is three-dimensional.

**tridimensional** sólido, o que tiene longitud, ancho y altura. Por ejemplo, los cubos son tridimensionales.

---

**trapezoid (exclusive)** a quadrilateral with exactly one pair of parallel sides.

**trapecio** cuadrilátero que tiene exactamente un par de lados paralelos.

---

**trapezoid (inclusive)** a quadrilateral with at least one pair of parallel sides.

**trapecio** cuadrilátero que tiene al menos un par de lados paralelos.

---

**tree diagram** a hierarchy diagram that connects categories and subcategories with lines to show how they are related.

**diagrama de árbol** diagrama jerárquico que conecta categorías y subcategorías por medio de líneas para mostrar cómo están relacionadas.

Triangles

Scalene    Isosceles

Equilateral

---

**triangle** a polygon with exactly 3 sides and 3 angles.

**triángulo** polígono que tiene exactamente 3 lados y 3 ángulos.

---

**two-dimensional** flat, or having measurement in two directions, like length and width. For example, a rectangle is two-dimensional.

**bidimensional** plano, o que tiene medidas en dos direcciones, como la longitud y el ancho. Por ejemplo, un rectángulo es bidimensional.

---

| English | Español | Example/Ejemplo |
|---|---|---|

## Uu

**unit cube** a cube with side lengths of 1 unit. A unit cube is said to have 1 cubic unit of volume, and can be used to measure the volume of a solid figure.

**cubo de unidad** cubo cuyos lados miden 1 unidad. Un cubo de unidad tiene 1 unidad cúbica de volumen y puede usarse para medir el volumen de una figura sólida.

unit cube

volume = 4 cubic units

**unit fraction** a fraction with a numerator of 1. Other fractions are built from unit fractions.

**fracción unitaria** fracción cuyo numerador es 1. Otras fracciones se construyen a partir de fracciones unitarias.

$\frac{1}{4}$

**unit square** a square with side lengths of 1 unit. A unit square is said to have 1 square unit of area, and can be used to measure the area of a plane figure.

**cuadrado de unidad** cuadrado cuyos lados miden 1 unidad. Un cuadrado de unidad tiene 1 unidad cuadrada de área y puede usarse para medir el área de una figura plana.

1 unit

1 unit

unit square

**unknown** the value you need to find to solve a problem.

**desconocido** el valor que se debe hallar para resolver un problema.

$18 - ? = 9$

## Vv

**Venn diagram** a diagram that uses overlapping ovals (or other shapes) to show how sets of numbers or objects are related.

**diagrama de Venn** dibujo que contiene óvalos u otras figuras que se superponen y muestra cómo se relacionan conjuntos de números u objetos.

Polygons

Quadrilaterals

Parallelograms

Hexagons

**vertex** the point where two rays, lines, or line segments meet to form an angle.

**vértice** punto donde dos semirrectas, rectas, o segmentos de recta se unen y forman un ángulo.

vertex

| English | Español | Example/Ejemplo |
|---|---|---|

**volume** the amount of space inside a solid figure. Volume is measured in cubic units such as cubic inches.

**volumen** cantidad de espacio que hay dentro de una figura sólida. El volumen se mide en unidades cúbicas como las pulgadas cúbicas.

Volume = 24 cubic units

## Ww

**weight** the measurement that tells how heavy an object is. Units of weight include ounces and pounds.

**peso** medición que dice qué tan pesado es un objeto. Las onzas y las libras son unidades de peso.

| Weight |
|---|
| 1 pound = 16 ounces |

**word form** the way a number is written with words or said aloud.

**en palabras** manera en que se escribe o se dice en voz alta un número usando palabras.

467,882
four hundred sixty-seven thousand, eight hundred eighty-two

## Xx

**x-axis** the horizontal number line in the coordinate plane.

**eje x** recta numérica horizontal en el plano de coordenadas.

x-axis

**x-coordinate** the first number in an ordered pair. It tells the point's horizontal distance from the origin.

**coordenada x** el primer número de un par ordenado. Indica cuál es la distancia horizontal del punto al origen.

x-coordinate

(4, 3)

(0, 0)

| English | Español | Example/Ejemplo |
|---|---|---|

# Yy

**y-axis** the vertical number line in the coordinate plane.

**eje y** recta numérica vertical en el plano de coordenadas.

y-axis

```
  y
8
7
6
5
4
3
2
1
O 1 2 3 4 5 6 7 8   x
```

**y-coordinate** the second number in an ordered pair. It tells the point's vertical distance from the origin.

**coordenada y** el segundo número de un par ordenado. Indica cuál es la distancia vertical del punto al origen.

y-coordinate

```
  y
5
4
3        (4, 3)
2
1
(0, 0)
O 1 2 3 4 5   x
```

**yard (yd)** a unit of length in the customary system. There are 3 feet, or 36 inches, in 1 yard.

**yarda (yd)** unidad de longitud del sistema usual de Estados Unidos. 1 yarda equivale a 3 pies o a 36 pulgadas.

3 feet = 1 yard
36 inches = 1 yard

# Acknowledgments

Common Core State Standards © 2010. National Governors Association Center for Best Practices and Council of Chief State School Officers. All rights reserved.

## Photography Credits

United States coin images (unless otherwise indicated) from the United States Mint

Images used under license from **Shutterstock.com.**

iii freedomnaruk; **iv** graphicmaker, PrimaStockPhoto; **v** timquo; **vi** Danielle Balderas, Istimages; **vii** Aila Images, Cartarium, jeep5d; 1 Peter Turner Photography; 8 Quang Ho; 14 FabrikaSimf; 17 Issarawat Tattong; 20 Y Photo Studio; 22 Mega Pixel; 23 Picsfive; 32 c12; 36 Africa Studio, heraldmuc; 37–38 Tibet Saisema; 39 Nadiia Korol; 40 Garsya; 41 HeinzTeh; 42 Stephen Rees; 43 Kitch Bain, M. Unal Ozmen, Patty Chan; 44 Nik Merkulov; 46 Beth Swanson; 54 Gruffi, Inc., ORLIO; 58 ananaline; 59 Olga Popova, 60 levgenii Meyer; 62 Creativestockexchange; 64 Ivan Kurmyshov; 68 Qwasder1987; 72 PhotoStock10; 73 Mathier; 76 Cory Thoman, Studiovin; 77 Konstantin Faraktinov; 80 Aluna1, Nerthuz; 81 sumire8; 82 freedomnaruk, Natasha Pankina; 84 kibri_ho; 86 Dr Ajay Kumar Singh, Liskus, Roblan; 87 Nertuz; 88 Nerthuz, Topform; 91 Lucie Lang; 93 Trong Nguyen; 94 Nares Soumsomboon; 96 Sharon Day; 98 Photka; 100 Steve Collender; 101 Evgeny Karandaev, Natasha Pankina; 102 Kleber Cordeiro, Natasha Pankina; 103 Africa Studio; 104 vitec; 106 Bernatskaya Oxana, vitec; 108 Natasha Pankina, Worker; 110 Sanit Fuangnakhon; 111 Tatevosian Yana; 117 Bubutu; 130 Jiang Hongyan; 131 Capslock, rCarner; 132 Elnur, Rica Photography; 137 rCarner; 145 Ivonne Wierink; 148 Africa Studio, Stefano T; 149 Edward Hardam, Photogal; 150 Masterchief_Productions; 155 Bezikus, mhatzapa; 156 PrimaStockPhoto; 160 Jeffrey B. Banke; 163 GrashAlex; 166 Ajt, jingdi, Odua Images; 167 Garsya, Pavel L Photo and Video; 170 Artmim; 171 neotemlpars; 172 pio3; 174 Eric Isselee; 175 Quang Ho; 176 Eric Isselee; 177 Jojje; 180 Julian Rovagnati; 181 649386629, 182–183 Yellow Cat; 185 Somboon Bunproy; 188 Krasowit; 189 Pete Saloutos; 190 Mny-Jhee; 192 Maxpro; 193 Craig Barhorst, Stockagogo; 194 Jojoo64; 196 Goran Bogicevic; 197 Andrey_Popov; 198 irin-k; 199 AVprophoto; 200 Ruslan Semichev; 204 Eric Isselee, r.classen; 205 Sari Oneal; 206 Mike Truchon; 208 3DMAVR, 209 Hue Ta; 210 Hong Vo; 212 AVprophoto; 214 fivespots; 218 inxti; 219 Maks Narodenko; 220 Y Photo Studio; 222 Moving Moment; 223 Vitaly Raduntsev; 226 1989studio, jiangdi, LAURA_VN, MaraZe; 227 Art65395; 228 Anastasia Prisunko; 230 HomeStudio; 231 Holy Polygon; 232 Holy Polygon; 236 Africa Studio; 237 Elvaisla; 240 JeniFoto; 242 gresei; 244 imfoto; 245 Your Design; 246 Baibaz; 247 MIGUEL GARCIA SAAVEDRA; 248 graphicmaker, pirtuss; 249 Kostsov; 250 Tish1; 252 Valzan; 253 Mariyana M; 255 Kiprej, kubais, Mariyana M; 256 Lunatictm; 258 artjazz, mhatzapa; 259 Nungning20; 260 3DMAVR, serazetdinov; 266 Ayman alakhras, Mega Pixel, Natasha Pankina; 267 Perun; 269 paulista; 270 Sirtravelalot, Tapui, Valzan; 271 Elena Zajchikova, Wk1003mike; 272 Wk1003mike; 274 Grey_and; 275 Alisafarov, 276 Ryzhkov Photography; 278 artnlera, Tim Masters; 280 George3973, Marionhassold; 281 DenisNata; 282 DenisNata; 284 marilyn barbone; 286 JeniFoto; 288 Victor Moussa; 289 liskus, oksana2010; 290 Picsfive; 291 Crepesoles, Natasha Pankina; 292 Natasha Pankina, Susan Schmitz; 294–295 Grafikwork; 296 Alina Demidenko, Marssanya; 297 Tsuguliev; 298 Marssanya, Vincent noel; 299 Africa Studio, stock photofan1, Kao; 305 Alex Staroseltsev; 308 EtiAmmos, LifetimeStock; 309 akiyoko; 312 Wira SHK; 313 Julia_Lelija; 314 D7INAMI7S; 316 Kletr; 318 artnLera, jantima14; 319 Nattika; 321 blue67design, JRP Studio; 324 Winiki; 325 mhatzapa, rsooll; 329 AlenKadr; 330 cubolabo, timquo; 332 James Steidl; 334 symbiot; 335 ducu59us; 338 Carolyn Franks; 340 liskus, SeDmi; 343 3d11z, 340 Andrey_Popov, Levchi Bohdan; 317 3oruntoro; 350 thodonal88; 351 Chayatorn Laorattanavech; chotchitima; 355 primiaou, Valentyna7; 357 Tiger Images; 358 Tiger Images; 360 Natasha Pankina, Sanit Fuangnakhon; 363 balabolka, cubolabo; 366 Keith Bell; 368 aarrows; 372 Africa Studio, Quang Ho; 373 JeniFoto; 374 Hong Vo, Photka, Tommy Atthi; 375 LoopAll; 376 Africa Studio; 378 Bscmedialc, timquo; 379 vincent noel; 380 Binh Thanh Bui; 382 Madlen; 384 Eric Isselee; 386 Sapnocte; 387 Africa Studio; 389 Cherdchai charasri; 394 Quang Ho; 400 Gencho Petkov; 401 STILLFX; 402 Rose Carson; 403 Bilevich Olga; 406 urfin; 407 Perlav; 410 Ed Samuel; 413 Dmitry Polonskiy, Hdcsislava, LukaKikina; 418 Tim UR; 424 Africa Studio, Mike Flippo; Lobachev, Birute Vijeikiene; 434 Dslaven; 435 Evikka, Mike Flippo; 436 COLOA Studio, Fablok, hitforsa; 437 Cunaplus unaplus; 438 Mayakova; 440 Maetisa; 441 Elvaisla; 442 Evikka; 443 Timquo; 444 Fotoearl; 447 KAMONRAT; 448 LanKS; 449 lenetstan; 450 Arthito; 451 Gino Santa Maria; 454 Lisovskaya Natalia; 455 Coprid; 456 Symbiot; 458 baibaz; 459 absolutimages, Natasha Pankina; 460 a_v_d; 462 tratong; 463 margouillat photo; 467 KucherAV; 468 Iriskana, Pixelbliss; 469 iamtui7; 470 9comeback, Laurelle; 471 a_v_d, advent; 474–475 Trinset; 476 Africa Studio; 478 Mike Flippo; 479 Africa Studio; 480 The_Pixel; 481 MaraZe; 482 Erik D. Monticello; 484 Nataliia Pyzhova; 485 Happy monkey; 486 Diana Taliun, smilewithjul; 488 IB Photography; 489 FakeStocker; 490 Pixelbliss, Stockforlife; 491 Viktar Malyshchyts; 494 Christoforos Avramidis; 496 Motorolka, Rangizzz; 497 Motorolka; 498 Danny Smythe, Vinicius Tupinamba; 499 Madlen; 505 Ariya Phornpraphan; 508 Lano4ka, vesna cvorovic, zorina_larisa; 509 Africa Studio; 510 akepong srichaichana; 512 Roxana Bashyrova; 513 Bennian; 514 Istimages; 516 mkos83, Natasha Pankina; 518 Eric Isselee; 519 Danielle Balderas, Feng Yu; 520 M. Unal Ozmen; 527 Bjoern Wylezich; 529 Barry Blackburn, Tapui; 530 wk1003mike, Wonderful Future World; 531 M Kunz; 534 Alexandr Korolev, Natasha Pankina; 535 PrimaStockPhoto; 536 kudla, olnik_y; 538 mlorenz Avramidis; 539 Voronina Svetlana; 540 Cipariss; 541 BERNATSKAYA OXANA, mhatzapa; 542 Bernatskaya Oxana, mhatzapa; 544 Vladimir Sazonov, mhatzapa; 545 Eric Isselee, qingqing; 546 kanashi, mhatzapa; 547 Nikolai Tsvetokov; 548 Mmaxer; 549 Africa Studio; 551 Jiang Hongyan; 552 Hong Vo; 553 LuXpics; 554 Paket; 555 Hurst Photo; 556 Juburg; 557 Julie vanec; 558 Nik Merkulov; 560 Mrs_ya; 561 Nik Merkulov; 562 Valentyn Hontovyy; 566 artnLera, Elena Schweitzer; 568 Garsya, Natasha Pankina; 569 Hans Geel; 570 Kuznetsov Alexey; 572 Duplass, olnik_y; 578 Galina Petrova; 582 MaxFX; 586 T. Dallas; 590 Peter Hermes Furian; 604 Butsaya; 607 Diana Taliun; 608 Gts; 610 Gts;

## Front Cover Credits

©Paul Bradbury/OJO Images/Getty Images

612 Kitch Bain; 614 Alexander Raths; 615 Natasha Pankina, Nearbirds; 621 Alexandru Nika; 625 M. Unal Ozmen; 626 Aila Images; 628 jeep5d; 629 Eric Isselee, Nantawat Chotsuwan; 634 MirasWonderland; 640 Milya; 646 Gjermund; 647 Cartarium; 669 Africa Studio, Nubenamo; 670 Joe Belanger; 672 M. Unal Ozmen; 674 Keith Homan; 677 Ifong; 680 Nuttapong; 681 Billion Photos; 682 Gresei; 684 Iriskana, Kitamin; 685 Cigdem; 686 Nata-Lia; 689 Africa Studio; 691 Ben Barnes; 692 Ben Barnes, liskus; 694 Ivan Anta; 696 JeniFoto; 701 marssanya, Mellutto; 704 Bedrin; 706 Swill Klitch; A5 Showcake; A13 Trinacria Photo

**Student Handbook, appearing in Student Bookshelf and Teacher Guide only: HB1** ArtMari, Rawpixel.com, Pixfiction, Disavorabuth; **HB1** Africa Studio, opicobello; **HB2** iadams; **HB3** Palabra; **HB5** Havepino; **HB6** Tatiana Popova; **HB8** Chiyacat; **HB9** Kyselova Inna, Markus Mainka; **HB10** ArtMari; **HB11** Disavorabuth; **HB12** ArtMari, Disavorabuth; **HB13–HB14** ArtMari; **HB16** Rawpixel.com